Service-Learning:
Applications From the Research

CONTRIBUTORS

Tom Berkas, Search Institute, Thresher Square West, 700 South Third Street, Minneapolis, MN 55415

Dale A. Blyth, Search Institute, Thresher Square West, 700 South Third Street, Minneapolis, MN 55415

L. Richard Bradley, Four District Consortium, 6489 Brookbend Drive, Columbus, OH 43235

Janet Eyler, Department of Human Resources, Vanderbilt University, Box 90GPC, Nashville, TN 37203

Dwight Giles, Jr., Human and Organizational Development Program, Box 67 Peabody College, Vanderbilt University, Nashville, TN 37203

Novella Zett Keith, Interdisciplinary Urban Education Program, College of Education, Temple University, Philadelphia, PA 19122

Bruce A. Miller, Rural Education Program, Northwest Regional Educational Laboratory, 101 Southwest Main Street, Suite 500, Portland OR 97204

Rebecca Saito, Search Institute, Thresher Square West, 700 South Third Street, Minneapolis MN 55415

Robert C. Serow, Educational Leadership and Evaluation, North Carolina State University, P.O. Box 7801, ELPE, Raleigh, NC 27695-7801

Robert D. Shumer, National Service-Learning Clearinghouse, College of Education, University of Minnesota, R-460 VoTechEd Building, 1954 Buford Avenue, St. Paul, MN 55108

Rahima C. Wade, Elementary Social Studies, University of Iowa, Lindquist Center N293, Iowa City, IA 52242

Alan S. Waterman, Department of Psychology, The College of New Jersey, Hillwood Lakes, CN4700, Trenton, NJ 08650-4700

Service-Learning:
Applications From the Research

Edited by

Alan S. Waterman
The College of New Jersey

NATIONAL YOUTH LEADERSHIP
COUNCIL

LEA LAWRENCE ERLBAUM ASSOCIATES, PUBLISHERS
1997 Mahwah, New Jersey   London

Lawrence Erlbaum Associates, Inc., Publishers
10 Industrial Avenue
Mahwah, NJ 07430

Library of Congress Cataloging-In-Publication Data

Service-learning : applications from the research/ [edited by] Alan S. Waterman.
      p. cm.
This volume grew from a conference held in Philadelphia in 1995 and convened annually by the National Youth Leadership Council (NYLC).
Includes bibliographical references and indexes.
ISBN 0-8058-2535-5 (C : alk. paper). —ISBN 0-8058-2536-3 (P : alk. paper)
1. Student service—United States—Congresses. 2. Student service—research—United States—Congresses. 3. Student volunteers in social service—United States—Congresses. I. Waterman, Alan S.
LC220.5.S456 1997   96-49391
370.11'5—dc21   CIP

10 9 8 7 6 5 4 3 2 1

For My Mother

Contents

Foreword

"Thought without practice is empty, practice without thought is blind."

—Kwame Nkrumah
Former President, Ghana

Linking research and educational practice for the benefit of both is not a new idea. If however, practice is a bold departure from the status quo, practice such as service-learning, research is not just beneficial—it is critical.

If schools are to become laboratories of democracy and entrepreneurship, and if students are to become engaged as partners in renewal of their communities, a research case must be made for service-learning. Does learning take place? Will other kinds of learning suffer? And what kinds of practice are most effective? Clearly, solid research is essential if this transforming way of teaching and learning is to be fully integrated into American schooling and youth development institutions.

The National Youth Leadership Council (NYLC) took a first step toward joining service-learning practice with research in 1983 when we chose to locate at the Center for Youth Development and Research, University of Minnesota. In 1991, NYLC created the Center for Experiential Education and Service-Learning in the University's Department of Work, Community, and Family Education, in the College of Education and Human Development. From this Center, NYLC has initiated and encouraged program evaluation, formative research that informs and improves practice, and summative studies that measure results. Moreover, NYLC has joined with the University to create a K–12 service-learning clearinghouse, tied to the ERIC system, which gathers and distributes research information from sources across the nation.

This volume, *Service-Learning: Applications from the Research*, grew from the National Service-Learning Conference convened annually by NYLC and a regional host organization. A day-long research seminar at the Conference brings together researchers to discuss latest developments among themselves and with practitioners. Papers from the 1995 Philadelphia Conference, which provided the basis for the chapters contained herein, were impressive in their range and rigor. Together they offer documentation and analysis useful to an emerging research knowledge base, a starting point for the evidence needed to firmly establish service-learning for K–12 age people as a widely accepted way of teaching and learning.

Service-learning has been tinkered with on the fringes of higher education for more than 20 years, and has been largely ignored by those in teacher education. Experiential educators however, inspired by young people in and out of the schools, and apart from mandates or special funding, have brought the current movement to life. Their major allies in launching service learning today have been advocates of national service and the federal Corporation for National Service (CNS).

Through 1990 and 1993 National and Community Service legislation, national service was redefined from a single program model for young adults to a developmental process that included K–12 service-learning, along with AmeriCorps and VISTA. CNS has funded hundreds of K–12 age school and community programs reaching more than 1 million students. In their wisdom, they have also invested in research including providing the key funding for the research seminars held at the annual National Service-Learning Conferences, and hence for this volume. Stepping up in a major way to fund service-learning research has also been the private sector, particularly the W. K. Kellogg Foundation.

Thanks to Dr. Alan Waterman and Dr. Harry Silcox, this edition, begun at the 6th Annual National Service-Learning Conference in Philadelphia, is not only available to inform the current reader, but its example has helped launch an ongoing series to be sponsored by NYLC under the title: *Studies in Service-Learning*. This series will include periodic research volumes shaped at the Annual Conferences. Our young people and our communities deserve nothing less!

—James C. Kielsmeier
President, National Youth Leadership Council

Preface

Service-learning is an experiential approach to education that involves students in a wide range of activities that are of benefit to others, and uses the experiences generated to advance the curricula goals. Service-learning is presently in wide use at the primary, secondary, and college levels, and its use is expanding more as states make service-learning and community service a part of their high school graduation requirements. There has been an active tradition of research on service-learning regarding its effectiveness in terms of increasing student attendance, promoting the development of academic knowledge and skills, fostering personal development among students, promoting civic responsibility, increasing community–school linkages and yielding valuable benefits to the community.

This research has been scattered in journals and books across a wide range of disciplines. Although there are efforts underway to keep track of this literature, as well as the several review articles published on it, a systematic treatment of the range of topics relevant to service-learning programs has not previously been published. This volume brings together the work of leading researchers in the area and has two principal objectives:

1. To review and evaluate the empirical research literatures on (a) the methodologies for assessing the nature and impacts of service-learning programs and what has been learned using different methods; (b) the characteristics of school-based programs, the variables affecting teacher involvement, and the motivations that students bring to their participation, as these affect the effectiveness of service-learning; and (c) the distinctive aspects of community contexts affecting program implementation.

2. To generate a range of recommendations derived from the empirical research literature that can be used in planning the implementation of new service-learning programs and the continuing improvement of existing programs.

This volume was developed for both an academic audience, including college and university faculty teaching in the fields of education (particularly in the areas of service-learning and educational research); psychology (particularly in the areas of child and adolescent development); community service and development; and for researchers and evaluation and training specialists, based outside of university settings, who are involved with service-learning programs or other forms of experiential education. This book is also intended for educational administrators at the state, school district, and project-director levels. Given the extent of service-learning programs currently in place and their rapid and continuing expansion, each of these groups can benefit from the compilation and review of the principal methodologies and current research findings on the various aspects of service-learning.

This volume can also serve as a text in undergraduate and graduate school courses in service-learning and educational research. Both with regard to the scope of the topics covered and the recommendations drawn from the empirical research literature, the contributors and I sought to make this volume a model of how research can be used in the continuing process of program development.

Acknowledgments

This book has its origins in an invitation I received from Dr. Harry Silcox, Director, Pennsylvania Institute for Service-Learning, to serve as the organizer and chair of the first day-long research session to be held at a National Service-Learning Conference. Harry served as Host and Chair of the 1995 National Conference held in Philadelphia, Pennsylvania. I am indebted to him not only for the invitation, but for the continuing encouragement he has provided to me over the years.

As President of the National Youth Leadership Council (NYLC), the sponsoring organization of the National Service-Learning Conferences, Dr. James C. Kielsmeier has played the central role in placing service-learning on the national agenda for education reform. Jim and Harry not only recognized the vital role research could, and should, play in the documenting of the impacts of service-learning and identifying ways to improve practice, they were also in the position to serve as catalysts for focusing attention to the theme of research. Through the efforts of Jim Kielsmeier, and others at NYLC, this volume is the first in a series of volumes to be sponsored by the Council dealing with research on service-learning.

I want to thank the Corporation for National Service for their financial support of the research session held at the 1995 National Service-Learning Conference. This support made possible the opportunities for discussion among researchers and practitioners, as well as the extended exchanges among the contributors that have added so much to the value of this volume.

I also wish to express my appreciation to the Lilly Endowment, Inc., and the staff of the Program on Youth and Caring, for grant support during the year prior to my work on this book. My efforts on the grant project contributed significantly to my thinking on the topic of youth service and helped to prepare me to take on this book project.

As a teacher of psychology who has invested more than 20 years in the practice of service-learning, I need to thank my students for the opportunities they afforded me to learn along with them.

And personally most important, my continuing gratitude to my family, my wife and colleague Sally Archer, and our sons Aaron and Jeremy, for all they do each day to enrich my life.

—Alan S. Waterman

1

An Overview of Service-Learning and the Role of Research and Evaluation in Service-Learning Programs

Alan S. Waterman
The College of New Jersey

We have been doing "service-learning" in our society for far longer than we have applied the label to this approach to experiential education. We have involved our children, adolescents, and young adults in service to the community through our schools, our religious institutions, and youth organizations (e.g., scouting). We have expected service experiences to promote responsibility, caring, citizenship, competence, and a practical knowledge of our communities, our nation, and our world. We have believed that service promotes these goals more effectively than other means, particularly standard classroom instruction. And we have found that in doing service, many of our students come to feel quite differently about that standard classroom instruction as a function of seeing its application in ways that make a difference in the lives of others.

AN OVERVIEW OF SERVICE-LEARNING

Defining Service-Learning

The term *service-learning* has come to be applied to a very wide range of activities with students from kindergarten through higher education. As the use of the term has expanded, there has risen a lively debate about what should and should not be considered educational practices under this label. Although there is potentially much to be gained from this debate in terms of the identification of parameters

1

potentially necessary for effective practice, this is not the forum to review the sometimes broad, but often subtle, distinctions offered from competing perspectives. Still, it is appropriate to provide some formal definition of service-learning, so as to identify the major defining features of this approach to education.

The Commission on National and Community Service has defined service-learning as follows: Service-learning is a method

> (A) under which students learn and develop through active participation in thoughtfully organized service experiences that meet actual community needs and that are coordinated in collaboration with the school and community;

> (B) that is integrated into the students' academic curriculum or provides structured time for the student to think, talk, or write about what the student did and saw during the actual service activity;

> (C) that provides students with opportunities to use newly acquired skills and knowledge in real-life situations in their own communities; and

> (D) that enhances what is taught in school by extending student learning beyond the classroom and into the community and helps to foster the development of a sense of caring for others. (National and Community Service Act of 1990)

The Roots of the Service-Learning

Contemporary programs in service-learning represent the confluence of two important historical traditions: (a) the American tradition of service to the community, and (b) the experiential approach to pedagogy (Alt & Medrich, 1994; Shaffer, 1993). The value and importance of service to the community is reflected in the writings of Thomas Jefferson and in the works of the American philosopher William James. James (1910) called for a program of national service for youth that would function as "the moral equivalent for war" (p. i). The circumstances of the economic depression of the 1930s spurred the creation of community service programs such as the Civilian Conservation Corps that involved millions of unemployed youth with benefits to the environment, the society, and the participants (Shaffer, 1993). More recently, John F. Kennedy and Bill Clinton promoted national and community service as a means of tapping the best potentials within individuals and integrating youth into the community and the nation.

The philosopher and educator John Dewey advanced the view that active student involvement in learning was an essential element in effective education (Dewey, 1956). Through experiential education, students are challenged to discover relationships among ideas for themselves, rather than merely receiving the information about such relationships from the authorities around them. Dewey viewed the community as an integral part of educational experiences, because what is learned in the school must be taken and utilized beyond its bounds, both for the advancement of the student and the betterment of future societies (Dewey, 1916).

The Distinction Between Service-Learning and Volunteer Service

Participants in the field of service-learning make an important distinction between service-learning and volunteer service. In both activities, individuals become involved in service projects that are believed to be of benefit to others, their community, or their environment and from which they derive no direct monetary or material benefits. In volunteer service there is no explicit focus on the educational value to be gained through involvement in the particular projects. In the case of service-learning, the projects are designed, enacted, supervised, and evaluated with the educational benefits of the experiences as one of the consciously held goals (Nathan & Kielsmeier, 1991). Consistent with the objectives of experiential learning, practitioners in service-learning endeavor to have the students develop expectations of what can or should be learned as a result of involvement in the project. Both during and after the activities that constitute the service project, attention is called to the learning objectives as a means of fostering the educational outcomes. Both during and after the service activities, time may be devoted toward having the students and others involved in the project reflect on the nature of what is taking place (or has taken place), and the reasons that events have transpired as they have. Further, explicit efforts are made to integrate what is taking place during the service project with elements of the more traditional in-class curriculum. Although there is a great deal that individuals may learn on their own from their personal involvement in volunteer service, the absence of a systematic focus on the educational possibilities of such service inevitably results in less utilization of those possibilities than can be achieved through service-learning.

THE OUTCOMES SOUGHT
THROUGH SERVICE-LEARNING

The benefits believed to be derived from student involvement in service-learning activities can be grouped into four broad categories: (a) enhancement in the learning of material that is part of the traditional in-school curriculum, (b) promoting personal development, (c) fostering the development of civic responsibility and other values of citizenship, and (d) benefits accruing to the community.

Enhancing Learning Through Action

It is a fundamental assumption underlying the practice of service-learning, as well as other forms of experiential learning, that students will develop a better understanding and appreciation of academic material if they are able to put that material into practice in ways that make a difference in their own lives and/or in the lives of other people. There is an abstract quality to the subject matter of most courses in which the academic material appears only in classroom and textbook contexts. Students quite naturally respond to the classroom-based curriculum with questions about its relevance for their lives outside of school. By integrating academic material from the classroom with service activities in the community, the relevance and application value of the class content become more readily evident. As important, the hands-on application of skills taught in the classroom provides a clearer, yet simultaneously more complex, perspective regarding those skills. What is experienced through action will be remembered more vividly than what is merely read, or heard in a teacher's class presentation.

Promoting Personal Development

In seeking to use service-learning as a means of promoting personal development, it should be recognized that there is a wide range of outcomes that are included under such a heading. Many of the personal development outcomes will be a direct function of the particular nature of the service projects in which students participate, whereas others may be more generic outcomes of such experiences. Furthermore, in a classroom, students participating in the same project may respond to it in a wide range of ways resulting in diversity of developmental outcomes.

The attitudes and values held by students participating in service-learning projects will tend to be specific to the nature of the project itself. We would expect students involved in environmental clean-up projects to become more reflective concerning issues pertaining to pollution, littering, and civic pride, whereas students involved in a project in a retirement or nursing home will become more reflective with respect to attitudes toward the elderly, and about abilities and disabilities. But both groups may experience developments regarding issues about the role of governments, and what can, and cannot be realistically achieved through governmental efforts. It should be noted here that from an educational perspective, the goal is to promote a reflective development of attitudes and values, not the forming of particular attitude or value contents.

Service-learning experiences at the high school and college levels may also contribute to students' thinking about their career preparation. One of the difficulties of school-based education is that career decisions are often made without any extensive information about how day-to-day activities in the work environment are actually carried out. By getting students into the community for service projects, they are likely to receive exposure to a wider array of work environments than might otherwise be possible. For some students this might suggest possible career directions, whereas for others it may confirm or disconfirm decisions previously made.

Another type of personal development outcome that is likely to occur across different types of service-learning experiences involves increases in feelings of self-efficacy and self-esteem. *Self-efficacy* refers to the perception that one has the ability to bring about desired outcomes (Bandura, 1977). Service-learning programs have as one of their points of focus the development of those skills necessary for the conduct of the service projects; skills that are then enacted to make a difference in the lives of other people or in the quality of the community or environment. Students are thus in a position to appreciate the value of their contributions in a way that is generally not available in the classroom. Self-esteem is a somewhat broader concept involving the overall value assessment one makes regarding oneself. Although there are educational programs that are designed to increase feelings of self-esteem apart from the behaviors one enacts, the effects of service-learning on self-esteem are mediated through self-efficacy. If students have a perception of higher levels of skills and competencies that contribute to desired outcomes, the level of their overall self-assessment will be increased. Of course, higher levels of self-efficacy and self-esteem will only result if the students experience themselves as making useful contributions to projects they believe are worth their efforts.

Fostering Civic Responsibility

Consistent with the American tradition of service to the community represented in the ideas of Thomas Jefferson and William James, education advocates of service-learning are seeking to promote feelings of concern, care, and responsibility for one's community and the nation, in terms of people, institutions, and ideals (Barber, 1991). Involving students in service to the community at a relatively early age is seen as a way for students to come to recognize that individual and collective action can make a difference in the quality of civic life. It is believed that this will increase the likelihood that individuals will be involved in community service in a sustained way through the adult years.

Service to the community is also seen as a way to promote an identification with and involvement in community institutions, including governmental agencies. Recognizing the interrelationships among the levels of government can promote a sense of the importance of voting, political involvement, and, under some circumstances, political protest.

Contributing to the Community

An integral part of service-learning as an educational framework is that the students are providing real service to their communities. Whereas it could be argued that benefits to the community are not, strictly speaking, *educational* outcomes, it is not likely that positive outcomes in the other categories could be achieved in the absence of evidence that the students' efforts result in contributions to the community. Also, when educational administrators and teachers weigh a decision as to whether to initiate a service-learning program, ancillary benefits to the community may be used as one factor in favor of the initiative, although it is not likely to be the determining factor.

THE RANGE OF SERVICE-LEARNING ACTIVITIES

Service-learning programs have been developed for all educational levels from kindergarten through higher education. It is beyond the scope of this chapter, and indeed this volume, to describe the myriad forms that service-learning can take with the diverse populations with whom it has been implemented. It will be useful however to draw attention to some of the principal dimensions along which service-learning programs differ, and to catalog some of the principal types of programs now in existence.

Service Within Versus Service Outside the School Environment

Service-learning projects that are of direct benefit to others can be carried out without the students having to leave the school environment. Tutoring programs across grade levels have been demonstrated to be of benefit to both the students receiving the tutoring and those providing it (Cognetta & Sprinthall, 1978). Providing the tutors with structured opportunities to reflect on these service experiences and integrating material emerging from the tutoring sessions into the tutors' academic courses, provides the service-learning elements to such tutoring programs. Similarly, participation in peer counseling programs at the secondary level can provide opportunities for both service and learning.

Another model for providing service to the community within the school context is offered by industrial arts and home economic courses in which goods produced in the classroom are donated to community agencies. Typically, a direct connection is established between the students producing the goods, for example, furniture and clothing, and the individual recipients.

The alternative model is for students to engage in service-learning projects outside of school, that is, directly in the community. Such projects may involve identifying sources of stream pollution, improvement of buildings within the community, or visiting with the residents in retirement or nursing homes. The organization of project experiences outside of school is inevitably a more complex undertaking than providing in-school service experiences. Arrangements for transportation and on-site supervision must be made. Coordination must be established with community administrators for the sites at which the students will be carrying out their project. And issues of safety and insurance must be addressed.

Service as an Element in Academic Courses
Versus Service as a Separate Course in the Curriculum

One model for service-learning is to have service as an element in a wide range of relatively traditional academic courses. For example, for a college class covering tax law, students may have a project in which they donate time to provide assistance to the poor or elderly in the preparation of their tax returns. The experiences generated in the field can then be brought back into the classroom for discussion. In this example, the service is likely to be a one-time experience in a course. Alternatively, the service element may be built into a course on an ongoing basis, as exemplified by an introductory psychology course that entails the students providing service as a volunteer at a social service agency for 3 hours per week throughout the semester.

An alternative model at the secondary school and college levels is for there to be separate service-learning courses not identified with any traditional curricular subject area. These courses may involve having students work at a single site for a specified number of hours during the school term or may have elements of a survey course in which a succession of projects are carried out at different sites. Whether one or more projects are performed, the students spend classroom time in school reflecting on their field experiences and considering the relationship between what they are learning in school subjects and what is being done in the field.

Service-Learning as a Curricular Requirement
Versus Service-Learning as a Curricular Option

In some school districts, community service is a curricular requirement, with a specified number of hours of service required for graduation. Such a requirement would only be considered as a service-learning requirement if some provisions are made to have the students reflect on their service experiences and to use those experiences to advance the type of educational objectives described earlier. An alternative approach to a curricular requirement for service-learning is to require students to enroll in a designated service-learning course.

In many school districts service-learning courses are available as a curricular option. Students may select such courses on the basis of their personal values and interest, the reputation of service-learning at the school, and scheduling considerations.

ON THE USE OF REFLECTION
IN SERVICE-LEARNING

A recurrent theme in the preceding discussion of service-learning has been the concept of reflection as a necessary component for the realization of educational objectives. The importance of reflective activity in learning was discussed by Dewey (1916) and it has been a continuing focus of the work in experiential education. It entails the ability to stand back from an experience, in this instance from the experience of providing service to the community, to discover the connections between actions and their effects (Silcox, 1993). These connections are concerned not only with what occurred, the descriptive level of analysis, but also with why the events are connected as they are, the explanatory level of analysis. Such a reflective analysis of events in which the students have been active participants provides a wealth of opportunities for incorporating concepts from the traditional academic curriculum, whether in math, science, social studies, English, or other fields, depending on the nature of the particular service projects giving rise to the experiences.

One of the traditional distinctions with respect to reflective activities concerns whether the focus is placed on personal development and/or on more structured classroom learning. A second distinction concerns whether this reflection is carried out orally, during class time, in the form of student questions and comments that draw on what they have observed and/or takes the form of a written assignment, whether as a log, journal, or formal report. In neither instance are the alternatives mutually exclusive.

Reflection for Personal Development and/or Academic Learning

Reflection activities that focus on the students' emotional reactions to their experiences or on the development of skills and the recognition of increased competencies can serve to promote personal development. Because service experiences often take place in contexts with which the students do not have prior experience, and call for activities that they have not previously performed, there is often a noticeable level of anxiety present prior to the start of a service project. With actual experience in a situation, the context and the activities become more familiar and the students come to recognize the capabilities they bring to the situation. Their skills generally will improve over time, resulting in a reduction in anxiety and an increase in confidence. Attitudes in specific areas may change as a consequence of the particular experiences each student has. The function of the reflection activities is to draw the students' attention to the types of personal changes they are experiencing in connection with their service projects. These activities will themselves help shape the nature of the changes that occur (Waterman, in press).

Promoting academic learning through reflection on service activities requires a more structured approach. Although gaining familiarity with educational concepts from the classroom and participation in the service project may take place within the same general timeframe, the connections spontaneously made by the students between the two are likely to be haphazard and incomplete. In order to maximize the educational potentials of service experiences, reflection exercises can be used to focus the students' attention on those connections. Tasks can be assigned to draw examples of concepts from the students' prior experiences on a project or they can be cued to look for examples in a project they are about to undertake.

Oral Reflection and/or Written Reflection

Both personal development and academic learning can be furthered using either oral or written reflection activities. Either in discussions in the full class, or in smaller units, oral reflection is likely to take place spontaneously. Students will ask questions concerning what they have done, or what they have observed, or what they might have done differently. They will offer examples from their experiences regarding academic material being taught to their class. The teacher is then in a position to have the students elaborate on the connections between their experiences and the class material. The teacher can provide feedback concerning the success of the students' efforts and can give such elaboration as well. Teachers can also take a proactive stance in this regard by asking students to think about particular ideas when they next go on their service project.

Written reflection on service experiences may be in the form of logs, journals, and topical reports. Logs are descriptive daily records of the students' activities while on a service project. As such, they are of limited value from a teaching perspective. Journals are more often structured to elicit the students' emotional feelings while engaged in their service projects. Journal assignments are likely to be successful as a vehicle for students to gain an increased awareness of their personal and skill development over the period of time in which they are engaged in a service project. Topical reports provide a means to have the students focus on particular ideas or themes that are part of the curriculum and that may be observed in action as part of a service project.

THE ROLE OF RESEARCH AND EVALUATION IN SERVICE-LEARNING

Although the concepts of research and evaluation clearly are interrelated, the distinction between them should also be made. With respect to education research on service-learning, the focus of research is on whether such programs are effective in meeting each of the objectives discussed earlier, the nature of the student populations most likely to benefit from such programs, and the identification of those program components that contribute most to success. The focus of evaluation activities is narrower, with the concern directed toward particular programs, including their planning, implementation, and outcomes. The primary audience for evaluation reports are the teacher–participants in the program, their administrative supervisors, and representatives of their funding sources, whether school district, state, federal, and/or private foundations. It is important to recognize that evaluation activities, considered across programs, can help to answer a wide range of basic research questions.

Knowledge about what program practices contribute most to successful outcomes of service-learning, and why they work, can be used in the development of new service-learning programs and the improvement of existing programs. When such knowledge is generated at the level of the individual program, it is referred to as formative assessment, and the recommendations made are specific to the program assessed. However, the broader research literature can be used to acquire information on principles and practices in order to reach decisions concerning initial program development or the revision of existing programs. Following the lead of Conrad and Hedin (1991), it is the intent of the contributors to this volume to provide the foundation for the improvement of practice by identifying potential applications from the body of existing service-learning research. In generalizing from this research base to a specific program in which principles and practices will be applied, it is necessary to consider the nature of the samples contributing the original research data and their similarity to the student groups for whom the program is intended. It is also important to ask the extent to which the goals and objectives of the program under development or revision are similar to the goals and objectives of the programs contributing data to the research literature. The closer the match on these points, the greater confidence can be held with respect to the generalization of the applications recommended.

The existence of an extensive body of research literature on service-learning, and its continuing expansion, will provide the basis for continuing improvement in the quality of the educational programs we provide to our students. It will also promote a climate within the education community conducive to the wider adoption of service-learning programs in school settings. For this reason, it is desirable that research on, and evaluation of, service-learning programs should be an integral part of the conduct of such programs, with the results contributed to our knowledge base through publication or other dissemination within the field.

THE PLAN FOR THIS VOLUME

The chapters that follow are divided into three sections. Part I covers themes related to the methodologies for the study of service-learning. In chapter 2, Robert Serow presents a model for holistic assessment of service-learning programs, including both qualitative and quantitative methodologies. The potentials for the different methodologies are explored with regard to their suitability for generating information on the effectiveness of service-learning programs and the aspects of the programs contributing to successful outcomes. The contributions obtained from the use of qualitative techniques in the area of service-learning are presented by Robert Shumer in chapter 3. In addition, the research literatures on career education, school-to-work programs and other forms of experiential education are analyzed with respect for their relevance for service-learning. Chapter 4, by Dale Blyth, Rebecca Saito, and Thomas Berkas, looks at the contributions obtained using quantitative techniques in a large scale study of 20 service-learning programs of a wide variety of types. Both perceived and actual changes in the participants are reported and the evidence for differential impacts based on program characteristics is considered.

Part II consists of three chapters with a focus on the research pertaining to the elements that contribute to effectiveness of service-learning programs. In chapter 5, Janet Eyler and Dwight Giles, Jr. evaluate the characteristics of service-learning programs that have been demonstrated to relate to the extent to which such programs meet their objectives. The program characteristics identified pertain to both the planning and the implementation of the programs. The focus of chapter 6, by Rahima Wade, is on the role of teachers in the area of service-learning. Both personal characteristics of the teachers and the school environments in which they work are discussed in terms of their impact for teacher initiatives in program development. In chapter 7, I consider the role of student motivations for involvement in service-learning, the personality characteristics associated with the level of student involvement in service activities, and the variables relating to the willingness to sustain such service over time.

Part III of this volume contains two chapters on the role environmental contexts play in the conduct of service-learning programs. In chapter 8, Bruce Miller looks at the unique aspects associated with conducting service-learning programs in rural settings. The contributions service-learning make to strengthening school–community linkages and the implications for community development are evaluated. These themes are discussed by Novella Keith in chapter 9, as they pertain to the conduct of service-learning programs in urban settings. The emphasis is placed on the utilization of school and community assets as a means to advance educational objectives.

This volume concludes with a chapter by Richard Bradley (chapter 10), drawing together and evaluating the diverse contributions from the research literature presented here. He writes from the perspective of the service-learning practitioner looking to utilize the existing knowledge for the purposes of program development.

REFERENCES

Alt, M. N., & Medrich, E. A. (1994). *Student outcomes from participation in community service* (Report prepared for the U.S. Department of Education, Office of Research). Berkeley, CA: MPR Associates.

Bandura, A. (1977). Self-efficacy: Toward a unifying theory of behavioral change. *Psychological Review, 84*, 191–215.

Barber, B. R. (1991, Spring). A mandate for liberty: Requiring education-based community service. *The Responsive Community*, 46–55.

Cognetta, P. V., & Sprinthall, N. A. (1978). Students as teachers: Role taking as a means of promoting psychological and ethical development during adolescence. In N. A. Sprinthall & R. L. Mosher (Eds.), *Value development as the aim of education* (pp. 53–68). Schenectady, NY: Character Research Press.

Conrad, D., & Hedin, D. (1991). School-based community service: What we know from research and theory. *Phi Delta Kappan, 72*, 743–749.

Dewey, J. (1916). *Democracy and education.* New York: Macmillan.

Dewey, J. (1956). *Experience and education.* New York: Macmillan.

James, W. (1910). *The moral equivalent of war.* New York: American Association for International Conciliation.

Nathan, J., & Kielsmeier, J. (1991). The sleeping giant of school reform. *Phi Delta Kappan, 72*, 739–742.

National and Community Service Act of 1990. Public Law 101–610, as amended.

Shaffer, B. (1993). *Service-learning: An academic methodology.* Unpublished manuscript, Stanford University, Palo Alto, CA.

Silcox, H. C. (1993). *A how to guide to reflection: Adding cognitive learning to community service programs.* Philadelphia: Brighton Press.

Waterman, A. S. (in press). Integrating volunteer service into a course in adolescent development. In J. P. McKinney, L. B. Schiamberg, & L. Shelton (Eds.), *Teaching the course on adolescent development.* New York: Garland Press.

Part I

Methodologies for the Study
of Service-Learning

2

Research and Evaluation on Service-Learning: The Case for Holistic Assessment

Robert C. Serow
North Carolina State University

BACKGROUND AND OBJECTIVES

The argument advanced in this chapter is based on two premises: First, that research and evaluation (R&E) can contribute significantly to the continued growth and improvement of service-learning; second, that this potential has so far gone largely unfulfilled. To be sure, worthy studies have been conducted, and, as indicated by other chapters in this book, some notable results have been achieved. Such instances, however, seem more the exception than the rule. Thus, the basic documents in the field, such as the Principles of Good Practice (1990), are derived mainly from theories of experiential education and from the accumulated wisdom of many years of practice, whereas the educational policies that have brought new attention to service-learning have been based more on expectations of potential impacts than on hard evidence of actual outcomes. As one recent review noted, service-learning is a field where "anecdotal evidence is stronger than empirical data" (Buchen & Fertman, 1994, p. 14).

There may well be other reasons that research and evaluation on service-learning have not been more influential, but surely one explanation is that investigators in this field have taken an unduly restrictive view of what constitutes good R&E. The literature on program impact in particular seems to consist disproportionately of studies grounded in a single approach—namely, the statistical analysis of responses to surveys of short-term attitude change. As is argued shortly, quantitative analysis can play a useful part in assessing the effects of service-learning on individual development and on community well-being as well. The problems come when we rely *exclusively* on quantification for our knowledge of the changes that occur in conjunction with a service-learning program. Some of these difficulties are technical, in that quantitative analysis entails rigorous standards for sample selection, instrument validation, and hypothesis testing that are likely to be met mainly by those whose projects are generously funded. Consequently, program managers, teachers, and many out-of-pocket researchers have been unable to produce empirical data of a quality likely to be widely disseminated and discussed; meanwhile, those who are blessed with adequate financial backing have generally taken little notice of the field, although that apparently is changing. Another factor that may have limited the visibility and influence of service-learning R&E is the frequently muddled character of its results. Presented repeatedly with studies that mostly yield nonfindings or mixed results (see, e.g., Cohen & Kinsey, 1994; Miller, 1994; Rutter & Newmann, 1989) some observers may have leapt to the conclusion that measurement outcomes are inherently ephemeral, varying with every minute wrinkle in program delivery.

More generally, the point is what we find depends on where, when, and how we look. The primary objective of this chapter is to introduce an alternative paradigm, known as *holistic assessment*. Although not previously recognized as a distinctive model of R&E, the core ingredients of holistic assessment appear with some regularity in otherwise diverse studies of national service, grassroots voluntarism, and student service. The label itself, holistic assessment, seems appropriate because the studies that exemplify this approach examine not just service-related activity but also the broader particulars of human lives. It is holistic, too, with respect to method, so that its outcomes encompass real-world behaviors as well as answers to psychometric questionnaires, qualitative as well as quantitative techniques, community as well as individual-level data, and the needs and interests of a variety of both academic and practitioner audiences.

This presentation of holistic assessment proceeds in two steps: illustration and amplification. First, there is an overview of studies that collectively exemplify the holistic paradigm, including journalistic and historical accounts of national service participants, psychological case studies of local volunteers, and sociologically oriented research on community service participation by college and university students. Thereafter, the objective is to review some of the substantive and methodological issues surrounding holistic assessment.

SOME ALTERNATIVE ASSESSMENTS
OF SERVICE PROGRAM IMPACTS

The studies included in this section vary widely in method and focus. The only link among them, it appears, is that they all testify to the vast potential for personal and social change that inheres in service work.

National Service

Some of the richest descriptive literature on the impact of service on individuals has centered on policies in which participant benefits were secondary considerations. Consider, for example, *Soil Soldiers*, Leslie Lacy's study of the Civilian Conservation Corps (CCC), a New Deal agency that devised one of the most effective job-creation programs ever implemented in this country. As described by Lacy, the principal intent behind the CCC was to hold down relief costs and defuse social tensions by creating work for unemployed young men between the ages of 18 and 23 and, in the process, to address some of the nation's most pressing environmental needs. It accomplished both objectives in spectacular fashion, employing up to 2 million Corpsmen and implementing some of the most effective conservation measures ever undertaken in this country (Lacy, 1976). As to the personal benefits, the CCC offered nothing more than room and board, health care, and $1 a day in wages, which was expected to be sent home to support one's family. Although a 10-week educational requirement was also written into the law, in hopes of promoting basic literacy and hygiene, in practice education "was an extra to be used if possible (and) to be ignored, if necessary" (Lacy, 1976, p. 197). The real payoff usually took a different form—namely, practical, hands-on work training and experience. In only 9 years, the CCC "managed to produce 45,000 truck drivers a year, 75,000 bridge builders, 2,000 bakers, and 1,500 construction workers"—all skills that would be needed during the nationwide economic boom that marked the quarter century following World War II (p. 197).

The postwar years also gave rise to the GI Bill of Rights, a law that made substantial housing, education, and medical benefits to some 15 million returning veterans. Although the GI Bill is usually regarded as the very model of a modern benefits-for-service policy, its original goal, according to the historian Keith Olson, was less to reward the ex-GIs for their sacrifices than to lubricate the American economic machinery, thereby forestalling the return of the Great Depression that had been widely forecast for the immediate postwar era. In this respect, Olson argued, the Bill was "an unqualified success" pouring $14.5 billion directly into the nation's economy during the life of the original legislation (Olson, 1974, p. 101). This sum was eventually repaid many times over through the increased productivity, earning power, and tax payments of the 8 million men and women who took advantage of the Bill's education and training provisions.

The third and final model of national service to be considered is the Peace Corps and its domestic counterpart, ACTION. Much more modest in scope than its predecessors, the Peace Corps did not produce the massive economic benefits associated with the CCC and the GI Bill. But it has sparked a small stream of accounts documenting the ways in which the Peace Corps permanently, and for the better, altered the lives of those who took part in it. These included, in many instances, a lasting interest in international affairs and a lifelong commitment to public service and pro bono work (Landrum, 1986; Luzzatto, 1986). Parallel results have been produced by at least one study of alumni of ACTION (Gansneder & Kingston, 1990).

Grassroots Voluntarism

Most of the service work that Americans do is carried out on a comparatively informal basis rather than under the auspices of the federal government. Accordingly, it is worth examining the personal growth observed among those who participate in grassroots voluntarism. Two well-known examples of research conducted in such contexts are Robert Coles' studies of veterans of the civil rights campaigns of the 1960s and Colby and Damon's analysis of "moral exemplars," that is, those habitually inclined toward large and small daily acts of compassion. One conclusion emerging from both of these inquiries is that personal changes associated with service work are often of a global nature and are thus difficult to define with precision. Coles' (1993) discussions with civil rights workers, for instance, led to his finding that "(m)any veterans of those social and racial and economic struggles attribute the nature of their current lives to what happened 'back then'—to friendships and activities that decades later continue to exert a strong and decisive influence" (p. 256). When one man told him that "What I *am* today started with what I *did* in Mississippi in 1964," Coles saw the basis for a more general understanding of individual change—namely, that "being (is) a consequence of doing" (p. 256). Thus, from Coles' perspective, it is entirely reasonable to see acts or episodes of service as the basis for diffuse personal development throughout the life span. Colby and Damon (1992) made a similar point, with an emphasis on the explicitly moral dimensions of personal growth. On the basis of their close study of 23 exemplary community activists and humanitarians, the authors concluded that:

> (O)ver the course of their lives, there is a progressive uniting of self and morality. Exemplars come to see morality and self as inextricably intertwined, so that the concerns of the self become defined by their moral sensibilities. The exemplars' moral identities become tightly integrated, almost fused with their self-identities. (p. 304)

Student Service

Because they have involved major, often full-time commitments, both the governmental and the informal service initiatives mentioned earlier probably represent the outer limit of program impact. By comparison, service-learning projects in schools and colleges are usually of shorter duration, are less intensive, and must be integrated into a larger curriculum, where they compete with other courses or activities for the participant's time and energy. For these reasons, it may be instructive to examine some of the small but growing holistic literature on student service. One question that looms large in these studies is whether the burgeoning of the community service movement over the past decade prefigures the resurgence of 1960s-style political activism. The most comprehensive treatment of this issue can be found in Paul Rogat Loeb's book, *Generation at the Crossroads*. Here, comparison is made among several distinct clusters or types, including issue-oriented activists, the compassionate but politically uncommitted, and sizable residual categories of the indifferent and the alienated. The point then is that no one profile fits all. Nevertheless, this volume contains compelling portraits of several students whose increasing grasp of social, economic, and political matters stemmed directly from their involvement in community-oriented voluntary organizations. Thus, what was once understood as a personal crisis—such as the threatened loss of the family farm for a University of Nebraska student—gradually came to be seen in the fuller context of the ongoing transformation of American life (Loeb, 1994).

Explicitly political studies such as Loeb's raise a host of issues about the desired ends of service-learning and the ways they are measured. Although Loeb is generally quite respectful of students whose views differ from his own, it is nonetheless clear that he conceives of personal growth largely as the movement toward certain highly egalitarian political and economic objectives. It is reasonable to inquire, then, whether researchers who develop criteria of program impact do not have an obligation to take into account the student's own goals and values. This seems especially important in view of the evidence that a large proportion of service providers are essentially apolitical. In my own research (Serow, 1991), only a handful of the hundreds of students interviewed or surveyed identified a serious commitment to a social or political cause as a galvanizing force in their own service work. Instead, what drew most of them to the soup kitchens, literacy campaigns, and other projects were two factors: the desire to help others deal with personal difficulties of some type, and the desire to be personally efficacious in so doing. Such motives are evident in the words of Alexandra, an architecture major, as she attempted to explain her reasons for spending 5 hours each week as a volunteer literacy tutor:

> I had a friend in education who tutored first-graders. That sounded like something I couldn't do. I was spending so much time in studio that I needed something different. Then I talked to someone working with the literacy group. Everyone was surprised when I did it. Architecture isn't a giving field, and 80% of my friends wouldn't be impressed ... I don't think of myself as idealistic and I don't really look forward to it, but I'm very glad I do it. There's one person who wouldn't come if I didn't show up every week. (Serow, 1991, p. 552)

I have called the combination of these motives the norm of personal assistance, and believe that it is best understood against the background of the increasingly bureaucratic quality of both higher education and the workplace.

> Viewed solely from the perspective of the participant, volunteer work offers a form of personal empowerment in which one not only acquires and displays competence but attempts to extend its benefits to others. For many young people service has thus become an attractive alternative to the passivity of the student role and to the marginality of part-time paid employment. (Serow, 1991, p. 556)

The suggestion, therefore, is that students seek out service-learning in hopes of finding opportunities for certain types of personal growth and experience that are not readily available elsewhere. If this conclusion is accurate, then service-learning does not so much complement or supplement the formal curriculum as compensate for its deficiencies.

SCOPE AND METHOD OF HOLISTIC ASSESSMENT

The reflections on the politics of service-learning R&E contained in the previous paragraph set the stage for further consideration of the substantive and procedural

issues surrounding holistic assessment. With respect to substance, it remains to be
determined how wide a scope we should employ when weighing the possible
impact of the service experience on individual lives and on communities. Metho-
dologically, the main issues have to do not only with the balance between quantitative and qualitative techniques but also with the use of portfolios and other
mechanisms of holistic assessment for communicating effectively with both internal and external audiences.

Causes and Effects

One of the most critical needs in impact assessment is separating effects directly
attributable to a specific program from all other influences, both preexisting and
contemporaneous (Campbell & Stanley, 1963). In the case of initiatives that
generate broad societal changes, the investigator must not only document the full
extent of the transformations, but also be able to describe in some detail the
processes through which the changes occurred. In the case of the CCC and the GI
Bill, for instance, Lacy (1976) and Olson (1974) tied subsequent macrolevel
economic changes to the job training and educational benefits that these programs
made available to millions of young American adults. Such structural changes can
only be recorded over an extended period of time. Indeed, the recent observance of
the 50th anniversary of the GI Bill has brought fuller acknowledgments than ever
before of its role as one of the pivotal social and educational policies of this century
(Greenberg, 1994; Kerr, 1994; Olson, 1994). Much the same point applies to
measuring the impacts of smaller programs on their local communities. Whereas it
is relatively simple to document service delivery, gauging the true effects of those
services would require a much more extensive effort—one that is likely to consume
months and, in many cases, years of observation.

Partly because of the complexity of macrosocial measurements, but mostly
because the focus of this book is on service-learning, our attention should be
directed principally toward individual-level educational outcomes. If the societal
consequences of a program are in some sense the aggregated effects of changes in
individual lives, does it not also hold that long periods of time must pass before we
can truly claim to understand how a person changes as a result of a particular
experience? The need for long-range studies of human development is well established. Coles (1993), for example, quoted from George Eliot's *Middlemarch* to
precisely that effect: "Who can quit young lives after being long in company with
them, and not desire to know what befell them in their after-years?" (p. 254). But
studies of individual lives do not necessarily have to be conducted longitudinally.
One approach that has gained renewed popularity among social scientists in recent
years is the life history technique (Bertaux, 1981). In essence, life history (also
known as assisted autobiography) involves a researcher working closely with a
subject to assemble oral and/or written information about the overall course to date
of the subject's life. The same technique may be applied to several individuals or
small groups, though in such instances the focus narrows to a particular experience
shared by all members. As exemplified by Colby and Damon's *Some Do Care*

(1992), this "topical" approach to life history acquaints the researcher with the details of individual lives before, during, and after participation in a particular program and thus places the investigator in a position to judge the extent to which changes in individuals' life circumstances can be attributed to that program.

The operative word in the preceding sentence, of course, is *judge*, for none of the research techniques presently available to the social sciences is capable of conclusively establishing the precise causation of an observed behavior. Judgment, in turn, often depends on knowing which questions to ask. In the case of service-learning, it is possible to conceive of a great many concrete facts that would have to be established before the investigator could draw clear conclusions. Often, however, questioning might be expedited by conceiving of the relevant issues in terms of categories of possible outcomes. For instance, the alternative assessments of service-learning that were reviewed in a previous section of this chapter might be interpreted as pointing to at least four broad types of personal outcomes: (a) changes in competence (such as the job skills acquired by CCC members), (b) participation (the lifelong activism of some civil rights workers of the 1960s [Coles, 1993]), (c) understanding (of self and society, as reported by many of the respondents in the studies by Colby and Damon [1992]), and (d) relationships (long-term networks formed among Peace Corps veterans [Landrum, 1986]).These categories, together with several examples for each, are displayed in Table 2.1. However, two provisos must be added. First, it should be obvious that this list is intended to be illustrative, not definitive or exhaustive. The point, rather, is to suggest that even in a relatively open-ended research process, some degree of structure is helpful. Second, we can not assume that students' testimony will by itself constitute adequate documentation of the outcomes. Consider once again Alexandra, the architecture major who relished the positive impact she believed her literacy tutoring was having on her client. Thus, one outcome was the enhanced sense of self-efficacy that Alexandra derived from tutoring. But what about her client? Note that Alexandra does not specify why the client so eagerly sought the tutoring. Was it because of her skill as a tutor? Or, as in so many cases (e.g., Coles, 1993), was the payoff for the client simply the opportunity for personal interaction that the weekly session afforded? The point, then, is that the search for program impact must also take into account the perspectives of instructors, supervisors, clients, and other community stakeholders.

TABLE 2.1
Service-Learning Outcomes for Individuals

Category	Examples
Competence	Academic achievement, occupational or leisure skills
Participation	Involvement in community affairs, political campaigns, voluntary associations
Understanding	Social attitudes, values, motives, self-perceptions
Relationships	Recurring interactions, networks, friendships, mentoring

Qualitative and Quantitative

A cardinal rule of holistic assessment is that the method should fit the task. As obvious as this might seem, methodological flexibility has not always been viewed as feasible or even desirable. Rossi (1994), for instance, contended that given the high degree of methodological specialization among researchers and evaluators, few are competent in both qualitative and quantitative techniques. Accordingly, they are advised to stick to what they know. Arguments of this sort seem to reflect the long-standing antagonisms between traditionalists in both camps rather than the new economic realities that dictate versatility and adaptability on the part of those whose professional success depends on a steady stream of grants and contracts. Today, the consensus seems to be clearly in favor of multimethod teams (see, e.g., Datta, 1994; Hedrick, 1994; Smith, 1994).

The need to choose between methods may be obviated by circumstances that point clearly to one approach. Consider, for example, that although any of the outcomes in Table 2.1 could be pursued either through open-ended interviews (a qualitative technique) or through survey research (and subsequent statistical analysis), the utility of the data yielded by each approach might be quite different. Datta (1994) suggested that if the researcher's interest is in understanding the meanings that participants attach to an experience, then qualitative methods are normally to be preferred; if, on the other hand, the goal is to examine competing explanations for certain outcomes, then a standard statistical test would probably be called for.

Service-Learning Portfolios

Holistic assessment, therefore, is inclusive with respect to methods. The argument made at the outset of this chapter, rather than signaling opposition to quantitative techniques, is more correctly understood as a statement of concern about their indiscriminate use in the study of service-learning outcomes. Properly applied, surveys and experiments can be indispensable in assessing program impacts in such matters as academic achievement, psychological maturation, and social attitude formation. There are other instances, however, where multiple-choice answers and bubble sheets are no substitute for gathering more direct, first-hand evidence of personal growth. This is especially true of creative and experientially based courses. The increasing popularity of such courses, along with the expanded amount of fieldwork that is now required in some preprofessional curricula, may help to explain one of the clearest recent trends in educational evaluation—namely, portfolio assessment.

In essence, portfolios are an enhanced version of the cumulative folder that schools and colleges have routinely maintained on each student. But instead of merely compiling the abstract symbols of academic achievement, such as standardized test scores and grade transcripts, portfolios are filled with artifacts that the students themselves have produced as a way of documenting their interests and accomplishments. They may include creative works (essays, drawings, photos, tapes, computer programs, etc.), scientific or scholarly projects, awards and other tangible indicators of time well spent. And because they are cumulative, portfolios are especially valuable in charting the progress that one has made over a particular span of time.

Portfolio assessment has great potential for enhancing our understanding of the dynamics of service-learning. In fact, it is already in wide use, as when college or high school students are required to maintain logs or journals as a way of documenting the services they provide and recording their reflections on the broader meanings of these activities. The existing use of portfolios within service-learning could also be extended to include testimony from instructors, supervisors, parents, clients, and others as to the impact of the service project. Thus expanded, the portfolio contents could serve several purposes. First, they could provide useful feedback to teachers and administrators about a project's most and least successful features. Second, they could provide a solid evidentiary base for service-learning R&E. To date, external evaluators and researchers have made only limited use of such documents. One obstacle is the legal and ethical quagmire that surrounds the privacy of student records. Yet, given appropriate incentives for cooperation and the growing understanding that researchers and the people who formerly were called research subjects are actually partners in seeking and producing knowledge, it should be possible to arrive at a resolution that benefits all parties.

One way to increase the likelihood of mutual satisfaction between R&E people and program personnel is to construct a permanent feedback loop. In return for being granted access to a full range of potential data sources, researchers should accept the obligation to produce usable information, that is, findings and conclusions that are relevant to curriculum and instruction. Even better, they should include students and practitioners as members of the study team throughout all phases of the project, with full rights to consultation on everything from design to reporting. Such steps cannot, of course, guarantee that results will turn out to be significant or even interesting, but if implemented, they would at least represent a step toward the integration of inquiry and practice.

Communicating With External Audiences

Program managers, teachers, and students constitute the internal audiences for service-learning R&E. But what about external audiences, such as institutional CEOs, funders, board members, legislators, and the media? Specifically, is there anything about holistic assessment that would make it an effective device for communicating the outcomes of service-learning to these makers and shapers of decisions? Such constituencies, after all, are notoriously skeptical of claims of success that are not solidly documented. They may also be dubious about the meaningfulness of outcomes and can be expected to raise the famous "so what" question about the findings of research and evaluation. In other words, we should be prepared to defend both the plausibility and the significance of our results.

Holistic assessment can be helpful in addressing these concerns. Most important, holistic assessment focuses more on actual behavioral outcomes than on attitudes or values. Recall that of the four outcome categories, three (competence, participation, and relationships), were primarily behavioral in nature. This is not to say that the fourth category (understanding) is unimportant. But from a policymaker's perspectives, it may be that values, motives, and attitudes are best understood as proxies and triggers for behavior. So, although it would certainly be desirable for a service-learning program to show that it boosted students' scores on standardized tests of social responsibility, most legislators or board members would probably be far more impressed to know that students who completed the program subsequently decided to spend substantial amounts of their own time working in soup kitchens or literacy campaigns. In this context, it is worth observing that members of the assessment community are increasingly being required to support any claims of program effectiveness by documenting changes in actual behaviors. To some extent, this can be accomplished through process evaluation, the purpose of which is to verify that services are being delivered as called for in the grant or contract. However, there is also a growing expectation, reflected in the evaluation guidelines for the AmeriCorps and Learn and Serve America national service programs (Corporation for National and Community Service, 1994), that outcome evaluations also include behavioral measures of individual change.

In addition to its focus on actual behaviors, holistic assessment lends itself to plain-language reporting. To the extent that students and teachers are viewed not simply as data sources but as partners in the research process, considerable pressure can be exerted on the investigators to avoid the excessive use of jargon and other stylistic deficiencies that so often hinder effective communications between R&E specialists and potential audiences. Even in cases where more esoteric language may be called for, as in conference papers or journal submissions, it might be useful to insist that a parallel document, written in ordinary language and emphasizing the practical significance of the study, be circulated among external constituencies.

CONCLUSION

Service-learning, like experiential education in general, poses problems for the assessor. More so than conventional classroom approaches, service-learning tends to be flexible with respect to goals and objectives; what one gains from the experience may depend less on an instructor's preconceptions about good and appropriate knowledge than on the actions and interactions in which the learner engages. Certainly, there must be some degree of structure and oversight through which teachers and field supervisors attempt to influence the quality of the outcomes. But what makes the assessment of service-learning so challenging is that it ultimately requires the evaluator or researcher not only to capture the essence of the experience itself, but also to show that students are converting that experience into other outcomes, among which are competence, participation, understanding, and relationships (to mention the four outcome categories identified in this chapter).

In sum, what is expected of a service-learning program is that it lead the student to an enhanced "participation in reality," the opportunity for which, as Bellah,

Madsen, Sullivan, Swindler, and Tipton (1991, p. 174) reminded us, is a hallmark of the good society. In his final book, *The Revolt of the Elites and the Betrayal of Democracy*, Christopher Lasch (1995) made much the same point when he wrote that democracy requires that a very large proportion of the citizenry have opportunities to become fully competent, both in their work and in civic or community affairs. Transmitting the cognitive and motivational bases for full participation in the workplace has long been recognized as a core goal of modern educational systems, just as providing opportunities to apply those attitudes and skills, and to be rewarded for doing so, is a fundamental underpinning of the economic system. In its attempts to advance the interests of the community, service-learning often aims at those corners of society that lie outside the mainstream of power and opportunity. It provides chances to ask questions about the overall shape of society and about our own efforts as individuals. Such situations do not always lend themselves to orderly or predictable outcomes, such as can be readily captured by off-the-shelf questionnaires. For all of these reasons, it is essential not only that the R&E specialists take a more holistic approach to assessment but also that instructors and program managers—whose support is vital—encourage them to do so. The end result, if all goes well, would be not only better research and evaluation, but better service-learning programs as well.

REFERENCES

Bellah, R., Madsen, R., Sullivan, W., Swidler, A., & Tipton, S. (1991). *The good society*. New York: Vintage.

Bertaux, D. (1981). *Biography and society: The life history approach in the social sciences*. Beverly Hills, CA: Sage.

Buchen, I., & Fertman, C. (1994). Service-learning and the dilemmas of success. *NSEE Quarterly*, *20*(2), 14–15, 20.

Campbell, D. & Stanley, J. (1963). *Experimental and quasi-experimental designs*. Chicago: Rand McNally.

Cohen, J., & Kinsey, D. (1994, Winter). Doing good and scholarship: A service-learning study. *Journalism Educator*, 4–14.

Colby, A., & Damon, W. (1992). *Some do care: Contemporary lives of moral commitment*. New York: The Free Press.

Coles, R. (1993). *The call of service: A witness to idealism*. Boston: Houghton Mifflin.

Corporation for National and Community Service (1994). *Principles for high quality national service programs*. Washington, DC: Author.

Datta, L. (1994). Paradigm wars: A basis for peaceful coexistence and beyond. In C. S. Reichardt & S. F. Rallis (Eds.), *The qualitative–quantitative debate: New perspectives* (pp. 53–70). San Francisco: Jossey-Bass.

Gansneder, N., & Kingston, P. (1990). A longitudinal study at the University of Virginia. In J. C. Kendall (Ed.), *Combining service and learning: A resource book for community and public service*, (Vol. 1, pp. 37–55). Raleigh, NC: National Society for Internships and Experiential Education.

Greenberg, M. (1994). The GI Bill: Reflections on the past and visions of the future. *Educational Record, 75*(4), 57–61.

Hedrick, T. E. (1994). The quantitative–qualitative debate: Possibilities for integration. In C. S. Reichardt & S. F. Rallis (Eds.), *The qualitative–quantitative debate: New perspectives* (pp. 45–52). San Francisco: Jossey-Bass.

Kerr, C. (1994). Expanding access and changing missions: The federal role in U.S. higher education. *Educational Record, 75*(4), 27–31.

Lacy, L. A. (1976). *The soil soldiers: The Civilian Conservation Corps in the Great Depression*. Radnor, PA: Chilton.

Landrum, R. (1986). The veterans. In M. Viorst (Ed.), *Making a difference: The Peace Corps at twenty-five* (pp. 87–96). New York: Weidenfeld & Nicolson.

Lasch, C. (1995). *The revolt of the elites and the betrayal of democracy*. New York: Norton.

Loeb, P. R. (1994). *Generation at the crossroads: Apathy and action on the American campus*. New Brunswick, NJ: Rutgers University Press.

Luzzatto, F. A. (1986). The vocation. In M. Viorst (Ed.), *Making a difference: The Peace Corps at twenty-five* (pp. 153–166). New York: Weidenfeld & Nicolson.

Miller, J. (1994). Linking traditional and service-learning courses: Outcome evaluation using two pedagogically distinct models. *Michigan Journal of Community Service Learning, 1*, 29–36.

Olson, K. (1974). *The GI Bill, the veterans, and the colleges*. Lexington: University Press of Kentucky.

Olson, K. (1994). The astonishing story: Veterans make good on the nation's promise. *Educational Record, 75*(4), 16–26.

Principles of good practice in combining service and learning. (1990). In J. C. Kendall (Ed.), *Combining service and learning: A resource book for community and public service*, (Vol. 1 pp. 409–412). Raleigh, NC: National Society for Internships and Experiential Education.

Rossi, P. H. (1994). The war between the quals and the quants: Is a lasting peace possible. In C. S. Reichardt & S. F. Rallis (Eds.), *The qualitative–quantitative debate: New perspectives* (pp. 23–36). San Francisco: Jossey-Bass.

Rutter, R. A., & Newmann, F. M. (1989). The potential of community service to enhance civic responsibility. *Social Education, 53*, 371–374.

Serow, R. (1991). Students and voluntarism: Looking into the motives of community service participants. *American Educational Research Journal, 28*, 543–556.

Smith, M. L. (1994). Qualitative plus/versus quantitative: The last word. In C. S. Reichardt & S. F. Rallis (Eds.), *The qualitative–quantitative debate: New perspectives* (pp. 37–44). San Francisco: Jossey-Bass.

3

Learning From Qualitative Research

Robert D. Shumer
University of Minnesota

OVERVIEW

Some people believe service-learning is a relatively new idea. The fact is, it has been around for a long time. Service-learning is built on a rich history of study, primarily found in the fields of experiential learning, career education, and school-to-work programs. Whereas many quantitative investigations on service and experiential learning programs have focused on outcomes, there are several qualitative studies worth reporting that provide insight into the process of service-learning. Studies to be highlighted in this report are based on detailed, in-depth observations of programs. The duration of the studies is usually greater than 2 months, and in some cases encompasses up to 3 years of work. The information compiled through this process paints a picture of complex human interactions framed in a context of rich learning environments. The reports covered were completed during the past 20 years.

Reference to qualitative study indicates that information was acquired primarily through participant observation, interview, review of documents, and so forth; almost any discovery method other than paper-and-pencil tests. The majority of work on these studies included observation and interview of participants, staff, and community sponsors. All have something important to contribute to the overall understanding of the service/experiential learning process.

CAREER EDUCATION

Studies conducted in the 1970s on career education programs revealed a great deal about the process of how students learn in community-based settings. Experience-Based Career Education (EBCE) programs were the service-learning "fad" of the decade. Heavily funded by the U.S. Department of Education, these secondary education programs were intended to connect students with people and situations in the community to learn about careers and about basic, academic, and life skills. Many of the programs included service-learning activities, with students working in hospitals, schools, day-care centers, and many social agencies. Students tied their community learning experiences to classes held on campus, usually as part of their regular academic program. In many ways, these EBCE programs were more integrated into the curriculum than most service-learning programs today. Credit was often issued through academic classes in English, math, or career education. Much of the funding came from vocational education sources, and four major research and development laboratories (Northwest, Far West, Research for Better Schools, and Appalachia) developed the model programs and disseminated them throughout the country.

Four year-long anthropological studies were funded to examine how these programs functioned and how closely programs followed the models developed (Anderson & Drucker, 1976a, 1976b; Durgin, 1976; Smith & Theophano, 1976). The four studies focused on aspects of the learning process in carrying out and evaluating learning activities, and in applying the inquiry process to the field-learning experiences. The major intent was to determine whether the basic elements of EBCE (basic skills, career development, academic skills, and inquiry skills) were, in fact, operational. Researchers knew the original goal was to teach academic subjects through a community-learning base. Certain program features were designed to assure learning could be organized and documented to meet the needs of students, the community, and the school districts. The ultimate purpose of these studies was to determine if the structures and processes were effective.

Drucker and Anderson (1976a, 1976b) compared two lab models (Far West and Appalachia) with actual programs operated by those labs in Oakland, California and Charleston, West Virginia. The goal of the studies was to describe the structures of the program and compare it with the theoretical design. They observed the programs for an academic year and made their evaluations based on students' perceptions, on staff perceptions, and their own observations. They focused on staff roles, primarily because this was considered the most important aspect of the program for future implementation. Their observations were based at the school site itself, with the researchers occasionally visiting the workplace to observe students and resource people. Although not spending a lot of time in the community, they acknowledged that the people who served as teachers in the community helped to structure what students learn. The research focused on attitudes of students at the time of entry, on the setting, and on activities planned for the program. They did several case studies to illustrate how the programs functioned. It is from these case studies that we discovered something about the learning process as it related to the program models.

Most significantly, the research determined that student learning in the workplace did not go as planned. Both the Far West and Appalachian models called for structured activities in the workplace—one via a Project Plan and the other through an Activity Sheet. Students did not use these planning devices appropriately; in fact, they saw them as obstacles. Many learning plans were written post facto, instead of before, and student planning often depended on the strength of their worksite supervisor.

School site personnel responsible for supervising these planning documents were often concerned as much with the quantity of activities as with the quality (Anderson & Drucker, 1976a). They would check things off in a perfunctory manner, and the opportunities to discuss these activities with the student to measure the learning was inconsistent or nonexistent.

In the Appalachia program, the Activity Sheet assignments were to include investigations into the inquiry process. Yet, efforts to help students learn how to learn were not observed. In fact, the researchers report they did not hear discussions of the inquiry process, either in general or relation to student activity (Anderson & Drucker, 1976b).

Other ethnographic studies of programs in Philadelphia (Smith & Theophano, 1976) and in Tigard, Oregon (Durgin, 1976) revealed similar observations. Program designs where students were supposed to plan activities and to evaluate or reflect on what was learned, experienced "breakdowns" in practice. The flow of learning that was supposed to take place was either interrupted or nonexistent in several instances. What was anticipated as a systematic approach to building reflection and inquiry into a secondary school program did not happen for all students.

TUTORING

In a study of the tutoring process, Cognetta and Sprinthall (1978) reported that tutoring provided important benefits to those tutored as well as those doing the tutoring. Using both quantitative and qualitative approaches, they found that the students serving in teaching capacities improved in ego and ethical maturity. Students in high school who taught seventh and eighth graders reported growth in many areas, including self-worth, communication skills, and sensitivity toward others. Students said they were more willing to take risks, were better able to communicate with adults, and simply felt important helping others. This study, which corroborated the benefits derived from tutoring programs done earlier, laid the foundation for future research that examined the personal and social benefits of peer and cross-age tutoring.

WORK-BASED PROGRAMS

In another study using ethnographic methods, Moore (1982, 1986) described the observations made during a 3-year project at an experientially based high school in an urban setting. The school set up internships in field settings and students spent most of their time (4 days per week) learning at the off-campus sites. Like the EBCE programs, many of these community sites provided opportunity for service-learning; in fact, many of the settings were in hospitals, museums, schools, and other settings that allowed students to do service as they earned their credit and completed their work.

In contrast to the EBCE programs, there was little attempt to plan the learning experiences of students. They were able to function in any way their sponsor directed them and there was, in fact, little contact between the school and the field site. Moore and his staff actually spent most of their time at the field sites observing the interactions of students in their off-campus environments.

Moore reported that the experiential learning observed revolved around "tasks." Students learned about organizations and about applications of knowledge by performing various tasks or jobs at the sites. He analyzed the task episodes as to how they were learned and how the tasks fit into the structure and purpose of the organization.

The analysis resulted in categories of activities that were common to all tasks: establishing, accomplishing, and processing. *Establishing* referred to the process of setting up the tasks, getting information from the environment, and defining criteria for judging performance. *Accomplishing* referred to the ways students used information, objects, and people to get their jobs done. *Processing* meant the series of activities where students got information from the environment and proceeded to "apply them to the task." Included in processing was learning to read other people, actually performing the tasks, and reexamining the problems and developing alternative strategies for solutions. Moore emphasized that these social means (three functions) were not locked into a specific sequence; they were carried out in various ways as task episodes were performed.

Moore (1982) discovered that reflection, thinking about experiences in broader terms, occurred occasionally in the workplace, but not as frequently as had been hoped. School programs that were looking to utilize the naturally occurring thinking and guidance were going to have to add structures that assured the process took place. He said:

> Reflection rarely occurs as a natural component of work experience; that it has to be added on by educators. Our observations suggest that opportunities for reflection actually turn up in the real work more often than one might expect, although clearly not enough to satisfy us as educators. Both feedback and reflection may be regarded to some extent as corrective processes ... locating and understanding naturally-occurring opportunities for reflection strike us as important goals for experiential educators since this might streamline and enhance the educational potential of our programs. (p. 9)

Thus, reflective practices need to be important and intentional elements of sound educational programs.

EXPERIENTIAL-LEARNING PROGRAMS

Some of Moore's findings are reinforced by the national study conducted by Conrad and Hedin (1982) on various experiential-learning programs. They studied 27 programs, including adventure education, volunteer community service, career internships, and community study/political action. They specifically excluded EBCE programs because they were already heavily studied by others. Although much of their study involved quantitative measures from paper-and-pencil tests on subjects related to social, psychological, and intellectual development, they did interview program participants, staff, and parents to explore qualitative issues. Interviews and case studies reinforced the quantitative findings that students felt they learned more in experiential programs and that such programs were more effective than classroom programs alone in promoting feelings of improved self-worth. Interviews with participants also supported the discovery that more effective programs tended to be longer in duration and more intense (more than an hour per day). Most important, they noted that programs with reflective seminars helped students to learn more than programs without such opportunities to process the experiences.

EVERYDAY LIFE SETTINGS

This role of reflection was further studied by anthropologists in everyday settings. Research in the area of "everyday cognition" revealed that students needed adults to structure learning experiences in nonschool settings. Commenting on experiments with mothers preparing their children on a memory test, it was reported that certain structures or "scaffolds" were needed to lead children from the unknown to the known (Rogoff & Lave, 1984). Creation of familiar contexts for learning helped the child to acquire skills in new situations. The learner took an active part in the instructional process and assumed more responsibility for the actions as he or she became more proficient in doing initial tasks.

Other research in everyday learning environments reported similar findings. In numerous studies (Rogoff & Lave, 1984) this scaffolding or gradual matching activity was observed. Students did not easily transfer from one problem or situation to another unless they noticed the underlying similarity between the two. Program structures that assisted students in locating these common links helped learning to occur.

MENTORING AND EMPOWERMENT MODELS

In another study of experiential programs, Hamilton (1981) described important contributions of community-based learning. Part of his purpose was to examine program models, where youths are placed as individuals in adult settings or whether they work primarily in adolescent settings. Studying the Learning Web, a mentoring program where youth are placed individually with adults in community settings such as veterinary medicine, botanical research, and counseling (all of which can have a service dimension), he discovered that one of the great contributions of such programs is the exposure of young people to adults and the adult world. Asking students to identify the "five most important adults in your life" revealed that Learning Web students were not only able to name more adults than the comparison groups, but that they named individuals who were part of the community experience. Thus adult relationships seem to be an important component and outcome of mentoring-type experiences.

Hamilton also studied the Idyllic Foundation project in New York, a model that closely followed Foxfire, a program where youth work together to produce a magazine of local history, folklore, and crafts. Such efforts also encourage youth to get involved in projects to help their community. In these programs, youth set their own goals and design their own projects. Not surprisingly, Hamilton found that youth gain opportunities to take responsibility and to make decisions—not often available to young people in adult-dominated settings. Such programs afford students the opportunity to become engaged in learning activities of their own making, helping them to achieve levels of involvement not ordinarily found in traditional school settings.

The overall study pointed to the differing outcomes of community learning models based on their program design and what students do in the learning process. Depending on whether youth work with adults or other youth, they learn different things. In addition, Hamilton discussed the inherent variability of learning for each youth as a function of the student and the community settings. Different students have different agendas for what they want from a program. They also have different kinds of experiences depending how they interact with people at the site, so the predictability of what is to be learned is greatly reduced in experiential programs.

These differences were also noted with regards to staff roles. In the Learning Web, school staff worked primarily as counselors, providing guidance and feedback to participants. Most of the learning "beyond identifying interest" occurred through the community experiences. On the other hand, Idyllic Foundation staff worked continually with participants on all aspects of the program. Hamilton further suggested that this role is much more like a regular classroom teacher, who has overall responsibility for organizing and ensuring that good learning happens. The implications of these findings are that teacher training programs for such community-learning programs need to recognize these varying roles and provide opportunities for school staff to participate in a variety of program designs.

Despite these differences, he did disclose that experiential programs, no matter what the design, help adolescents to learn about themselves and help them to improve their self-image. Such improvement is based partly on the ability of youth to perform tasks of responsibility, where what they do matters to someone else.

Hamilton's (1981) final comments in the study focus on the wide variation of experiences found in community-based learning programs. This variation places great challenges for those who must evaluate such programs, especially when concerned about examining the internal changes in each student for areas such as affect and cognition. He suggested that "only long-term longitudinal studies following participants and comparable non-participants into adulthood and assessing career achievements and citizenship activities could demonstrate these kinds of effects" (p. 31).

Thus we learn about the challenge of assessing experiential-learning programs. One major difficulty is developing strategies that capture the varying agendas of the participants and the programs, as well as the nature of the community experiences and the assistance provided by community personnel. This is a very dynamic process to study that requires the utmost in design flexibility and sensitivity to individual experiences.

SCHOOL–COMMUNITY RELATIONSHIPS

Various themes raised by Hamilton were explored in a 6-month study of a magnet high school program in a large urban area. Shumer (1987) studied the role of school staff in operating a community-based learning program, as well as how high quality learning experiences were developed and monitored. In this study, seven learning sites in a medical facility were observed, with the researcher functioning as a participant–observer in both the community settings and in the school. Beside observations, interviews were conducted with students, school personnel, and community site sponsors. The focus was on how and what learning occurred and what role the school and community personnel played in ensuring good learning. The predominant activities were considered service-learning; curriculum for the field sites were developed by school personnel and tied into academic classes.

The study described various roles of the school personnel, depending on whether staff were teaching in classrooms or monitoring student learning as field-site coordinators. School staff integrated the learning from the field experiences into classes depending on individual styles and values. Those teachers who believed the community experiences were important to the overall program frequently provided assignments that included application and discussion of the field experiences in class activities. The English teacher, who probably included more site-related work than any other teacher, was herself previously a laboratory technician. She frequently talked about the value of the community experiences and had students write about them in journals and essays.

Teachers who monitored the field work usually spent minimal time at the sites and were concerned more with the regularity of attendance and general behavior of students than with the knowledge gained at the site. They often returned to the school campus (located across the street from the medical facility) to do more preparation for their traditional schoolwork rather than stay at the sites to further develop the educational program.

The researcher, who also worked as a school monitoring staff member, spent long periods of time at the observational sites and became involved in the development of the learning activities. Based on that experience, it was hypothesized that the quality of learning could be enhanced by school personnel if, indeed, they spent more time at the sites. This hypothesis was supported by follow-up observation and interview, where site staff talked about the level of involvement of school personnel necessary for good learning to occur. One of the conclusions of the study was that the quality of learning at the community site could be enhanced by the behaviors of the school supervising personnel if their attitude was that of being a teacher at the site, not just a coordinator.

It was also found that the quality of learning at the site was dependent on the level of responsibility given to students. This conclusion was similar to that of several other studies (Conrad & Hedin 1982; Owens & Owen, 1979; Moore, 1982). However, in this study it was discovered that the level of responsibility was actually earned by the interest, attitude, and behavior of the student—as perceived by the site staff. Tasks, as Moore (1982) referred to them, were assigned based on what the site supervisor thought of the student during the first few visits. If they thought the students were interested, capable of doing good work, and serious about the learning, they assigned them to more responsible activities. If the perception was the opposite, then students frequently found themselves performing routine work, the kind that was reported as being boring in studies done by Conrad and Hedin and Owens and Owen. Thus student behavior and attitude had some bearing on the quality of the learning.

It was also noted in this study that the curriculum developed for the community sites was best implemented by the site staff actually involved in writing the material. All the sites in this program had curriculum developed by school staff, the researcher, and by site staff collaboratively. However, only in sites where the community staff both developed the material and worked on it with students was there more effective implementation of the educational activities. At sites where the curriculum was transmitted by someone else, the quality level of learning (specifically related to the academic content outlined) was of lesser quality. Students would be as likely to be doing some nonacademic activity or something unrelated to the objectives of the site. There was even a noticeable difference in how site staff checked on student attendance, with those involved in writing the curriculum more involved in supervising the students than those who did not produce the materials.

DROPOUT PREVENTION PROGRAMS

A study conducted on an experiential/service-learning program designed for potential dropouts produced important information about the value of community experiences for student retention and school success (Shumer, 1990, 1994b). Conducted at a K–12 magnet school in a large city, quantitative and qualitative data were collected on student attendance and grades, as well as program components which were valued by students. Several case studies were conducted on students in the experimental and comparison programs. Interviews and observations were collected over a period of 4 months. Although the focus of the program was on community-based learning, many of the experiences of the students were service-learning activities conducted in such settings as schools, hospitals, and nonprofit community agencies.

Results of the study indicated that students in the community learning program made significant improvement in their attendance and their grade averages, as reported by both quantitative data and by interviews and observations. Students, who also rank ordered program components, reported that it was the community experiences, related to careers and to service, that kept them in school. They felt such experiences help provide meaning and context for their learning, allowing them to connect classroom activities with learning about life, careers, and citizenship.

The most important influence on their learning came from the college students who taught and tutored them in various subjects. Students reported they were more comfortable with these tutors who were closer in age than their official teachers; it was more "like working with a friend than a real teacher." College students also helped teachers to individualize instruction and to provide extra assistance in the classroom, promoting the community-based components of the program.

Like studies before it, case studies reinforced the value of the program in helping students grow in self-confidence, risk taking, and connections with the adult world. Students reported that they were better able to try new things and felt more comfortable working with adults. In fact, one of the key values of the program seemed to be the connections with the tutors and the community site sponsors. Human connections were what was desired by students in the classroom, in the community, and among peers. Students spoke about how much they valued the opportunity to learn about future careers from interested adults in the community and how much they appreciated learning their school subjects from concerned college students. Indeed, the ultimate value of the program was connecting young people with adult figures to assist in the adult development process. As did the students in the Hamilton study reported earlier, these students valued the relationships between their teachers, their peers, and the college and community people who were assisting in the educational process.

A PRACTITIONER-DIRECTED STUDY

In a unique study done by a practicing teacher, Mara Beth Gross (1991) followed four students involved in a community service program at Central Park East Secondary School in Manhattan. She wanted to give the students a voice in describing their own experiences Through observations and interviews she collected data on their development throughout the 1988–1989 school year.

Based on these data, she developed five themes about their experiences. First, she found that community service made students feel good about themselves. All four individuals explained how the community experiences of helping others improved feelings about themselves. Second, she found community service experiences exposed students to a world beyond their normal life. They were brought face-to-face with people outside of their school and families. Third, the community service experiences gave students responsibility and placed them in positions where others depended on them. The service activities put students in situations where they had to perform real tasks in the community—do things where consequences mattered to others. Fourth, the exposure to people and situations in the community allowed the students to meet new people and to learn how other people face challenges in life. This broad exposure to the adult world helped them to see the world from a new and different perspective. Fifth, the community experiences provided opportunities for students to be successful. Because some of the students had not felt good about their high school experiences, the service activities allowed them to interact with people and programs in such a way that they felt they accomplished things. Student self-esteem grew as a consequence of doing well in community activities.

EXEMPLARY PRACTICES

A key study of exemplary practices in service-learning was sponsored by the Corporation for National and Community Service in 1993. With funding provided to the Center for Experiential Education and Service-Learning at the University of Minnesota's Department of Vocational and Technical Education, studies of five service-learning programs were conducted, in addition to a teacher education program in a rural community (Berkas & Maland, 1993; Gorak, Huang, & Shumer, 1993; Huang & Shumer, 1993; McPeak & Shumer, 1993; Shumer, 1994b). The studies lasted 4 months and involved observations and interviews in both school and community-based service-learning programs. Programs included a K–8 Open School, a 9–12 Comprehensive High School, and three Girl Scout troops. Data were aggregated for all the studies, with general patterns and themes identified.

The first finding was that all programs were initiated by individuals who valued the use of the community for learning. Teachers or administrators started the school-based programs, and interested leaders began the Girl Scout efforts. What was significant was they all had a strong individual who started the program and convinced others to support it. In the case of the high school, the program was begun by a strong, progressive principal. He wanted students to have an experience similar to a domestic peace corps, so he worked with the social studies instructor to develop a service-learning class. The course has been offered for more than 20 years, with the same teacher conducting it. His enthusiasm for the class, supported by the school principal and the school board, has made a difference in the attitudes and behaviors of the students, and in the longevity of the program. The program continues because of the teacher. In fact, he is attempting to start a new program that combines English with his social studies class on service-learning. In addition, he plans to include more choices so students can gain even more control over their service-learning site.

Beside being started by individuals who believe in the principles of service-learning, exemplary programs demonstrate good communication between all parties, especially between the school personnel and the community sponsors. Such communication involves regular discourse between the two groups and a willingness to talk through problems as they arise. Like any good relationship, discussion between the parties becomes the watchword of success. In the high school program cited earlier, community sponsors mentioned the reason they continued with the program was the school personnel contact and support provided by the staff. Because there were two service-learning programs in this city, sponsors could choose to work with both, either, or neither. The fact is they decided the poor communication and lack of support from the other program was not worth the effort and discontinued participation with them. Thus, the constant communication and support made a difference in this community.

Another discovery of these studies is that youth participate in service-learning programs because they are fun. Youth of varying ages described fun differently. For first graders, fun meant they got to do things. For middle schoolers, fun meant they got to do things with their friends and the things they did helped others. It made them feel good about what they could contribute. For high school students, fun meant they were able to assume adult roles and to be responsible for things. When a substitute teacher in an elementary school relied on the high school aide for guidance and allowed the aide to run the class, this was fun ... and a challenge. Even community-based programs such as the Girl Scouts had youth agreeing that they participated in the service activities because they were fun ... they were social activities and they were things that placed youth in responsible roles. Thus the motivational aspects of service-learning, the enjoyment and pleasure, seemed to be essential elements of these supposedly exemplary programs.

Another common theme of these studies was that service-learning (and experiential learning) is holistic. When students described what they learned from the service experiences, it was always more than just about subject matter: it was about many things. They learned about themselves and their skills and abilities (which reinforces Hamilton's and Conrad and Hedin's conclusions); they learned about the world of adults and adult behaviors; they learned about careers and about occupations and activities they may or may not want to do; they learned about how subjects were applied in real-world settings, such as using math or language skills to compute the calories consumed by a senior citizen or to write letters to the families of seniors. Perhaps most important, they learned about how they fit in the world—how they could connect with others to accomplish things in a social setting.

Focus groups held with teachers at the middle school and high school in a rural community revealed that attempts to integrate service-learning into the curriculum had mixed results. Teachers noted increased motivation on the part of the students, increased sensitivity to others, and improved ability to apply learning to new contexts. They also commented on the increased motivation, initiative, and leadership shown by students who traditionally had not demonstrated such traits previously. Teachers noted changes in their own behaviors, working together more frequently on planning and implementing units, using community resources more, and generally having more engagement with students. They even saw general improvement in their enjoyment of the teaching process.

However, they also noted general problems with implementing service-learning programs. Such programs require more planning time, more coordination with community organizations and partners, more administrative support in terms of transportation and logistical assistance, and more administrative cooperation and direction in terms of evaluation of all the reform initiatives promulgated by districts and state departments of education. In other words, they need relief from traditional evaluation systems in order to feel comfortable trying new teaching approaches.

CONCLUSION AND DISCUSSION

With 20 years of research and evaluation behind us, what do we really know about service-learning? The answer is simple: a lot. In contrast to major quantitative studies that generally helped us to answer "what" questions, qualitative studies have helped us to understand the "how" of service-learning: how programs are initiated, how programs are operated, how students learn effectively in community settings, and how different programs produce varying results and require different roles for adult participants.

We learned in 20 years of study that individuals tend to initiate these programs on their own. They frequently have administrative and community support from both individuals and organizations.

Successful operation of programs is based on regular, open, communication between community sites and educational staff. Such communication ensures more attention to the learning taking place and encourages site sponsors to become more engaged in the process of connecting communities to classrooms.

Service-learning is fun. Participants routinely report what they did in the service project not only helped them to learn, but had a positive effect on their attitude toward learning and group behavior. Students at all levels reported service-learning to be an enjoyable experience, from just "doing things" as an elementary student, to taking on adult responsibility and contributing things of real value in high school. They also claimed the experience helped eliminate the monotony of school by providing breaks in time and by providing learning opportunities away from campus.

The central organizing learning component in community-based programs is the task. How tasks are established, accomplished, and processed is important; the nature of tasks performed is a primary determinant of the quality of learning experienced in community settings.

The quality and complexity of tasks assigned is dependent on the attitudes, behaviors, and skills of the students. Site personnel, alone, do not determine how work is assigned; they assign work based on perceptions of student attitudes and skills.

Efforts to plan and control student learning are not always successful. The process of learning frrom experience is dynamic; it requires methods of reflection and feedback to continually monitor its flow and direction.

School personnel, especially those assigned to supervise and/or monitor community settings, can influence the quality of learning at the sites. They can influence the quality of experiences if they perceive their role to be that of a teacher rather than simply a supervisor concerned with issues of attendance and general behavior.

Tutoring programs have positive effects on students' attitudes toward self-worth and provide opportunities for increased self-confidence. As the most prevalent form of service-learning in the country, such programs allow youth to serve their own school communities, working directly with teachers and other students. The results of these efforts undeniably help both tutor and tutee alike.

Program design has been shown to influence outcomes and other program characteristics. Programs where youth are placed with adult mentors in community settings tend to develop better relationships among and between youth and adults. Programs where youth work together show improvement in individual initiative and in ability to problem solve through group processes.

It is clear that qualitative studies in the past 20 years have uncovered a great deal about the experiential/service-learning process. We have learned how programs get started, how programs are developed and implemented, and how good learning occurs in community settings. Although we understand a lot, there is still much more to learn. We need to understand the long-term effect of service-learning on social and civic behavior. Do people who practice service activities while in formal schooling continue on as a regular practice throughout life? If so, how and why is it done? How are program purposes carried out so that outcomes are achieved (or is experiential learning not very predictable)? How do people in schools responsible for establishing and monitoring service-learning programs actually perform their jobs and ensure the program quality one expects from professionals? What is the benefit to communities in having service-learning programs and how does the benefit manifest itself?

Much remains undone. But rest assured, qualitative researchers will continue to contribute important information to our continuously increasing knowledge base on service-learning.

REFERENCES

Anderson, S., & Drucker, C. B. (1976a). *Experience based career education in Charleston, West Virginia: An anthropological perspective. External evaluator's final report on EBCE programs,* (Volume 2). Berkeley, CA: Educational Testing Service.

Anderson, S., & Drucker, C. B. (1976b). *Experience based career education in Oakland California: an anthropological perspective. External evaluator's final report on EBCE programs,* (Volume 3). Berkeley, CA: Educational Testing Service.

Berkas, T., & Maland, J. (1993). *Excellence in action: the community service learning program.* St. Paul: Center for Experiential Education and Service-Learning, Department of Vocational Education, University of Minnesota.

Cognetta, P. V., & Sprinthall, N.A. (1978). Students as teachers: Role taking as a means of promoting psychological and ethical development during adolescence. In N. A. Sprinthall & R. L. Mosher (Eds.), *Value development ... as the aim of education.* Schenectady, NY: Character Research Press.

Conrad, D. & Hedin, D. (1982). The impact of experiential education on adolescent development. *Child and Youth Services,* 3–4.

Durgin, E. C.(1976). *An ethnographic account of (CE)/2:; EBCE in Tigard, Oregon. External evaluator's report on the Experience Based Career Education Programs.* (Volume 5). Berkeley, CA: Educational Testing Service.

Gorak, K., Huang, G., & Shumer, R. (1993). *Exemplary practices in service-learning at an open school in an urban setting.* St. Paul: Center for Experiential Education and Service-Learning, Department of Vocational and Technical Education, University of Minnesota.

Gross, M. B. (1991). *Reflection in action: A practitioner's study of four high school students' experiences in community service.* Unpublished doctoral dissertation, Columbia University Teacher's College, New York.

Hamilton, S. F. (1981, Summer). Adolescents in community settings: what is to be learned?, *Theory and Research in Social Education. 9*(2), 23–38.

Huang, G., & Shumer, R. (1993). *A service-learning program: the Girl Scouts—Scenic Valley.* St. Paul, MN: Center for Experiential Education and Service-Learning, Department of Vocational and Technical Education, University of Minnesota.

McPeak, G. & Shumer, R. (1993). *Exemplary practices of service-learning in two girl scout troops.* Center for Experiential Education and Service-Learning, Department of Vocational Education, University of Minnesota.

Moore, D. T. (1982). *Students at work: Identifying learning in internship settings* (Occasional Paper #5) Raleigh, NC: National Society for Internships and Experiential Education.

Moore, D. T. (1986). Learning at work: Case studies in non-school education. *Anthropology and Education Quarterly, 17.*

Owens, T., & Owen, S. K. (1979, Winter). Enhancing the quality of community learning experiences. *Alternative Higher Education. 4*(2).

Rogoff, B., & Lave, J. (Eds.) (1984). *Everyday cognition: Its development in social context.* Cambridge, MA: Harvard University Press.

Shumer, R. (1994a). Community-based learning: humanizing education. *Journal of Adolescence, 17,* 357–367.

Shumer, R. (1990). *Community-based learning: An evaluation of a drop out prevention program.* Report submitted to the City of Los Angeles Community Development Department. Field Studies Development, UCLA.

Shumer, R. D. (1987). *Learning in the workplace—An ethnographic study of the relationship between schools and experience-based educational programs.* Unpublished doctoral dissertation, University of California, Los Angeles.

Shumer, R. (1994b). *A report from the field: Teachers talk about service-learning.* Center for Experiential Education and Service-Learning, University of Minnesota, Department of Vocational Education.

Smith, D., & Theophano, J.(1976). *The academy for career education: an ethnographic evaluation. external evaluator's final report on the EBCE programs,* (Vol. 4). Berkeley, CA: Educational Testing Service.

4

A Quantitative Study of the Impact of Service-Learning Programs

Dale A. Blyth
Rebecca Saito
Tom Berkas
Search Institute

Over the last 5 years Search Institute has been involved in evaluating the National Service-Learning Initiative and the Generator Schools Project. These efforts are managed by the National Youth Leadership Council and its regional partners, with funding from the Kellogg Foundation and the Dewitt Wallace–Reader's Digest Fund. Although most of our evaluation efforts have focused on the impact of training and the processes these initiatives used to implement quality service-learning, we also developed a set of *Learning Through Service* surveys designed to explore the impact of service learning on youth.

The surveys were specifically designed to assess the following factors:

- The nature of the service experiences themselves (nature of service activity, hours of service performed, with whom, and with what level of adult guidance).
- The characteristics of youth in the service programs (levels of preservice activities, service, risk behavior, and grades).
- The youths' perceptions of their service-learning experiences relative to their other classes.
- The extent to which youth changed their engagement in and disengagement from school and the learning process.
- The extent to which youths' attitudes and behaviors changed in such areas as personal and social responsibility, intent to serve, acceptance of diversity, and self-efficacy.

These surveys were made available free or at reduced rates to a wide variety of programs during the 1993–1994 school year. The schools that completed the surveys neither represent a random sample of service-learning programs nor a set of programs preidentified as being of high quality. It is the results from these surveys, administered to this voluntary sample of schools who participated in the study—most of which are neither Generator Schools nor directly involved in the National Service-Learning Initiative—that are reported in this chapter. Virtually all the school programs lack data from a comparable control group so that the results focus only on what happens to youth in service-learning programs and the youth's perceptions of these programs.

The current study, based on the limited literature available at the time, was designed to use the *Learning Through Service* surveys in an effort to get systematic data on the outcomes of as wide a variety of service-learning programs as was possible with limited funding. This chapter examines the data from these surveys on a mixed sample of service-learning programs to initially address four critical questions that face the field of service-learning:

1. What is the nature of the service-learning programs in operation?
2. What are youth's perceptions of their service-learning experiences?
3. What changes in attitudes and behaviors do youth in service-learning programs experience?
4. Are any of these changes related to any specific program characteristics?

After briefly summarizing the literature on impact and describing the various service-learning programs that responded and the number and type of youth involved, the data bearing on each question shall be presented.

LITERATURE ON IMPACT

In 1992, when this impact study was initiated, there was a variety of literature that described the impacts of doing experiential education (Cognetta & Sprinthall, 1978; Conrad & Hedin, 1978, 1981; Hamilton, 1980, 1981; Hedin, 1983; Hursh & Borzak, 1979; Moore, 1981) and of doing community service (Boyte, 1991; Calabrese & Schumer, 1986; Conrad & Hedin, 1982, 1989, 1991; Delve, Mintz, & Stewart, 1990; Hamilton & Fenzel, 1988; Hamilton & Zeldin, 1987; Hedin, 1987, 1989; Hedin & Conrad, 1987; Luchs, 1981; Newmann & Rutter, 1983, 1986; Rutter & Newmann, 1989; Williams, 1990). However, there was very little literature on the impact of the new generation of service-learning programs—particularly based on pre–post analysis of quantitative data. The literature that did exist (e.g., Caskey, Cairn, Kielsmeier, & McPherson, 1991; Conrad & Hedin, 1991) was not very conclusive about either the magnitude or nature of potential impacts. Often the research was based on either one specific, often intense, program (e.g., Calabrese & Schumer, 1986; Hamilton & Zeldin, 1987) or on a variety of experiential education and community service programs (e.g., Conrad & Hedin, 1982; Hedin, 1983; Williams, 1990).

A brief summary of the literature that describes the quantitative analysis of the impacts of experiential education, community service, or service-learning on the students doing the education, service, or learning finds Cognetta and Sprinthall (1978) indicating increased self-confidence, Cognetta and Sprinthall and Conrad and Hedin (1982) finding more principled moral reasoning, and Hursh and Borzak (1979) and Conrad and Hedin (1989) noting increases in self-understanding. Luchs (1981), Conrad and Hedin (1982), and Hedin (1989) found increases in self-esteem. Luchs and Conrad and Hedin also found increases in social efficacy. Luchs, Conrad and Hedin (1982), and Giles and Eyler (1994) all found that students improved their attitudes toward adults and to the people and organizations with whom they worked. Conrad and Hedin (1982) and Newman and Rutter (1983) both found that service programs can at least modestly increase students' sense of personal competence. Conrad and Hedin, Newman and Rutter, and Hamilton and Fenzel (1988) all found gains in social responsibility. Newmann and Rutter (1983) also found gains in social competence. Conrad and Hedin (1982) found that students increased their problem-solving abilities. Luchs (1981) and Calabrese and Schumer (1986) found fewer disciplinary problems, and increases in grade point averages. Calabrese and Schumer (1986) also found reduced levels of isolation and alienation. Conrad and Hedin (1982, 1989) found increases in intellectual growth. Hedin (1987) showed increases in math and reading scores for those students who have done tutoring while Conrad and Hedin (1982) and Hamilton and Zeldin (1987) explained gains in factual knowledge in the areas most directly related to the field experience. Conrad and Hedin (1989) also found increases in self-understanding. Finally, Markus, Howard, and King (1993) and McCluskey-Fawcett and Green (1992) found improvement in the integration of theory and practice.

Although there is now more literature (e.g., Alt & Medrich, 1994; Batchelder & Root, 1994; Burke, 1993; Cohen & Kinsey, 1994; Dewsbury-White, 1995; Giles & Eyler, 1994; Kraft & Krug, 1994; Markus, Howard, & King, 1993; McCluskey-Fawcett & Green, 1992; Miller, 1994; Switzer et al., 1995; Yates & Youniss, 1996) and at least one major new systematic study of the impact of K–12 *Serve America* programs (Melchior & Orr, 1995), these results were not available when the present study was initiated. Furthermore, such research is complicated by the wide variety of programs that are described as service-learning and the very different goals such programs may have—from improving achievement (Markus, Howard, & King, 1993) to improving civic responsibility (Rutter & Newmann, 1989) to promoting healthier psychosocial development (Switzer et al., 1995). The present study is designed to add to our understanding of impacts for different types of programs.

THE SEARCH INSTITUTE STUDY

In the spring of 1992, Search Institute sent out materials describing our study and asking people in service-learning programs from around the country if they would be willing to administer a set of three *Learning Through Service* surveys. The set consisted of a pre- and a postservice-experience survey designed for 6th- through 12th-grade youth as well as a staff survey designed to get a description of the service-learning program from the perspective of the person most directly responsible for its operation. The invitations went to more than 100 schools, many who had been affiliated with the Generator School Program, the National Service-Learning Initiative and its regional efforts, or who had received training in service-learning from the National Youth Leadership Council. Depending on the nature of the relationship to the funded programs, the survey and results were offered free of charge or on a sliding-fee scale. Sites that indicated they were able to provide a control or comparison groups were also offered a discount.

More than 15 service-learning programs replied, including some with multiple classrooms within some programs. Surveys were sent to each site and were to be administered by school staff. Surveys were anonymous but with a linking code to permit an analysis of individual change. Unfortunately, many schools found the youth surveys too long or failed to administer the postservice survey. In the end, only 10 programs provided data that were useable and where a majority of the pre- and postsurveys could be linked. This loss of data, and all comparison groups, is truly unfortunate and probably a direct result of two factors—the length of the surveys and the difficulties teachers have in conducting such studies in their classrooms with only minimal instructions and no special support.

The present analysis consists of data from 369 youth who completed both the pre- and postsurveys. This sample reflects a matching rate of 62%. These youth come from 10 different service-learning programs and 25 different classrooms:

- Two classes from two different middle school programs.
- 16 ninth-grade classes in a mandatory service-learning program.
- Six classes from six different senior high school programs.
- One class from a program for high school seniors only.

Although the results will occasionally be presented by program type or by a characteristic describing the service-learning experience (e.g., presence of reflection), this analysis generally combines all youth into one group for analysis because the intent was to find any broad impacts common to a variety of programs. The wisdom of this broad-based analysis approach is discussed further in the final section.

WHAT CHARACTERIZES SERVICE-LEARNING PROGRAMS AND THE YOUTH INVOLVED IN THEM?

Nature of Service Experience

The nature of the service-learning experiences varied considerably in this sample based on youth's responses to a series of questions about the nature of their service experience. Youth could answer yes to more than one question. Most of the youth (51%) were involved in environmental or beautification projects. Forty-nine percent were in service activities directly helping others such as tutoring or working in a nursing home. Forty-one percent of all youth indicated they did general volunteer work—helping out an organization by answering phones, typing, and so forth. Thirty-five percent were engaged in educational or specific prevention presentations to others. Only 19% indicated their activities were "political" (e.g., working to change laws or getting signatures on petitions).

When asked specifically about whether most of their service activities helped others directly, indirectly, or were of some other type, 40% of youth reported service experiences directly helping other people, 25% reported their service experiences indirectly helped people, and 35% reported experiences of a noninterpersonal kind (e.g., recycling cans). More than half of the youth (56%) in environmental types of projects saw these efforts as not directly helping other people.

Hours of Service

Forty-four percent of youth reported that they performed more than 40 hours of service in their program with another 15% doing between 21 and 40 hours, and 20% doing between 5 and 20 hours. However, fully 20% of youth did less than 5 hours of service during their entire service-learning experience. Staff perceptions of the hours of service performed tended to be higher than those reported by youth. The ninth-grade mandatory service program reported the highest number of service hours and the middle school programs tended to involve fewer hours of service than the high school programs. This last finding is consistent with the Abt Associates and Brandeis University study of Serve America programs (Melchior & Orr, 1995).

Length of the Service-Learning Programs

Staff reported that the length of service-learning programs varied with the grade levels involved. Middle school programs tended to be just several weeks in duration whereas high school programs (other than the ninth-grade mandatory program) were typically a full year in length. The ninth-grade mandatory programs were reported as either semester- or quarter-long efforts. The length of a program was not directly related to the total number of service hours youth performed.

Amount and Nature of Reflection Activities

In general, teachers tended to report more reflection activities than youth recognized. Fifty-nine percent of the staff reported devoting at least 20% of their time to reflection activities and only 1 of 10 said they did not do any reflection at all. By contrast, twice as many students (21%) reported they engaged in no reflection activities (i.e., time spent after the service activity talking or writing about your experience). Another 25% of students reported only a little time spent in reflection. A majority of students noted they spent some (34%) or a lot (21%) of time on reflection. The amount of reflection reported by both teachers and students varied widely at all grade levels and even by students within the same program. The mandatory ninth-grade service-learning program tended to involve somewhat more reflection according to student reports.

The type of reflection activities reported by teachers focused heavily on written assignments including using papers (72%), journals (62%), and other projects

(53%). Discussion was also very common with 91% of teachers reporting some form of whole class discussion, 64% noting small group discussions, and 52% saying they discussed the experience on a one-to-one basis with students—especially in the ninth grade and high school programs. Youth were not asked about the nature of the reflection in which they engaged.

Characteristics of Youth in These Service-Learning Programs

Fifty-eight percent of youth in these programs were females and about one third had mothers and/or fathers with some college education. As a group, 17% did 6 or more hours of homework a week (compared to 23% in general samples of youth, reported in Benson, 1993), and 28% did less than 1 hour per week. Approximately 54% spent 6 or more hours a week in various music, sport, and club activities (about the same as in general samples of youth). Fifty-five percent reported above average grades (As and Bs) compared to 47% of youth in a general survey. Forty-three percent reported no involvement in drug or alcohol use, vandalism, stealing, or fighting whereas 21% engaged in at least three of these six behaviors in the last 12 months. No directly comparable figures for a general sample are available but these would appear to be modest levels—they are neither particularly high or low. Finally, at the time of the pretest survey, 77% of the youths report less than 1 hour of volunteer work per week. This level is roughly similar to that in other studies we have done of youth in grades 6 through 12 (Benson, 1993).

In summary, the youth in these service-learning programs do not appear to be very different from youth in the general population. They may be somewhat more likely to be females, have slightly higher grades, and be involved in somewhat less high-risk behavior but they are clearly not exclusively highly involved, service-oriented students who only get above average grades. This diversity of youth provides a good general test of the benefits of service-learning in the areas to be explored next.

HOW DO YOUTH PERCEIVE THEIR
SERVICE-LEARNING EXPERIENCE?

In order to assess how youth perceived their service-learning experience along a variety of dimensions, the survey completed after the experience included a number of questions. Some were about the nature of relationships youth formed whereas others asked youth to agree or disagree with a series of statements about their service-learning experiences.

Perceived Impact on Relationships With Others

One benefit of participating in service-learning efforts is that youth may get to know better the people they help, the adults who run the program, and the variety of other youth in the program. Building positive relationships in constructive contexts is an important part of healthy adolescent development. In this study, 42% of the youth reported they got to know the people they helped very well or somewhat well during their service experience. Because 21% of youth did not work with other people, this means over half (52%) of youth who worked to help people got to know them at least somewhat well. These are often people they would not otherwise have come to know at all. Furthermore, more than half the youth (54%) reported getting to know the adults who run the program very well or somewhat well. Although these are often teachers they already have, they may now see them in a new, more holistic context. Finally, 68% of youth report the service experience helped them get to know the other youth involved in the activities very well or somewhat well. To the extent that these are youth from a single class they are probably not youth who would have gotten to know each other very well in a traditional classroom. These results are encouraging because positive relationships and getting to know other people in new ways and in new contexts is helpful in an era when too many youth are isolated from adults and people who are different than they are.

Perceived Involvement and Impact on Community

Overall, 54% of youth strongly agreed or agreed with the statement that they "felt highly involved in what they were doing." Only 15% disagreed with the statement. More high school youth than middle school youth felt this way, with the ninth graders in the mandatory service program in the middle.

Youth also felt their service made a difference in the community. When asked to agree or disagree with the following statement—"My service activities did *not* make any difference in improving my community"—47% disagreed or strongly disagreed. Only 18% agreed or strongly agreed. Once again the high school programs, and to a lesser extent the mandatory ninth-grade program, felt they had more impact on their communities. As was the case for personal involvement, about one third of the youth neither agreed nor disagreed with the statements.

These results suggest that most youth, although not a majority, see their service experiences as engaging them and helping them make a difference in their communities. Few (less than one in five) felt uninvolved or that their efforts made no difference.

Perceived Impact on Feelings, Skills, and Thinking

A majority of youth (56%) agreed or strongly agreed with the statement that "My service activities showed me how good it feels to help people." Only 14% disagreed or strongly disagreed and 30% neither agreed nor disagreed (most of whom did not even work directly helping people). The high school programs were especially strong in this area (with over 60% of youth agreeing) compared with the ninth-grade and middle school programs. To the extent that increasing the value of helping others is often a goal of service-learning programs, this data suggests that most youth feel good about helping others after their service experience.

The data on perceived increases in basic academic skills and thinking are intriguing. More youth disagreed (37%) than agreed (26%) with the statement that "My service experience improved my basic academic skills (like reading, writing, and math)." Thirty-seven percent neither agreed nor disagreed. In contrast to this, 50% of youth agreed or strongly agreed that their "service experience made me think harder about things I normally do not think about." Only 17% disagreed with this statement. Youth also were much more likely to agree than disagree that their service experience "showed me how much more can be done when people work as a team" (58% vs. 13%) and that as a result of their service experience "I feel better prepared to plan a project from beginning to end" (46% vs. 15%). Furthermore, as shown below, youth were more likely to disagree than agree with a statement that says they "learned less through my service experience than ... regular classes."

Taken together, these data are remarkably similar to conclusions drawn by 40 experts at the Service-Learning Summit held in September 1995 (Blyth & Kroenke, 1996). At that summit, experts were split on the importance of emphasizing or de-emphasizing changes in basic academic skills. They preferred placing greater emphasis on improved critical thinking and problem solving as likely outcomes of service-learning programs. The strength of quality service-learning experiences may have more to do with how they help youth think and work together in teams than in how they help youth improve basic academic skills. Given the importance of critical thinking, project planning, and teamwork in today's business world, these types of changes may be exactly what many leaders desire. As we see later, service-learning may also affect the willingness of youth to engage in learning.

Youths' Perceptions of Service Classes
Relative to Their Regular Classes

The survey contained seven statements about how the youth's service classes compared with their other regular classes. Table 4.1 summarizes youth's reactions to these statements. In brief, students felt their service-learning classes were somewhat more enjoyable (38% vs. 27%), less boring (47% vs. 21%), more related "to my life outside of school" (40% vs. 24%), and that they learned more (39% vs. 25%) than in their regular classes. Youth did not, however, feel their service-learning classes made them work harder (29% vs. 33%), become more interested in their other classes (30% vs. 28%), or talk more with others about what they did (31% vs. 31%) than their regular classes. In all three of these areas there were essentially no differences in the proportions who agreed or disagreed. For all questions, many youth (typically more than one third) did not report any differences between their service-learning classes and their regular classes. These results, taken as a whole, suggest that whereas about a third of youth in a wide range of service-learning experiences do not see their service-learning experiences differently than their regular classes, those that do more often respond positively to the experiences than negatively.

TABLE 4.1
Youths' Perceptions of Their Service-Learning and Regular Classrooms

Statement	Percent Who ...		
	Strongly Agreed or Agreed	Had No Opinion	Disagreed or Strongly Disagreed
I enjoy my regular classes more than my service experience.	27%	35%	38%
My service experiences are boring compared to regular classes.	21%	32%	47%
The things I learn through my service experience do not relate any more to my life outside of school than my regular classes do.	24%	36%	40%
I learned less through my service experience than I have in my regular classes.	25%	36%	39%
I work harder in my regular classes than in my service experiences.	33%	38%	29%
My service experience made me more interested in my other classes.	30%	42%	28%
I talk more with others about my service experience than about my regular classes.	31%	38%	31%

WHAT CHANGES IN ATTITUDES AND BEHAVIORS DO YOUTH IN SERVICE-LEARNING PROGRAMS EXPERIENCE OVER TIME?

The two youth surveys contained identical items in 13 domains to assess whether there were significant changes over the course of the program (either a semester or a full academic year). Scales were created within five basic areas: attitudes toward social responsibility for service and the intent to serve (in three different domains); the nature of youth's engagement with at-risk behaviors and disengagement from school; youth's engagement in academic tasks and learning more broadly; personal development; and the acceptance of diversity. The internal reliability of the scales are reported in terms of Cronbach's alphas. Each of these domains are examined separately.

Changes in Social Responsibility for Service and the Intent to Serve

Social responsibility for service and the likelihood or intent to serve in the future was measured in three broad domains—environmental issues, civic involvement, and service to others. Three or four item scales were created to measure all six constructs. All had alpha levels over .74 except for social responsibility for service to others (where the alpha was .63). The scales are adapted from those created by Conrad and Hedin (1981). Changes over time were tested for significance through a regression approach that uses change scores as the dependent variable with the time one score included as a predictor.

Environmental Issues.   In general, youth in service-learning programs reported less socially responsible attitudes to the environment over time. This was significant overall ($p = .03$) and in one of the six specific programs in which there were enough students responding to test for an effect within the program. Although surprising, this result appears to be primarily a function of unusually high, socially responsible attitudes in this area early in the programs (9.5 on a scale that ranges from 3 to 12). This type of ceiling effect is not unusual in areas where there is widespread agreement on socially desirable ways to respond or where the programs may especially emphasize such attitudes early in their programs as may be the case here. Furthermore, although there was no overall change in the intent to serve the environment in the future, the same school program which showed decreased social responsibility earlier also experienced a decreased interest in future service to the environment. However, it is also important to state that, across all programs, those youth actually involved in environmental activities for their service project were more likely to say they would engage in future environmental activities than those whose service was not related to the environment. A similar difference was not found with respect to a sense of social responsibility for the environment, which was high in both groups at the beginning of the study and did not change differentially.

Civic Involvement.   With respect to social responsibility for civic involvement, there was no significant change overall. In looking at particular programs, one program changed attitudes significantly in a positive direction and another changed significantly in a negative direction. Most showed little change at all. There was a slight and almost significant ($p = .07$) increase in the overall intent to become civicly involved. There were positive changes in this scale in three of the programs and negative changes in only one. These results indicate both the potentially negative impact of some service-learning programs on civic involvement and the need to examine what particular programs are doing that accounts for these differences. For example, it is worth noting that the one program with negative consequences in both aspects of civic involvement was also the only program to have consistently negative impact in multiple areas—including social responsibility toward the environment, reduced academic engagement, increased disengagement from school, and increased risk behaviors. Unfortunately, why this particular program had these effects can not be determined from the present data.

Others in Need.   Finally, with respect to social responsibility for others in need, youth reported a significantly lower sense of responsibility after the service projects than before ($p = .02$). Once again, this unexpected finding appears to be due to very high (6.2 on a scale that ranges from 2 to 8) scores at Time 1. This interpretation is supported by the fact that only one program showed a significant reduction in responsibility and it had the highest Time 1 scores (7.2). There was no overall change in the intent to help others and none of the individual programs changed significantly.

Unlike the scales for the environmental issues, youth in programs that involved helping others showed no differences in either the responsibility or intent scales when compared to those youth who were not doing helping activities. However, when we examined those youth who reported they actually got to know the people they helped, we found they were more likely to serve others in the future than other youth. The formation of a relationship with those helped, rather than the performance of the service per se appears to make a difference.

Summary.   Changes in youths' attitudes about social responsibility and the intent to serve in three domains appears to be a function of how high the attitudes already were early in the program and the specific nature of the service program and activity. Where the actual service experience directly relates to the domain investigated, or where youth actually get to know the people they helped, significant differences in the expected direction were often found. These results have implications for more closely aligning expectations for impact with program goals and content rather than searching for a broad array of effects—an observation also made by many experts at the Service-Learning Summit (Blyth & Kroenke, 1996).

Youth Engagement in Risk Behaviors and Disengagement From School

Overall, there was no mean change on a scale assessing six at-risk behaviors. Two programs showed small but significant increases in at-risk behaviors but because there is no comparison group these may simply be due to the general increases in these at-risk behaviors over time. Similarly, the fact that the at-risk behaviors did not increase overall may be a good sign.

Youth in the service-learning programs examined did become slightly more disengaged ($p = .001$) from school (i.e., they skipped a class or day of school, or were sent to the principal's office, or were suspended slightly more often). Only two programs showed this pattern, one a high school and one a middle school. There were no differences in the other programs. The findings in one of the two schools may be partially explained by the higher potential for an overall increase in disengagement from school in inner-city areas.

The results in this area are mixed to negative although the scales have adequate internal reliability (alphas of .69 and .74). Without adequate control or comparison groups and with a tendency for these problems to increase with age, it is impossible to interpret the findings clearly. Further work is clearly needed in this area.

Engagement in Academic Tasks and Learning

The surveys also included a series of items about the extent to which youth were engaged in regular academic activities (e.g., trying hard, coming to class prepared, and really paying attention) as well as learning more broadly (relating learning to life outside of school, getting excited about learning, thinking in new ways, seeking out extra materials, and talking to others about it). These scales had alphas of .70 and .68 respectively.

Overall, there was a significant decrease over time in academic engagement for youth ($p = .001$). This unfortunate change was found in three of the programs but, as noted earlier, may be a function of the general tendency for youth to become less engaged in schoolwork over time and especially in the spring when most of the final surveys were completed. There was no significant overall change in the broader engagement in learning although one program did show a positive change whereas two others showed negative changes.

As noted earlier, the absence of real comparison groups makes it difficult to know what is happening as a result of the service-learning classes. One hypothesis for the negative findings in this area is youth become dissatisfied with regular classes after taking classes using a service-learning approach. There is some evidence of this dissatisfaction noted above in youth's comparisons of their regular and service-learning classes.

Changes in Personal Development

Two scales were used to assess changes in personal development: a five-item global self-esteem scale (alpha = .72) and a three-item measure of self-efficacy (alpha = .60). These scales measure how youth feel about themselves and whether they believe they can influence what happens to them.

Overall, self-esteem decreased slightly but significantly ($p = .02$) over the course of the year. This change is primarily the result of changes in one inner-city school. For the self-efficacy scale we found no changes either overall or for particular schools. Because we lack comparison groups, it is again difficult to interpret these changes.

Changes in the Acceptance of Diversity

The youth's acceptance of diversity was measured by an 11-item scale with an alpha of .79. The items ask about being bothered by or enjoying people who are different in terms of age, race, looks, and physical abilities. Interestingly, although there were no overall changes in this measure, there was a significant and sizable favorable change in one program located in the sixth grade of an elementary school. Perhaps service-learning programs for younger children may have a greater impact on attitudes about diversity than similar programs for older youth whose attitudes are more fully formed. It is also possible that this program approached the issues more directly or effectively than the other programs.

WHICH PROGRAM CHARACTERISTICS, IF ANY, INCREASE THE IMPACT OF SERVICE-LEARNING PROGRAMS?

In this section we seek to address the issue of what it is about service-learning programs that make them more or less effective in different areas. For example, we noted earlier that social responsibility for and intent to serve the environment in the future were differentially affected by whether the service activities involved the environment. Here we address whether three program characteristics—reflection, the number of hours of service, and the ways in which youth are involved—alter the nature of the program's impact. For each characteristic, people have hypothesized that the benefits of service-learning are improved or greater when done in these ways. In order to address these questions and not confound other aspects of the programs (such as the grade levels involved), we only analyze data from ninth graders in the mandatory service program. Whereas this constrains the ability to generalize the results, it provides for a less ambiguous interpretation within this special case.

Does Reflection Matter?

Part of the reason service-learning is different than general volunteering or community service more broadly is the belief that reflecting on the service is a fundamental key to learning and impact. In the programs we studied, 53% of youth reported little or no reflection activities. Do youth who do not reflect on their experiences report any worse outcomes than those who do more reflection activities in their programs?

The amount of reflection youth report is related to 7 out of the 13 indicators of change reported earlier. When reflection, as reported by either the youth or the staff member, is absent or low, there are some undesirable impacts. When reflection is present in some form, there is little change in most indicators. Thus, the amount of reflection does matter but in a complex and interesting way. Some examples will serve to illustrate this effect.

Youth who did not reflect on their service experience were more likely over time to express less socially responsible attitudes toward the environment, toward civic involvement, and toward serving others and they were also less likely to report the intent to help others or the environment in the future. There was additional evidence that those who reflected the most were less likely to disengage from school and that those that did not report reflecting on their experiences became more disengaged from school.

These findings strongly suggest that the amount, and probably the nature of reflection activities, are related to desired outcomes. Without reflection, service activities would appear to have even the potential for detrimental impact (although this cannot be assessed without a comparison group). Among practitioners, this might be described as the importance of placing the service experience in a larger context from which it draws its meaning. Without this reflection on the nature and context of the experience, the experience may be more negative in its impact than anticipated. Service alone is probably not enough, particularly if it is mandatory as it was in this program.

Does the Number of Hours of Service Matter?

Next we examined whether the amount of time youth were involved in service activities had a differential impact on the outcomes under study. We compared those who did less than 20 hours, between 20 and 40 hours, and more than 40 within the ninth-grade service-learning program studied. Results indicate that those who did more than 40 hours reported less at-risk behavior over time; a greater increase in social responsibility for civic involvement, and less disengagement from school. However, we also found that self-esteem increased most for those doing less than 20 hours of service as did engagement in regular academic tasks. Ironically, attitudes about social responsibility for helping others decreased among those doing more than 40 hours although most of these were not actually helping others in their service experience. Imposing service may affect youth's attitudes toward helping others in negative rather than positive ways without some important factors being present. Undoubtedly, as any quality practitioner would tell you, a number of factors other than the sheer number of hours are important in determining the nature of the impact. Thus, the field should be very cautious in implementing service programs that require or mandate so many hours of service in the absence of teaching methods that allow students to interpret and learn from the experiences they encounter.

Do the Ways in Which Youth Are Involved Matter?

We explored the impact of three different levels of youth involvement in their service-learning activities—doing the service alone, doing the service with others but without active group planning, and doing everything from planning to the actual service as a group.

The analyses revealed that, among the ninth graders in the mandatory service program, those who worked alone on their service project, were more likely to accept diversity, report higher self-efficacy levels, and became more engaged in academic tasks. Those who worked as a group on both the planning and execution of the service experience were more likely to gain a sense of responsibility for civic involvement, were less likely to lose a sense of responsibility for helping others and for the environment, and were more likely to express the intent to serve others and be civicly involved in the future.

These findings suggest that how youth are involved in the creation, planning, and execution of the service does affect the nature of the outcomes one might expect. The more group oriented the service project is the more impact on social responsibility and intent to serve. The more personally responsible the youth is for their own service experience the greater the chance it affects them personally—assuming they reflect on the activities in a structured way. Practitioners need to keep these factors in mind when seeking to create service-learning programs that are intended to have specific psychosocial or developmental outcomes. A good deal more research is required to further clarify these basic findings.

DO YOUTH AT RISK BENEFIT DIFFERENTIALLY FROM SERVICE-LEARNING?

In order to answer this question, we used all youth in the study and examined whether those who were engaged in risk-taking behaviors at Time 1, or were already disengaged from school, benefited differentially from being involved in a service-learning program.

In general, youth who were most engaged in risk-taking behavior at Time 1 were more likely at Time 2 to see service class as less boring than regular classes and to believe that what they did contributed to the community. These are important changes that can help youth who are at risk reengage in learning and the community. Furthermore, youth at risk initially also showed differential changes over time in that they became more accepting of diversity and more engaged in academic tasks. They unfortunately did not get to know either peers or adult staff better than their less at-risk peers.

With respect to those youth who at Time 1 had higher levels of disengagement from school (e.g., skipping class, suspended), we found they were more likely to think the service activities related to real life, were less boring, and that they had contributed to the community. With respect to changes over time, the youth who were most disengaged became significantly more engaged than they were in both academic tasks and general learning.

In summary, this study provides some clear evidence that in some very concrete ways, service-learning programs can help youth at risk or who are already starting to disengage from school. A more detailed analysis of these benefits needs to be undertaken in other studies.

CONCLUSIONS

Although this study lacks a comparison group and that limits its ability to draw clear conclusions about the benefits, or problems, associated with service-learning programs for 6th through 12th graders, it provides a number of insights into how youth perceive their programs and change over time within such programs. Three findings in particular have implications for practitioners.

First, many youth in these programs see the benefits of these types of classes and projects over their regular classroom activities. They see them as less boring, requiring harder thinking, and more related to real life. This evidence should encourage teachers to try these new methods to reach their students in new ways.

Second, it is clear that the nature and type of service programs can make a difference in some outcomes if they are designed to do so. The impact of service-learning would appear to be more focused than generic especially when it comes to changes over time. Including reflection, a standard of good practice, receives clear support in this data although more because its absence leads to problems than because of clear benefits from its inclusion.

Finally, this study affirms the utility of service-learning activities as a strategy, to be used in regular classrooms, that can help youth at risk and those already disengaged from school from falling further away. The evidence does not argue for separating out youth at risk and running special programs for them. Such labeling of youth may create more difficulties than opportunities.

Although much remains to be learned about the quantitative impact of different types of service-learning programs on different types of outcomes, we hope this study contributes to a more effective search for best practices and a strengthening of the case for quality service-learning programs.

ACKNOWLEDGMENTS

This study would not have been possible without the support of the Kellogg Foundation and the Dewitt Wallace–Reader's Digest Fund and their multiple efforts to improve the practice of service-learning and furthering our understanding of how it works. We are particularly grateful to the National Youth Leadership Council and its regional and national partners who helped recruit many of the schools who participated in this study and who selected us to evaluate their efforts. Several colleagues from Search Institute have been particularly helpful in designing, conducting, and analyzing the data for this chapter. In particular we wish to thank Melanie Majors and Vicky Mackerman for their administrative help, Candyce Kroenke and Richard Gordon for their technical assistance, and Michael Donahue who helped to create the surveys and did much of the initial scaling work. Finally, we wish to thank the schools, teachers, and youth who gave of their time and talents to participate in this study—often with little or no direct benefit to themselves.

REFERENCES

Alt, M. N., & Medrich, E. A. (1994). *Student outcomes from participation in community service* (report prepared for the U.S. Department of Education, Office of Research). Berkeley, CA: MPR Associates.

Batchelder, R. H., & Root, S. (1994). Effects of an undergraduate program to integrate academic learning and service: Cognitive, prosocial cognitive, and identity outcomes. *Journal of Adolescence, 17*(4), 341–355.

Benson, P. L. (1993) *The troubled journey: A portrait of sixth–twelfth grade youth.* Minneapolis, MN: Search Institute.

Blyth, D. A., & Kroenke, C. (1996). *Proceedings from the September 9–10, 1995 Service-Learning Summit.* Minneapolis, MN: Search Institute.

Boyte, H. C. (1991). Community service and civic education. *Phi Delta Kappan, 72*(10), 758–760.

Burke, J. (1993). Tackling society's problems in English class. *Educational Leadership, 50*(7), 16–18.

Calabrese, R. L., & Schumer, H. (1986). The effects of service activities on adolescent alienation. *Adolescence, 21*(83), 675–687.

Caskey, F., Cairn, R.W., Kielsmeier, J. C., & McPherson, K. (1991). A rationale for service-learning: Outcomes for students, schools and community. In R. W. Cairn & J. C. Kielsmeier (Eds.), *Growing hope: A sourcebook on integrating youth service into the school curriculum,* (1st ed., pp. 18–35). Roseville, MN: National Youth Leadership Council.

Cognetta, P. V., & Sprinthall, N. A. (1978). Students as teachers: Role taking as a means of promoting psychological and ethical development during adolescence. In N. A. Sprinthall & R. L. Mosher (Eds.), *Value development as the aim of education* (pp. 53–68). Schenectady, NY: Character Research Press.

Cohen, J., & Kinsey, D. (Winter, 1994). "Doing good" and scholarship: A service-learning study. *Journalism Educator,* pp. 4–14.

Conrad, D., & Hedin, D. (1978). Are experiential learning programs effective? *NAASP Bulletin, 62* (421), 102–107.

Conrad, D., & Hedin, D. (1981). National assessment of experiential education: Summary and implications. *Journal of Experiential Education, 4*(2), 6–20.

Conrad, D., & Hedin, D. (1982). The impact of experiential education on adolescent development. *Child and Youth Services, 4*(3/4), 57–76.

Conrad, D., & Hedin, D. (1989). *High school community service: A review of research and programs.* Madison: National Center on Effective Secondary Schools, University of Wisconsin-Madison.

Conrad, D., & Hedin, D. (1991). School-based community service: What we know from research and theory. *Phi Delta Kappan, 72*(10), 743–749.

Delve, C. I., Mintz, S. D., & Stewart, G. M. (Eds.). (1990, Summer). Community service as values education. *New Directions for Student Services (50),* 7–29.

Dewsbury-White, K. E. (1995). Service-learning project models and subject matter achievement of Middle School students. *Michigan Middle School Journal, 19*(2), 7–10.

Giles, D. E., & Eyler, J. (1994). The impact of a college community service laboratory on students' personal, social, and cognitive outcomes. *Journal of Adolescence, 17*(4), 327–339.

Hamilton, S. F. (1980). Experiential learning programs for youth. *American Journal of Education, 88*(2), 179–215.

Hamilton, S. F. (1981). Adolescents in community settings: What is to be learned? *Theory and Research in Social Education, 9*(2), 23–38.

Hamilton, S. F., & Fenzel, L. M. (1988). The impact of volunteer experience on adolescent social development: Evidence of program effects. *Journal of Adolescent Research, 3*(1), 65–80.

Hamilton, S. F., & Zeldin, R. S. (1987). Learning civics in the community. *Curriculum Inquiry, 17*(4), 407–420.

Hedin, D. (1983). *The impact of experience on academic learning: A summary of theories and review of recent research.* Boston, MA: Institute for Responsive Education.

Hedin, D. (1987). Students as teachers: A tool for improving school climate and productivity. *Social Policy, 17*(3), 42–47.

Hedin, D. (1989). The power of community service. *Proceedings of the Academy of Political Science, 37*(2), 201–213.

Hedin, D., & Conrad, D. (1987). Service: A pathway to knowledge. *Community Education Journal, 15*(1), 10–14.

Hursh, B., & Borzak, L. (1979). Toward cognitive development through field studies. *Journal of Higher Education, 50*(1), 63–78.

Kraft, R. J., & Krug, J. (1994). Review of research and evaluation on service learning in public and higher education. In R. J. Kraft & M. Swadenert (Eds.), *Building community: Service learning in the academic disciplines* (pp. 199–213). Denver: Colorado Campus Compact.

Luchs, K. P. (1981). *Selected changes in urban high school students after participation in community-based learning and service activities.* Unpublished doctoral dissertation, University of Maryland, Baltimore.

Markus, G. B., Howard, J. P. F., & King, D. C. (1993). Integrating community service and classroom instruction enhances learning: Results from an experiment. *Educational Evaluation and Policy Analysis, 15*(4), 410–419.

McCluskey-Fawcett, K., & Green, P. (1992). Using community service to teach developmental psychology. *Teaching of Psychology, 19*(3), 150–152.

Melchior, A., & Orr, L. (1995) *Final Report: National Evaluation of Serve America.* Prepared for the Corporation for National and Community Service. Washington, DC.

Miller, J. (1994). Linking traditional and service-learning courses: Outcome evaluations utilizing two pedagogically distinct models. *Michigan Journal of Community Service Learning, 1*(1), 29–36.

Moore, D. T. (1981). Discovering the pedagogy of experience. *Harvard Educational Review, 51*(2), 286–300.

Newmann, F. M., & Rutter, R. A. (1983). *The effects of high school community service programs on students' social development. Final report.* University of Wisconsin, Wisconsin Center for Educational Research: Madison.

Newmann, F. M., & Rutter, R. A. (1986). A profile of high school community service programs. *Educational Leadership, 43*(4), 65–71.

Rutter, R. A., & Newmann, F. M. (1989). The potential of community service to enhance civic responsibility. *Social Education, 53*(6), 371–374.

Switzer, G. E., Simmons, R. G., Dew, M. A., Regalski, J. M., & Wang, C. (1995). The effect of a school-based helper program on adolescent self-image, attitudes, and behavior. *Journal of Early Adolescence, 15*(4), 429–455.

Williams, R. (1990). The impact of field education on student development: Research findings. In J. C. Kendall & Associates (Eds.), *Combining service and learning.* (Vol. I, pp. 130–147). Raleigh, NC: National Society for Internships and Experiential Education.

Yates, M., & Youniss, J. (1996). A developmental perspective on community service in adolescence. *Social Development, 5*(1), 85–111.

Part II

Research on the Elements of
Effective Service-Learning

5

The Importance of Program Quality in Service-Learning

Janet Eyler and Dwight Giles, Jr.
Vanderbilt University

One of the tensions between practitioners and researchers in service-learning is that they seem to ask different questions. As we immerse ourselves in the practice and the research literature, we are reminded of the task of digging a tunnel under a mountain with crews starting at each end and finally breaking through at what they hope will be the same point in the middle. In this chapter we try to link the practice and the research literature so that the questions of "why" and "how," which appear most frequently in the practice literature, can be linked with the "what" or the question of outcomes raised most often by researchers.

Because there is no single literature on program characteristics that lead to quality experiences for students in service-learning, we review several related bodies of literature in this chapter. These are:

- the practice literature on principles of good practice in service-learning.
- the related experiential education literature that is derived from learning theory.
- the research literature on student growth and development outcomes.

PRINCIPLES OF GOOD PRACTICE

Because service-learning has largely been a practitioner enterprise, the earliest expressions of quality were statements of principles of good practice. These were developed by practitioners and were based on a combination of beliefs of what "ought" to be and years of reflection on what worked in practice. The earliest of these were the three principles articulated by Robert Sigmon (1979):

1. Those being served control the service(s) provided.
2. Those being served become better able to serve and be served by their own actions.
3. Those who serve also are learners and have significant control over what is expected to be learned.

Whereas all three principles relate to program characteristics, only the third relates directly to the experience of the student participants.

The next evolution of principles of good practice in service-learning came as the result of a Wingspread conference where a group of practitioners codified 10 principles that had been developed, critiqued and endorsed by 77 organizations in the field (Honnet & Poulsen, 1989). Although these 10 principles represent an expansion and elaboration of Sigmon's original three principles, in the Preamble they state very clearly the fundamental proposition of service-learning as educational philosophy and pedagogical approach: "Service, combined with learning, adds value to each and transforms both." (Kendall & Associates, 1990, p. 39).

In the introduction to the principles, there is a series of claims about the results of this combination related impacts on participants. Key among these are that students:

- Develop a habit of critical reflection on their experiences, enabling them to learn more throughout life.
- Are more curious and motivated to learn.
- Understand problems in a more complex way and can imagine alternative solutions. (Kendall et al., 1990, p. 38)

The major emphasis in the *Principles of Good Practice* is on the process of combining service and learning and general program characteristics; as such all are standards of quality. However, for the purposes of this chapter there are three that seem to link program characteristics and outcomes in terms of quality. These are: providing critical reflection (Principle 2); matching servers and service needs (Principle 6); and including training, supervision, monitoring and assessment (Principle 8).

The standard work in this field is the two-volume set compiled and edited by Kendall et al., (1990) that reviews philosophy, practice, and some research. Review of these encyclopedic volumes yields a few ideas about program quality and student outcomes. The first is Stanton's (1990) argument that experiential learning and service are necessary to meet the goals of liberal arts such as critical thinking and citizenship development. Next is Levison's (1990) conclusions about his national study of community service programs in independent schools. Levison concluded that quality programs provide *engagement* rather than just *exposure*. This engagement is intellectual understanding of problems and issues and not just "feeling badly" about those needing service. The key program characteristic of programs providing engagement is clear and concrete specification of objectives and outcomes (Levison, 1990).

Also in this volume is the commentary by former university presidents Kennedy and Warren on Campus Compact's national survey of its member campuses on the faculty role in public service. They argued that one of the three main findings is that the most important role of faculty in service programs is an instructional one where they "assist students to learn from their service experience and connect this learning with academic study" (Campus Compact, 1990, p. 472).

EXPERIENTIAL LEARNING THEORY AND PRACTICE

The question of how to make experience educative goes back to Dewey (1938) and is the focus of his work that is often cited in this field, *Experience and Education*. Implicit in most of Dewey's writings is a theory of how experiential programs ought to be organized to meet the outcome goals of growth and development.

Elsewhere we have argued that Dewey's theory is useful for undertaking service -learning research (Giles & Eyler, 1994b). He put forward four criteria that were necessary for projects to be truly educative:

1. Must generate interest.
2. Must be worthwhile intrinsically.
3. Must present problems that awaken new curiosity and create a demand for education.
4. Must cover a considerable time span and be capable of fostering development over time. (Dewey, 1933)

These criteria lend themselves well to being operationalized as both program characteristics and as student outcome indicators. Also useful in Dewey is the emphasis on growth and development as the goal of experiential education. He envisioned experiential education as being a continuum of experiences for the learner and an activity in which there was an interaction between the external experience and the developmental experiences of the individual. From this view he developed the two principles of continuity and interaction (Dewey, 1938; Giles & Eyler, 1994b).

This developmental view suggests that duration is an important element in program quality; a program or a sequence of experiences needs to be of a long enough duration to have a developmental impact. This view is often echoed in the practice literature. Observers have noted that the nature of the tasks that students do in field placements changes and becomes more complex over time (Moore, 1981; Moore, 1986; Suelzle & Borzak; 1981). One model of development focused explicitly on service learning has five phases and requires experiences over a relatively long duration in order for students to move through the phases (Delve, Mintz & Stewart, 1990).

Perhaps the most often appropriated element of Dewey's thinking about expe- riential leaning is the concept of reflection or "reflective activity" (Dewey, 1938). Through reflection, action and thinking are linked to produce learning that leads to more action. This is central in the literature that is practice oriented (Honnet & Poulsen, 1989; Silcox 1993), and as illustrated later in this chapter, one of the key areas of inquiry in the research literature.

In his recent volume on reflection, Silcox (1993) argued that reflection is necessary when students are to make sense of information so that they can know what it means. It is the processing of experience through reflective teaching that Silcox argued is the characteristic of service-learning programs that teach students *how* to learn. One expression of this view is the set of "Standards of Quality for School-Based Service-Learning" developed by the Alliance for Service-Learning in Education Reform. One of the key principles of these standards is that quality programs include preparation and reflection as essential elements (see Appendix 1 in Silcox, 1993).

In the mid-1980s, the National Society for Internships and Experiential Education (NSIEE, now NSEE) undertook a national program to strengthen experiential education in American postsecondary education. In the volume that resulted from this project, one of the chapters was devoted to quality (Kendall, Duley, Little, Permaul & Rubin, 1986). The core of this chapter is based on the work of John Duley (1979) in defining quality learning outcomes in college level experiential learning. Among the higher order outcomes listed are dealing with data through synthesis, coordinating, analyzing, and comparing. People skills include mentoring, negotiating, instructing, supervising, and persuading (Kendall et al., 1986).

The program characteristics necessary to achieve these outcomes are presented by Duley and the other members of this project as a series of tasks related to linking experience and learning: these characteristics of quality programs are:

1. Well established course or program goals.
2. Identification of service sites with students having the primary responsibility for securing positions in the field.
3. Help students establish educational objectives.
4. Recruiting students for sites.
5. Prepare students for learning and the field experience.
6. Monitor and support the learning.
7. Evaluate and assess the learning.
8. Report the learning on transcripts (Kendall et al., 1986, pp. 71–74).

Reflection, as developed in the service-learning practice literature seems most closely related to tasks 3, 5, and 6 in the NSIEE list.

Several emphases emerge from these two bodies of literature that are practice and or theory-based. Some of these emphases are also echoed in the service-learning research literature reviewed in the next section. As we noted at the beginning, the literature based on beliefs or the practice-derived "oughts" focused on the processes and inputs in service-learning programs. By contrast, the service-learning research literature focused on outcomes and with only a few exceptions, paid little attention to differentiating the processes and practices that might be associated with these outcomes (see Giles, Honnet, & Migliore, 1991). Themes that are not reflected in the empirical literature but are predominant in the theory and practice literature are the importance of student choice, community voice, and client control of service. Another theme is that successful service-learning or other experiential learning leads to the desire for new learning. One theme that emerges in the empirical literature that is not emphasized in the practice literature is the nature of the task and how the individual student experiences the task and the service or field setting.

Although there are differences in focus between the practice and empirical literature, several shared themes emerged. These are: the importance of program duration for developmental impact, and the central role of reflection in promoting learning.

EMPIRICAL LITERATURE LINKING PROGRAM QUALITY AND STUDENT OUTCOMES

As we have seen, there are many reasons for thinking that the quality of service-learning programs might make a difference in what students get out of them. And although the empirical research is spotty, there is growing evidence that program characteristics do make a difference, particularly on students' social and intellectual development. Empirical studies that explore program characteristics and link them to student outcomes focus on: qualitative differences between service-learning and more conventional classroom learning experiences; variations in the structure of service-learning programs themselves; and differences in individual student experiences within programs.

Qualitative Differences Between Service-Learning and Traditional Classroom Learning

When students participate in service-learning programs they are plunged into environments that differ substantially from most of their traditional classroom experiences. Some of the early empirical studies in service-learning focused on describing these differences. These differences include: the nature of the tasks they are asked to perform; the social relationships with other service providers and clients; the student's role as service provider; the way in which knowledge is sought and applied; and the nature of the feedback students receive for their efforts.

Both Conrad and Hedin (1980) and Hamilton (1981) noted community placements move high school students out of an "adolescent ghetto" and into positive peer relationships with adults. Moore (1981) and Heck and Weible (1978) also observed that students developed greater confidence in working with adults in their internships and service placements. Rubin (1983) noted that service-learning plunges students into a different set of cultural norms for knowledge acquisition; whereas students in the classroom obtain information from authorities, students in the field acquire it through observation, questioning, and chance. Moore agreed, noting that the tasks performed in the field required greater creativity and flexibility than those typically faced in the classroom and that they required understanding of the task in the context of an organization. He also found that the students' conception of tasks became increasingly complex and contextualized with continued service in the field. Pataniczek and Johansen (1983) also observed that students in field placements took on new roles as learners including learning by doing, collegial relationships with agency personnel, setting their own goals, and giving as well as receiving feedback. Faculty also found their roles changing to facilitators of learning and liaisons between campus and community. Eyler (1993b) analyzed student journals from a policy class and followed up with a later analysis of journals from the same students during their full-time internship. As interns, these students expressed a greater sense of ownership of the work they were doing. Where the students had focused on feedback from the professor in the classroom, they were much more likely to weigh their success in terms of accomplishing a task when they worked with organizations in the community. Hursh and Borzak (1979), in studies of college students in service placements, accounted for the changes in how students in the field defined themselves as learners by noting the role discontinuities involved in moving from the classroom to doing real and meaningful work in the community.

The changes in learning processes and roles noted by these qualitative researchers are consistent with the processes of effective experiential education identified by practitioners and theorists. Students polled about the characteristics of field experiences that helped or hindered their learning selected program elements consistent with these observations as well (Owens & Owen, 1979). Eyler (1993b) found that these qualities were more likely to be present in full-time rather than part-time field placements.

Thus qualitative studies have demonstrated that service-learning placements do provide many of the learning opportunities advocated by practitioners and experiential learning theorists and that more intensive experiences may provide more of them. What is needed is empirical evidence that helps identify which characteristics are most important for achieving the goals of service-learning.

The Association of Program Characteristics and Student Outcomes

Student community service programs are organized in vastly different ways. Some are purely volunteer experiences and others are tied to the curriculum. In some, students participate in frequent and carefully structured reflection; in others little or no reflection is built in. Some are carefully designed to match sites and activities to learning goals for students, others are rather haphazardly assigned. Some offer a one-time experience, others offer an articulated sequence of service activities over several semesters. Some immerse students in intense all-consuming experiences, others involve 1 or 2 hours a week. In some, students work with people in the community to plan and deliver services, others seem to operate with little community input. We are beginning to have some evidence about which program elements make a difference.

Program Type.   Few attempts have been made to compare different program types and where that has been done, not much evidence has been found to suggest that it makes a difference in student personal, social, or intellectual growth. Conrad and Hedin (1980) compared four types of field-based high school programs: community service, community study, career internships, and outdoor adventure. Their sample included 27 programs that involved 1,000 students; there were six control programs including at least one for each program type. They examined the impact of programs on personal development including moral development and self-esteem; social development including attitudes toward service as well as career development; and intellectual development including self-reports of learning and measures of problem solving.

They found that although field-based programs did lead to student growth, general program types did not make a difference. Initial differences favoring community service programs for their impact on social and intellectual growth disappeared when analyses controlling for other program and student characteristics were performed. They attribute this lack of differential impact to the fact that the kinds of characteristics that do make a difference were found in some programs of each type. For example, research on social issues, originally thought to be the defining characteristic of community study programs was also found in some career and community service programs. The things that make a difference in social and intellectual outcomes are the particular activities that students participate in regardless of general program type and one of the more promising characteristics seems to be the extent to which the service activity is integrated into the curriculum or provides opportunities for student reflection.

Reflection and Integration.   The old joke about the teacher who claimed 20 years experience teaching the first grade, but actually only had 1 year's experience 20 times, taps a basic truth about experiential education. An experience only becomes educative when students do something with it. Experience becomes experiential education when students are engaged in intrinsically worthwhile activities that awaken curiosity and stimulate reflection (Giles & Eyler, 1994b). Although reflection may occur naturally in field placements (Moore, 1986), often it does not. Reflection can be spontaneously initiated by the individual student or be the result of careful program planning, but there is a growing body of literature to attest to its centrality to the process of learning through experience.

For Conrad and Hedin (1980) the single most important, observable program factor in predicting student outcomes was "the presence of a formal, and at least weekly, seminar" (p. 36). Rutter and Newman (1989) found that high school service program participants who had a weekly reflective seminar were more likely to report positive interactions with community members during their service, than those who did not.

Linking service to particular classes would seem to assure some level of reflection and the growing number of controlled studies showing student learning in service-learning classes supports this assumption. Markus, Howard, and King (1993) found that students assigned to a political science section that included service achieved higher exam grades than those who did not; Batchelder and Root (1994) found that students in service-learning sections showed a significant increase in use of complex multidimensional perspectives in essays they wrote analyzing a social problem compared to those in regular class sections; Eyler, Giles, and Braxton (1996) examined the impact of service on students in liberal arts classes at 20 colleges and found that those who participated in service-learning showed significant increases over the course of a semester in political action skills, ability to identify social issues, tolerance, personal efficacy, belief that the community can solve social problems, sense of connection to community, support for requiring service and support for volunteering, valuing a career helping people, valuing service in their own lives, valuing the importance of influencing the political structure, perspective taking ability, openness to other points of view, commitment to social justice, belief in the importance of changing public policy and perception that problems are systemic rather than the fault of individuals who need service. Boss (1994) compared two sections of an ethics class and found the class that included service showed significant increases in moral reasoning over the course of the semester whereas the students in the nonservice section did not. Waterman (1993) compared seniors who participated in the Philadelphia High School Literacy Corps with a class of senior English students who did not participate in service. The students who participated in the service that included a reflective seminar increased in self-esteem and attitudes of social responsibility, whereas the others did not.

In one of the few studies that contrasts volunteer service without a systematic reflection component with service as part of the curriculum, Myers-Lipton (1994) tracked students in a college program that integrates service and learning over a 2 year period. He found that students in the integrated service-learning program increased in international understanding and civic responsibility and decreased in racial prejudice over the 2 years. Comparable changes did not occur in the students who participated in service without the reflection component or in no service. These changes also did not occur in the experimental group over the course of a single year; extensive and continuous integration of service and learning was necessary in this group to bring the change about.

Eyler (1993a) also found that extensive reflection is necessary in a field-based program if students are to transfer learning from the curriculum to use in new settings or tasks. She compared three groups of college interns completing full-time semester-long internships as the capstone to their interdisciplinary major in human and organizational development; some students were in service placements, others in business organizations. Two of the internship semesters immersed students in weekly intensive reflective seminars and required them to complete written assignment and projects and make oral presentations in which they analyzed their experience and organization using concepts that they had learned in the classroom. These groups were designated the "high reflection" treatment. One group completed a pattern of reflection more typical of internships and service-learning placements; they met occasionally to share feelings and discuss issues and concerns and they kept journals in which they received occasional written feedback. This group was designated "moderate reflection." When these interns completed "letters of advice to a friend entering a complex organization," only the interns in the high treatment groups drew on the information and theories they had studied for 4 years as well as on their own internship experience; the students in the moderate reflection group relied on general cliched advice like "be yourself" similar to the advice offered by freshmen who had yet to complete the curriculum or the internship. The fact that this transfer of learning did not occur among students with a strongly applied curriculum based on experiential learning theory without the additional element of extensive reflection on field experience, suggests how critical it is to have a clear conception of program goals and very explicit strategies for reaching them.

Preliminary results from a current study of the impact of service-learning programs on college student outcomes provides additional support for the importance of structured reflection. The Comparing Models of Service-Learning project surveyed 1,500 students at 20 colleges at the beginning and end of the spring semester 1995 and also gathered data from faculty and program directors; about 1,100 of these students were involved in service and about 400 were not. The students were in a variety of service-learning programs including internships, professional courses, volunteer programs, and alternative spring breaks as well as in traditional liberal arts courses. In one analysis, program characteristics identified by faculty teaching service-learning classes in the liberal arts and by researchers are used to predict perceptions by the 626 students in liberal arts classes that these classes were superior to their nonservice classes and the specific benefits they obtained from service-learning. The students in classes where the service was central to classroom activities were significantly more likely to report that the class was higher in quality than their nonservice classes and that they were motivated to work harder, they learned more and they were more intellectually stimulated than students in classes where the service was less well integrated into the curriculum. Oral complexity, which included students making oral presentations linking theory to their practice, was also linked to higher quality, learning and intellectual stimulation. The centrality of service to the class was also a significant predictor of students' perceptions that they had learned subject matter, attained personal growth, increased their commitment to the community, increased interpersonal skill and developed specific skills. Oral complexity was a predictor of subject matter learning and personal growth and written complexity was a predictor of social commitment. Classes in which reflection about service was consistently integrated into the class were consistently viewed as more powerful intellectually than those where service was performed but not well integrated (Eyler, Giles, & Braxton, 1995).

Greene and Diehm (1995) found that college students who received frequent written feedback on their service journals rather than a simple check mark were more likely to credit the elderly people whom they were serving with contributing to their education. They indicate that the feedback appeared to motivate students to reflect on their experience and to show an increased level of personal investment.

Evidence suggests that reflection is important and that the quality of that reflection makes a difference. Certainly one element of quality is a close match between course goals and content and the service activities for students.

Matching Placement With Learning Goals.   Although there is evidence that service placements may facilitate learning because they motivate students (Cohen & Kinsey, 1994), there is also evidence to support the view that placing students in settings in which they will deal with situations and issues related to the content of the course will help assure that the experience enhances learning.

We know that college students placed in political internships increased their understanding of the political process compared to students who studied the legislative process in an advanced political science class (Eyler & Halteman, 1981); that journalism students report greater understanding of communication concepts through their service (Cohen & Kinsey, 1994); and that students show somewhat greater problem analysis complexity on problems related to their service (Batchelder & Root, 1994).

The importance of matching service to the focus of the class has also been observed among high school students. The students observed by Hamilton and Zeldin (1987) learned more when the issues discussed in the legislative sessions they were observing matched those being discussed in the class seminar and they also found that preparation on the issues before their observations led to greater satisfaction with the legislative experience. Wilson found that students involved in political or social action became more open-minded as compared with students in other types of service (Alt & Medrich, 1994). The students in Conrad and Hedin's study (1980) showed the greatest increase in problem-solving skill when they experienced problems in their field placements similar to those in the problems they were asked to solve on the skill test and when they actually participated in problem analysis activities in the field. Moderate amounts of experience and instruction were linked to moderate growth in skill and students whose placements lacked experiences with such problems and also had no instruction in problem solving actually showed a decline in measured problem-solving skill. There have been a number of studies showing that tutors increase their learning in the subjects that they teach (Alt & Medrich, 1994). Matching service to course content appears to facilitate learning.

The kinds of tasks that students undertake during their service and the environmental context in which they work should also make a difference. Cohen and Kinsey (1994) involved 217 of 220 journalism students in a mass communication class in service activities. Some students were involved in direct contact with clients in the community, for example, teaching elementary school students about such media issues as stereotyping or violence in cartoons, whereas others prepared material for clients such as public relations brochures but did not work directly in the community. Whereas all students were positive about the experience and indicated enhanced learning in the key content areas of the course, the students who interacted with people in the community were more positive about the usefulness of the assignment in placing their course content in a meaningful context and were also more positive about the experience in their understanding of mass media audiences and messages.

Relationship With Community Members.   Although Cohen and Kinsey (1994) found interaction with community members important to student motivation and learning, other studies have noted that in even rather brief service projects, close involvement with people who need service can have an impact on how students view the clients of social services. In a community service laboratory where students spent 3 hours a week for seven weeks in a volunteer agency, 75% of a group of 57 students changed from negative to positive description of the people to whom they provided service as a result of their service. Only 4% changed from positive to negative and the remainder were positive both before and after the service; several in this category commented that their views had not changed as they had worked with people with similar problems before (Giles & Eyler, 1994a). Ostrow analyzed journals kept by students who spent a day of service in a soup kitchen for the homeless and came to similar conclusions. His focus was on the process by which students come to change their perceptions of homeless people and the role of self-consciousness in this process (Ostrow, 1995). For many students, a brief service project may be the first time they are confronted with people whose life experiences are very different from their own, and such an experience may be very emotionally powerful.

It would be helpful to practitioners to have more empirical research that explores the link between the kinds of tasks students perform during their service, and what is learned. Among the more easily studied dimensions of service are its duration and intensity; there is growing evidence to suggest that service over a lengthy period is desirable.

Duration and Intensity.   Many service programs are brief in duration; some as brief as a single afternoon event tied to club activities or campus orientation. The majority are probably of relative short duration and involve 2 or 3 hours a week in the field. There is evidence that a more intense program is more likely to provide the higher levels of the qualities associated with effective service-learning than a less intense one, that is, challenging and varied tasks, opportunities to make important decisions, sense of ownership, collegial relations with professionals in the field, opportunities to apply content from the classroom to the placement and vice verse, and to make a real contribution to the community. When 42 college students evaluated characteristics of their 3 to 6 hours-per-week service practicum and then later performed a similar assessment of their full-time internship, the levels of all these quality related variables were significantly higher for the higher intensity experience (Eyler, 1993b). Rutter and Newman (1989) compared opportunities for challenge such as making difficult decisions and being confronted with new ideas and found that students who participated in community services reported more of these challenges than those who did not.

The Comparing Models of Service-Learning study found that intensity was a predictor of students belief that their service-learning course was of higher quality than other courses and that they worked harder, learned more and were more intellectually stimulated than in nonservice courses. This was true for the 1,131 students in a variety of service programs, as well as for the 636 who were in liberal arts service-learning classes (Eyler et al., 1995).

There is more evidence for the effect of duration; in fact some suggest that the lack of findings in the service-learning literature may be due to the relatively short and low intensity experiences that have been studied (Clayton-Pedersen, Stephens, & Kean, 1994; Kraft & Krug, 1994; Kraft & Swadener, 1994). Given the theoretical literature on stages of service (Delve, Mintz, & Stewart, 1990) and the qualitative studies showing students undertaking increasingly more complex tasks as their time in the field increases (Moore, 1981), we would expect programs that involve students over a long period of time to be more powerful. Kraft and Krug studied all of the K–12 Serve America programs, the Youth and Conservation Corps, and the Higher Education programs funded by grants from the Commission on National and Community Service to the Colorado State Commission. They used multiple methodologies to try to assess the impact of service on attitudes, behavior, and institutional impact. Over 2000 students and staff from middle school through higher education responded to their survey. They found no impact of service experience on attitudes toward civic participation and community service or on other outcomes they examined. They noted that most of these programs were of 6 to 8 weeks in duration and involved field work about once a week for a few hours and suggested that this limited experience was not powerful enough to affect the measured outcomes. In an evaluation of the Break Away alternative spring break programs, there was also no impact on social attitudes as a result of the week-long experience; evaluators felt that both the initial strongly positive attitudes toward social service and social justice issues coupled with the brief duration of the experience left little room for growth on this measure (Clayton-Pedersen, Stephens, & Kean, 1994). The findings in these two studies of college students are consistent with Conrad and Hedin's (1980) landmark study of high school students, in which they found that duration of the program was significant especially in programs of a semester or longer.

Myers-Lipton (1994), in his study also completed in Colorado, found that students in a program that integrated service and learning over a 2 year period showed few changes in international understanding, civic responsibility, and racial prejudice after a single semester, or even at the completion of the first year, but differed significantly from control groups of service volunteers and nonservice involved students at the end of a 2 year period.

One of the phenomena noted by Astin (1991) in his studies of college students is that there is a dramatic fall off in participation between high school and college. One effect of even brief service programs of limited intensity, may be to reconnect students with their desire to perform community service and with an infrastructure to connect with a new community in their college town. Giles and Eyler (1994a) found that students in a community services laboratory in which they studied community agencies and then volunteered for 8 weeks for 2 or 3 hours a week indicated a commitment to continue with volunteer service in subsequent semesters.

About 81% of the 57 students had been active in service during high school, but only 39% had been active the previous semester in college. At the end of their service, all but one student indicated an intention to continue service; 71% of the group indicated they would continue with the current placement and 78% indicated a specific commitment of hours. Duration should not be thought of only in terms of particular programs, but also in terms of the chance to create a series of opportunities for students to serve in both volunteer and class-based service activities. If programs of limited intensity or brief duration succeed in connecting students with further service activity, then they have had an important impact.

There is a need for more research linking objective assessments of the structure of programs and experiences within programs to desired outcomes. But even in carefully planned programs, the actual experience of each student will differ. And we know that these idiosyncratic experiences and perceptions of students make a difference.

Linking Students' Perceptions
of Program Quality to Student Outcomes

Much of what we know about effective programs is based on students' perceptions of their experiences. Students in the same program will not necessarily have the same quality experience. Part of this difference will stem from actual differences in the sites or types of assignments, but students also bring their unique backgrounds and personalities to the field. Some students arrive at a site with a long history of service and are ready to contribute at a sophisticated level; for some students, the most important thing that happens will be coming face-to-face with distressing social conditions for the first time. Some students will take initiative and seek out challenge; others will passively do as they are told to meet a requirement. And even where students participate in the same program and experience, they may perceive those experiences differently as a result of their own backgrounds, motivations and personalities. Waterman summarizes the role of these student characteristics in his chapter "The Role of Student Characteristics in Service-Learning" (chap. 7, this volume.)

There is also considerable evidence that students who choose to do service or service-learning differ before their service on the attitudes and values that are desired outcomes of service-learning. In both the pilot sample of 150 students and the large survey sample of 1,500 students in the Comparing Models of Service-Learning study, college students who participated in service-learning were significantly higher than nonservice students in nearly every dependent variable pretest measure (Eyler et al. 1995; Eyler et al., 1996).

There are two large survey studies that attempt to link students' assessment of program characteristics to outcomes. These are Conrad and Hedin's (1980) landmark study of high school service and other experiential programs and the Comparing Models of Service-Learning study of service-learning programs in colleges and universities. The Comparing Models project is still in process but some results have been reported from the first year pilot with 150 students, and the second year survey of 1,500 students. (Eyler & Giles, 1995; Eyler et al., 1995) Results of both studies suggest that practitioners are right to be concerned about the design of their programs.

Quality of Service Experience.   Conrad and Hedin (1980) found that by far the most powerful predictor of student personal and social development was the students' perceptions of the quality of their experience. Whereas such objectively measured program characteristics as the presence of a reflective seminar accounted for about 5 to 8% of the variance on outcome measures, students idiosyncratic experiences of quality accounted for about 15 to 20%. The quality variables that make a difference are similar to those that the students studied by Owens and Owen (1979) identified as important for a quality program.

Among the elements that made a difference were: having important adult responsibilities; being involved in varied tasks; making a real contribution; and having freedom to explore their own interests. These echo the findings of qualitative studies of the special characteristics of service placements discussed earlier; the student who can take on a more adult role and do real and important work is most likely to develop stronger attitudes of social responsibility. Autonomy, that is, doing things instead of observing, challenging tasks, and freedom to use one's own ideas tended to be most associated with development of self-esteem and efficacy. Conrad and Hedin were, however, unable to link these characteristics with growth in problem-solving ability.

Data gathered during the first year of the Comparing Models study, linked students' perceptions of program quality to social responsibility and citizenship skill outcomes. Students in nine college service-learning classes and six alternative spring break projects completed surveys in which they assessed program characteristics of their service as well as pre–post outcomes measures including social responsibility and citizenship skills.

Quality of the experience, which included such elements as having important responsibilities, challenging tasks, varied tasks, acting rather than observing and having one's opinions challenged, was consistently a significant predictor of growth in social responsibility outcomes including: the importance of influencing public policy, of personally taking leadership positions in the community, of believing both citizens and they personally should volunteer, and of believing service provides personal as well as social benefits. Also, when students felt they had made important contributions during service, there was growth on all social responsibility measures (Eyler & Giles, 1995).

This link between doing meaningful work, that is, making a contribution and outcomes was also found in the survey of 1,500 college students. In both the larger sample of all students doing some type of service-learning and the subsample of those in arts and science service-learning courses, making a contribution was a predictor of students' belief that the service-learning experience was of higher quality than regular classes and that they worked harder, learned more and were more intellectually stimulated. It was also associated with student belief that the service contributed to learning subject matter, personal growth, social commitment, interpersonal skills, and specific task related skills. Students who found their service experiences to be interesting were also more likely to report these same outcomes (Eyler et al., 1995).

Collegiality and Social Relationships.   There is also support for the view that the chance to work as a peer with professionals in the field, as well as to interact with service clients, faculty, and other volunteers, contributes to the impact of service-learning. Conrad and Hedin (1980) found that placements that encouraged collegial relationships with adults including discussion with teachers, family and friends and those they worked with at the site contributed to social responsibility outcomes.

In the Comparing Models survey, students who reported high levels of collegiality including attention from those at the site were more likely to report personal growth and the development of specific task-related skills during their service-learning. They also reported greater personal growth, social commitment, and interpersonal growth if they were in a setting where they worked with people of different ethnic and racial backgrounds. Frequent discussion with faculty and peers was associated with interpersonal growth (Eyler et al., 1995).

Reflection and Integration.   Students surveyed in the Comparing Models study were asked a number of questions about reflection activities including amount and complexity of writing, discussion, presentation, and journaling. These were combined into a variable called "structured reflection." They were also asked about the applicability of what they did in the field to their studies and vice versa. For the total sample, structured reflection was a predictor of student perceptions that the service experience was of higher quality and that they worked harder, learned more and were more intellectually stimulated than in regular classes. It was also a predictor of student belief that they had learned subject matter, and experienced personal growth, social commitment, interpersonal growth, and specific task skills as a result of their service. For the liberal arts subsample, it was a predictor that they learned more and were more intellectually stimulated as well as increased in subject matter learning, personal growth, interpersonal growth, and specific skill development.

Application of service to study and study to the service experience also led to a belief that the service-learning was superior to regular classes on quality, hard work, learning, and intellectual stimulation, as well as to positive outcomes on nearly all of the other learning variables (Eyler et al., 1995). In the pilot study, application was a consistent predictor in the growth of students' assessment of their skillfulness from pretest to posttest. Application predicted growth in participation skill, communications skill, tolerance, and interest in social issues (Eyler & Giles, 1995).

There is thus, a growing body of support for the views of practitioners and experiential education theorists that the quality of the program will have an impact on outcomes. Program impacts, however, have been rather modest. Any service experience, no matter how well designed, is just one small aspect of the complex set of experiences that each student has. We should not be expecting dramatic changes, but looking for the types of program activities that best contribute to what is a long developmental process.

WHAT RECOMMENDATIONS FOR PROGRAM PLANNING CAN WE TAKE FROM THE RESEARCH LITERATURE?

Although much remains to be learned, there are some consistent findings. Some of these recommendations are easiest to implement in curriculum-based service-learning programs, but all have implications for learning.

Duration

How long does a program have to last to be effective? It depends on the effect that we hope to achieve.

• For most program objectives, students should be in their service-learning placements for extended periods of time. If service can be built into classes over the course of 1 year or more, it will have a more powerful effect on students than single-term experiences. And to the extent that schools can create volunteer service centers that support continuous student involvement, some of these goals can be achieved through extracurricular programs as well.

• If a service project is of short duration, it can still be useful in helping students change their stereotypes of people receiving the service. To accomplish this, it is important that students have a chance to work with the service clients directly and a chance to reflect on that experience.

• A service project of short duration can help students connect with service organizations and opportunities and continue as volunteers for longer periods. Organizers of single-day or short-term projects should make a special effort to encourage further service work and to help students identify and hook up with appropriate volunteer organizations.

Reflection

There is good evidence that students benefit from service experience when they think about it and how it relates to their other experiences. In fact, the term service-learning is commonly taken to refer to service programs that incorporate a reflective component. Different types of programs present different challenges to planners trying to facilitate effective reflection activities.

• All programs, whether volunteer service or curriculum-based should include regular opportunities for group discussion of the experience.

• Extracurricular volunteer programs sometimes find resistance to reflection activities that are formal or "classroom" like. Directors of these programs should try to create norms and techniques to encourage informal reflection. Student leaders can encourage and structure discussion "in the van" as they return from service sites or students might be encouraged to create a group journal of insights and comments that students have a chance to read, respond to, and pass along. Asking students to develop and make presentations to school or community groups can also encourage examination of the meaning of their experience.

• In classes where service is designed as an add-on enrichment activity for some students, be aware of what the volunteer students are doing and ask them to contribute examples to class discussions. In some cases, case studies or other presentations from the service may enrich the experience of the whole class. Application is central to effective service-learning.

• Where service is part of a class or curriculum, structure student assignments so that they can apply what they are learning in class to the field and vice versa. Assignments should require students to continuously observe and draw inferences from their experience. Where journals are used, structure the task so that students analyze and evaluate their experience using insights from their academic study and linking insights from their experience.

• Reflection activities should be designed to challenge students. Move from simple tasks like sharing feelings and descriptions to more complex tasks like analysis of assumptions and application of theory to practice.

Site and Task Selection

How sites are selected and managed makes a difference in the quality of the experience that students will have.

• Place students in situations where their service can make a real difference and they will receive feedback so that they know it is important. For example, when students work with the same child over 1 semester they can see the impact of their tutoring; when a community organization uses materials they have created, students feel a sense of accomplishment.

• Develop sites where organizational staff are willing to engage students as peers or colleagues and allow them significant responsibility. In long-term placements this should include varied tasks and assignments and limited amounts of gopher or routine work.

• Use classroom assignments associated with the service-learning project to help shape the service experience. Site staff need to be aware of the academic demands on the student and help to create meaningful projects to meet client and classroom needs. Developing a contract between student and site director can be a way of assuring that these needs are met and avoiding use of the student for undemanding tasks.

• Match the nature of the service assignment to curricular objectives. Chemistry students can tutor high school chemistry students or do demonstrations; students in a political science class might work with legislative committees or with community groups trying to influence policy.

REFERENCES

Alt, M. A., & Medrich, E. A. (1994). *Student outcomes from participation in community service* (report prepared for the U.S. Department of Education, Office of Research). Berkley, CA: MPR Associates.

Astin A. W. (1991, March). *Student involvement in community service: Institutional commitment and the Campus Compact.* Paper presented at the Wingspread Conference on Service Learning Research, Racine, WI.

Batchelder, T. H., & Root, S. (1994). Effects of an undergraduate program to integrate academic learning and service: Cognitive, prosocial cognitive and identity outcomes. *Journal of Adolescence, 17,* 341–356.

Boss, J. A. (1994). The effect of community service work on the moral development of college ethics students. *Journal of Moral Education, 23*(2), 183–198.

Campus Compact (1990). Action steps from a president's perspective: The faculty's role in the public service initiative. In J. C. Kendall & Associates (Eds). *Combining service and learning: Volumes I and II* (pp. 461–472). Raleigh, NC: National Society for Internships and Experiential Education.

Clayton-Pedersen, A., Stephens J., & Kean, G. (1994). *Breakaway evaluation for the Ford Foundation.* Nashville, TN: Center for Education and Human Development Policy, Vanderbilt Institute for Public Policy Studies.

Cohen, J., & Kinsey, D. (1994). Doing good and scholarship: A service-learning study. *Journalism Educator, 48*(4), 4–14.

Conrad, D., & Hedin, D. (1980). *Executive summary of the final report of the experiential education evaluation project.* University of Minnesota, Minneapolis. Center for Youth Development and Research.

Delve, C., Mintz; S., & Stewart, G. (1990). *Community service as values education.* San Francisco: Jossey-Bass.

Dewey, J. (1933). *School and society.* (2nd ed.). Chicago: The University of Chicago Press.

Dewey, J. (1938). *Experience and education.* New York: Collier Books.

Duley, J. (1979). The national institute of social sciences' project in field experience education. *Alternative Higher Education, 3*(3), 161–168.

Eyler, J. (1993a). Comparing the impact of two internship experiences on student learning. *Journal of Cooperative Education, 29*(3), 41–52.

Eyler, J. (1993b). From pedagogy to andragogy: The role of internships in the transition to adult learning. *Experiential Education, 17*(4), 5–7.

Eyler, J., & Halteman, B. (1981). The impact of a legislative internship on students' political skill and sophistication. *Teaching Political Science, 9,* 27–34.

Eyler, J., & Giles, D. E., Jr. (1995). *The impact of service-learning on citizenship development.* Paper presented at American Educational Research Association conference, April San Francisco.

Eyler, J., Giles, D. E., Jr. & Braxton, J. (1995). *The impact of alternative models of service-learning on student outcomes.* Paper presented at National Society for Experiential Education [NSEE] conference, New Orleans, LA.

Eyler, J., Giles, D. E., Jr., & Braxton, J. (1996). *The impact of service-learning on students' attitudes, skills and values: Preliminary results of analysis of selected data from FIPSE sponsored comparing models of service-learning project.* Paper presented at American Educational Research Association conference, April, New York.

Giles, D. E., Jr., & Eyler, J. (1994a). The impact of a college community service laboratory on students' personal, social, and cognitive outcomes. *Journal of Adolescence, 17,* 327–339.

Giles, D. E., Jr., & Eyler, J. (1994b). The theoretical roots of service-learning in John Dewey: Towards a theory of service-learning. *Michigan Journal of Community Service-Learning, 1*(1), 77–85.

Giles, D. E., Honnet, E. P., & Migliore, S. (Eds.). (1991). *Research agenda for combining service and leaning in the 1990s.* Raleigh, NC: National Society for Experiential Education.

Greene, D., & Diehm, G. (1995). Educational and service outcomes of a service integration effort. *Michigan Journal of Community Service Learning, 2,* 54–62.

Hamilton, S. F. (1981). Adolescents in community settings: What is to be learned? *Theory and Research in Social Education, 9*(2), 23–38.

Hamilton, S. F., & Fenzel, L. M. (1988). The impact of volunteer experience on adolescent social development: Evidence of program effects. *Journal of Adolescent Research, 3,* 65–80.

Hamilton, S. F., & Zeldin, R. (1987). Learning civics in community. *Curriculum Inquiry, 17,* 407–420.

Heck, S. A., & Weible, T. (1978). Study of first year college students' perceptions of career choice based on exploratory field experience. *Journal of Educational Research,* 272–276.

Honnet, E. P., & Poulsen, S. (1989). Principles of good practice in combining service and learning (Wingspread Special Report). Racine WI: The Johnson Foundation.

Hursh, B. A., & Borzak, L. (1979). Toward cognitive development through field studies. *Journal of Higher Education. 50*(1), 63–77.

Kendall, J. C. & Associates (Eds). (1990). *Combining service and learning: Vol. I and II.* Raleigh, NC: National Society for Internships and Experiential Education.

Kendall, J. C., Duley, J. S., Little, T. C., Permaul, J. S., & Rubin, S. (1986). *Strengthening experiential education within your institution.* Raleigh, NC: National Society for Internships and Experiential Education.

Kraft, R., & Krug, J. (1994). Review of research and evaluation on service learning in public and higher education. In R. Kraft & M. Swadener (Eds.), *Building community: Service learning in the academic disciplines* (pp. 197–212). Denver: Colorado Campus Compact.

Kraft, R. J., & Swadener, M. (Eds.) (1994). *Building community: Service learning in the academic disciplines.* Denver: Colorado Campus Compact.

Levison, L. (1990). Choose engagement over exposure. In J. C. Kendall & Associates (Eds). *Combining service and learning: Volumes I and II,* (pp. 68–75). Raleigh, NC: National Society for Internships and Experiential Education.

Markus, G. B., Howard, J., & King, D. (1993). Integrating community service and classroom instruction enhances learning: Results from an experiment. *Educational Evaluation and Policy Analysis, 15*(4), 410–419.

Moore, D. T. (1981). Discovering the pedagogy of experience. *Harvard Educational Review, 51*(2), 286–300.

Moore, D. T. (1986). Knowledge at work: An approach to learning by interns. In K. Borman & J. Reisman (Eds.), *Becoming a worker.* Norwood, NJ: Ablex.

Myers-Lipton, S. (1994). *The effects of service-learning on college students' attitudes towards civic responsibility, international understanding, and racial prejudice.* Unpublished dissertation, University of Colorado, Boulder.

Ostrow, J. (1995). Self-consciousness and social position: On college students changing their minds about the homeless. *Qualitative Sociology, 18*(4), 357–375.

Owens, T. R., & Owen, S. K. (1979). Enhancing the quality of community learning experiences. *Alternative Higher Education, 4*(2), 103–112.

Pataniczek, D., & Johansen, C. (1983). An introduction to internship education: New roles for students and faculty. *Journal of Experiential Education, 6*(2), 15–19.

Rubin, S. (1983). The internship process: A cultural model. *Experiential Education, 6*(4), 22–25.

Rutter, R., & Newman, F. (1989). The potential of community service to enhance civic responsibility. *Social Education, 53*(6), 371–374.

Sigmon, R. (1979). Service-learning: Three principles. *Synergist, 8*, 9–11.

Silcox, H. (1993). *A how to guide to reflection: Adding cognitive learning to community service programs*. Philadelphia: Brighton Press.

Stanton, T. K. (1990). Liberal arts, experiential learning and public service: Necessary ingredients for socially responsible undergraduate education. In J. C. Kendall & Associates (Eds), *Combining service and learning: Volumes I and II*, (pp. 175–189). Raleigh, NC: National Society for Internships and Experiential Education.

Suelzle, M., & Borzak, L. (1981). Stages of fieldwork. In L. Borzak (Ed.), *Field Study* (pp. 136–150). Beverly Hills: Sage.

Waterman, A. (1993). Conducting research on reflective activities in service-learning. In H. Silcox (Ed.), *A how to guide to reflection: Adding cognitive learning to community service programs*, (pp. 90–99). Philadelphia: Brighton Press.

6

Teachers of Service-Learning

Rahima C. Wade
University of Iowa

Teachers are central to the practice of service-learning in American schools. Whereas some districts mandate service-learning, more often teachers have the option whether to infuse service in their curriculum. Even in service-learning programs that are promoted by an enthusiastic administrator or facilitated by a district coordinator, invariably teachers have the primary responsibility for guiding their students in serving the community and learning from the process of doing so. At every level of schooling, the ultimate success of a service-learning project depends, at least in part, on the skill, knowledge, and creativity of the classroom teacher (Nathan & Kielsmeier, 1991).

Given the significance of the teacher's role in service-learning activities, it is important to understand what factors motivate teachers to begin and continue their service-learning efforts. Who are the teachers who choose to engage in service-learning? What are their beliefs about teaching? Do they have a history themselves of community involvement? Who do they involve in their service-learning activities? How much time do they spend on service, related learning, and reflection? What do they find rewarding or problematic about their service-learning experiences? These are the questions that guide the discussion in this chapter. The answers prove useful not only for teachers, but also for teacher educators, in-service trainers, program coordinators, and others who work with teachers in service-learning programs.

Whereas there have been a number of articles published on preservice teachers' service-learning involvement (Anderson & Guest, 1994, 1995; Erickson & Bayless, 1996; Root, 1994; Selke, 1996; Wade, 1993, 1995a, 1995b; Wade & Anderson, 1996), only a few studies have focused on public school teachers' experiences of service-learning (Seigel, 1995; Shumer, 1994; Wade & Eland, 1995). The primary sources for the information presented in this chapter are in-depth interviews with 10 teachers and surveys completed by an additional 74 elementary and secondary teachers from rural, suburban, and urban public school districts in the midwest. The diversity of these 84 teachers, in terms of grade level, geographic location, career phase, and personal background, contributes to a rich and varied description of teachers' experiences with community service-learning. In an effort to place these findings within the context of what we know about teachers' work lives, this chapter begins with a brief literature review on teachers' responses to curricular changes.

TEACHERS' RESPONSES TO CURRICULAR CHANGE

Most school-reform advocates place teachers in a central position in regards to school change (Flinders, 1988). Teaching is a highly contextualized enterprise and teachers' work lives are shaped by a variety of forces and factors including policy, the political–social climate, school structure, organizational factors, administrative arrangements, career paths, and professionalism (Rosenholtz, 1989). In addition, each teacher brings a unique combination of personality factors, life experiences, beliefs, and values to the teaching enterprise. "A teacher's-eye view sees teaching as an integrating activity, intertwined and interdependent with students, subject matter, and features of the workplace environment" (Paris, 1993, p. 81).

The literature on teachers' responses to implementation of innovations attests to the difficulties inherent in curricular change. First of all, most teachers are inundated with routine and overload and little time is provided for planning, discussion, and reflection (Fullan, 1991). Rarely is initial use of a new curriculum or teaching strategy a smooth enterprise. At the classroom level, teachers complain of unsuccessful attempts to "do it right," continuous cycles of trial and error, and difficulties in finding time for both the new pursuit and core academic activities (Huberman & Miles, 1984). Backsliding and freezing new practices at weak levels of implementation are all too frequent occurrences (Huberman & Miles, 1984). Many teachers cope by becoming merely efficient and compliant (Greene, 1978).

Despite these and other problems, significant classroom level changes in practice can and do result from attempts to introduce new programs, projects, or organizational arrangements (Little, 1990; Rosenholtz, 1987). When proposed changes involve a sense of mastery, excitement, and accomplishment, the incentives for trying new practices are powerful (Huberman & Miles, 1984). Fullan (1991) asserted that "good change processes that foster sustained professional development over one's career and lead to student benefits may be one of the few sources of revitalization and satisfaction left for teachers" (p. 131).

Although the school improvement literature focuses predominately on the institutional factors and types of assistance necessary to sustain and enhance implementation (Berman & McLaughlin, 1977; Clandinin & Connelly, 1991; Fullan, 1991; Huberman & Miles, 1984; Rosenholtz, 1989), a growing literature on the teacher as curriculum maker attests to the vital role of teacher agency (Paris, 1993). Paris defined teacher agency as the ability and willingness to engage in active construction of the curriculum and the learning environment. The skills of agency are acquired through active engagement with the curriculum. Teacher agency is oriented toward practical interest, for example, making curricular decisions that value individual growth toward understanding rather than "correct" ones based on published curriculum guidelines (Grundy, 1987).

In part, teachers' curricular choices are shaped by what Doyle and Ponder (1977–1978) refer to as "the practicality ethic." There are three aspects of this ethic: congruence, instrumentality, and cost. Congruence refers to the teacher's best estimate of how students will react to and learn from the change and how well the innovation appears to fit the teacher's situation. Instrumentality concerns the how to's of implementation, and cost can be defined as the ratio of investment to return as far as the individual teacher is concerned. When teachers assess if they should put effort into a particular change or not, they question the need for the change and the potential for student interest and achievement as well as the personal effort and potential benefits for themselves.

The notion of teacher agency is particularly important when innovation is an option rather than a mandate, as is often the case with service-learning activities. Teachers are often invited to incorporate a new pedagogy or topic into their teaching repertoire through in-service workshops, university courses, or pilot programs. Efforts focused on understanding the workplace and personal factors that contribute to teachers' willingness to seek out opportunities for professional development and to persist through the trial and error phase to commitment to the innovation are sorely needed.

In this chapter, I discuss the experiences of 84 teachers who have chosen to become involved in service-learning. Some of these teachers are very new to service-learning; others have practiced this teaching strategy for years, usually without having known the term "service-learning." Many have persisted through a trial-and-error phase with service-learning and attest to their commitment to continue to provide their students with opportunities to serve the community and learn in the process.

TEACHERS OF SERVICE-LEARNING: WHO ARE THEY?

Before examining the teachers' experiences with service-learning, I first discuss their personal backgrounds and their beliefs about service, teaching, and learning. The questions guiding this discussion are the following: Who are the teachers who choose to become involved with service-learning? What do they indicate as their motivation to become involved? Do they have a history of service experience in their own lives? How does service-learning fit with their philosophies of teaching and learning?

Teacher Characteristics

The 84 teachers in this study range in age from 26 to 59 years old and have taught between 2 and 34 years. The distribution is almost evenly spread between early, midcareer, and late career teachers. Many are new to service-learning. For about half, this was their first time implementing service-learning in the classroom. Almost all the teachers have been involved for 4 years or less; just a few have been long-time practitioners of service-learning for 15 years or more. Most are elementary school teachers; 17 are secondary teachers. Seventy-four of the teachers are white females. The population includes only six males, all white, and four female teachers of color. The teachers work in a variety of rural, suburban, and urban settings in the Midwest.[1]

Many of the teachers work in school districts that have formal yet voluntary service-learning programs. Of the 84 teachers, 74 were invited to participate in service-learning in conjunction with a university-sponsored program that provided them with training, curriculum materials, teacher education student assistance, and limited funds for transportation and project supplies. I coordinate this program overall; site managers are involved at two other universities as well. The support provided through external funding and personnel assistance clearly affects the teachers' service-learning experiences. This factor is discussed in more detail later in this chapter.

Motivation to Get Involved

When asked why they decided to participate in service-learning, teachers referred to a variety of factors. Many cited the importance of instilling a sense of caring, social responsibility, or self-esteem in their students. A few of these teachers asserted that they wanted to get involved as a way of increasing their own personal contributions to the community. Some knew other teachers who had tried it and had a positive experience. For example, one teacher wrote that she "saw it work successfully with two other teachers in my building." A few referred to the fact that they had been involved in service-learning for a long time without knowing the term. Involvement in the university-sponsored program gave one junior high teacher "a way to do a project I'd been thinking about for a long time."

The most common response involved reference to the compatibility between service-learning and the teachers' beliefs about teaching and life. For example, a first-grade teacher wrote, "I believe it is vital. Service will always be needed in the world of tomorrow. This is constant. Caring for and about others is essential." An elementary school teacher/counselor stated:

> I think there's a lot of pride that kids can get from making a contribution back to a school or community ... It's exciting to see kids as members of a community and as members of society ... and contributing in ways, whether it's entertainment or helping or hospice road races or volunteering at community centers or senior centers or whatever. I just think there are lots of opportunities in this community and we need to be teaching kids about what they are and how they can take advantage of them.

---

[1]More are elementary teachers simply because the university sponsored program targeted this level. The small number of secondary teachers in this study does not reflect lack of interest in service-learning among secondary teachers in general.

A few teachers mentioned the connections they saw between service-learning and their students' academic development. A sixth-grade teacher wrote that students have much to gain from service-learning. In addition to the self-esteem and personal skills there is a good deal of incidental learning along the way. These things put together with the planned academics certainly create a productive learning environment. A middle-school language arts teacher summed up the importance of service-learning to her academic goals in the following statement:

> It made so much sense that part of growing up as thinkers and listeners, that they be linked somehow with the community. ... One of the things that I talk with them (the students) about is the fact that I cannot provide for them within the context of the classroom, the kind of language experience that will be useful to them in interacting with the community and the world outside these walls. One of the things that I know about readers and writers is that they are constant observers and I want them to be in the community observing what is going on and coming back and talking and writing about it. It is a springboard for a lot of the writing.

A few teachers also referred to the support offered through the university-sponsored grant program. Particularly for teachers new to service-learning, it is likely that the project money, personal stipend, in-service training, or teacher education student assistance were motivating factors.

Prior Community Service Experience

Although most teachers did not say so overtly, it is also likely that prior experiences with community service were motivating factors for these teachers. Over three forths of the teachers indicated they had some prior service experience as a child in their family, community, or school or as an adult. Unfortunately, no comparative data exists about the prevalence of service experience in the teaching population as a whole so it is impossible to conclude that their early service experiences differ significantly from those teachers who choose not to become involved in service-learning. However, many of these teachers referred to the importance of community service activities in their growing up years. The importance of this experience is supported by a large-scale national study that found early community service experience to be a significant factor in predicting adult community service involvement (Hodgkinson & Weitzman, 1992).

The teachers mentioned experiences in their families and communities more often than school-related service activities. More than half of the teachers had engaged in service with their families or in their communities, for example, through church youth groups, 4-H, or Girl Scouts. A few teachers mentioned that they helped others as a normal part of their family activities by making meals for ill community members, visiting the elderly at a local care center, or participating in community clean-up projects. One elementary school teacher reflected on how much she appreciated being involved as a child in her community's service effort:

> I remember very clearly my whole town building a swimming pool because we needed a swimming pool, and being able to be involved. People were not telling me you can't help because I was a kid. The town raised money and then just with whatever expertise the people in town brought, we built the swimming pool. ... I remember tying reinforcement rods in the bottom of the pool together with these little wires when I was in junior high. I wanted to swim in the swimming pool, I wanted it as bad as anybody else. I didn't think it was something that just the adults had to have their fingers in. Fortunately, they let me help.

Some of the teachers specifically mentioned opportunities they had for engaging in service as part of their kindergarten through college experience. A few mentioned that their public school fostered a helping ethic, where older students would tutor younger students or everyone would engage in school clean-up activities. One teacher recalled making mittens for poor children in conjunction with a mitten tree in her school during each winter holiday season. A few mentioned high school service experiences helping preschool children or visiting the elderly in a nursing home. One referred to conducting service-learning projects in an inner-city student teaching assignment. Only four teachers mentioned being involved in service activities during college.

Some of the interviewed teachers, although not initially recognizing a connection between their service-learning involvement and their earlier service activities, did realize a relationship between the two through the course of the interviews. One fifth-grade teacher was not sure where she got the idea to have her students visit the nearby nursing home as part of a language arts "Grandparents" unit, until she remembered that she had spent many college vacations visiting her grandmother at a retirement community in Florida. A high school teacher who facilitates a service-learning program involving cross-age tutoring recalled her own experience tutoring others. "When I grew up I went to probably the very last country school in Iowa. For 9 years. A couple of years I was the only girl and other years there were just two of us. So for all those years I was the teacher for everybody else. So the tutoring business—I grew up tutoring. I guess you could say that was service because I did a lot of that."

Whereas other connections between early service experiences and teachers' current involvement in service-learning may have remained hidden, the information here supports the notion that many teachers are able to identify service experiences with their families, in their communities, and in their schooling that have contributed to their belief in the importance of service-learning and their willingness to engage in service-learning projects with their students.

Current Community Service Involvement

Of the 10 teachers interviewed, only 1 is extremely active in her community, having recently run for the state legislature and winning her seat there. Two others mentioned activities they used to participate in, such as giving blood and helping out with church-related projects. Less than half of the teachers in the survey sample indicated that they were currently involved in community service. Examples of the wide range of community activities for those who are involved include donating to shelters and the food bank, helping with meals at the free lunch program, working with Habitat for Humanity, serving on the board of a community agency, staffing a suicide hot line and volunteering at the public library, the hospital, the historical museum, and other community sites.

Again, no comparative data exists to assess whether these teachers are more or less involved in the community than their nonservice-learning-involved counterparts. However, it appears that not all service-learning teachers, despite their expressed beliefs in the importance of giving to the community, take the time to be involved personally outside of their school day. It is important to note, as mentioned previously, that some of the teachers saw the facilitation of their students' service-learning activities as their personal way of being involved in the community as well.

TEACHERS' EXPERIENCES OF SERVICE-LEARNING

Teachers' descriptions of their service-learning activities with students reveal that service-learning is at once both rewarding and problematic. The teachers' stories evidence the satisfaction they feel from seeing students motivated to learn and help others. Their experiences also highlight challenges with planning, finding the time for service-learning, and making contacts with community agencies. Of particular concern to the success of service-learning projects are teachers' approaches to planning and working with others in the school and the community. Following a discussion of teachers' experiences with planning and working with others, I explore further the rewards and challenges of service-learning practice for public school teachers.

Planning Service-Learning Projects

The midwestern teachers approach the planning of service-learning projects in very different ways. Some plan the project themselves and inform the students of what they will be doing. Others engage in a collaborative planning process with students and some involve other school faculty or community members at the planning stage as well. These differences appear to be connected to many factors including teaching style, age of students, type of project, extent to which the teacher is integrating the project in the curriculum, time spent on planning, and time allotted for service-learning during the school day.

Part of the variance in how teachers plan service-learning activities may also be connected to how project ideas originate. In some cases, students approach their teachers with ideas for service-learning activities. Other times, the project idea is generated from a topic of current interest in the community. Yet another approach is that the teacher will think of a project idea that is particularly suited to his or her academic curriculum.

A few examples from the teachers' interviews will serve to illustrate these differences. For example, in a fourth-grade science class, one girl pleaded with her teacher to do a unit on the rain forest. This "go-getter" student then formed a nature club and approached the media center staff about getting some books on recycling. Finally, the teacher said okay, that she would see what she could find on the rain forest. After acquiring materials from journals, conferences, and the local university curriculum lab, the teacher felt she had enough materials to put together the unit. The success of this student-initiated project was dependent on the teacher's flexibility. "I do have a little leeway," she stated in our first interview: "I have several places I can fill in with units I am interested in teaching."

Examples of teachers' choosing the service-learning project include a second-grade teacher's intergenerational project. Because the care center is near the school and the teacher is good friends with the director there, she opted for this service-learning project. She also chose the project because she immediately saw the connections she could build between service with seniors and her language arts curriculum goals. Whereas she acknowledges that she chose the basic project, she allows her students to decide what they would like to do with the seniors each month they visit.

Regardless of how the project idea is initiated, many teachers recognize the importance of student ownership to the success of service-learning activities. Students who have some input in the project are much more likely to be motivated and engaged in the activities and related academic learning. Recognizing this fact, two sixth-grade teachers emerged enthusiastically from a 3 day service-learning workshop with the following question, "We know what we want to do for our service-learning project! Now how do we get our students to think that it was their idea?"

Sometimes a constellation of factors congeal into a service-learning experience. This was the case for one fourth-grade teacher whose class had made and sold a calendar the previous year to raise money for the local food pantry at the invitation of another teacher in the school. She described how a similar service-learning project "kind of fell together" the following year:

> My kids read the book *Fly Away Home* by Eve Bunting (about the homeless) and they got to talking and they said 'let's do something.' They had just read about the man last year who died in the dumpster. ... A lot of kids clipped this story and they were really concerned about it. It was just a whole combination of things and I had the calendar sitting out from the previous year that the others kids had done and they wanted to do a project too. It just kind of evolved that way.

If there are generalities to the teachers' planning experiences, they involve the use of time and materials. Many of the teachers agreed that planning for service-learning takes more time than traditional, textbook-based subjects.[2] The teachers used a wide variety of materials to plan their projects. In addition to service-learning curricula provided by the university, most teachers used additional resources from their classroom and school libraries, public libraries, or local community agencies.

Rarely did teachers take an idea directly from a curriculum and put it in place in their classrooms. More often, teachers used their creative skills to construct a service-learning project. A junior high health teacher stated, "I took some of the

[2]The exception to this finding was in the group of teachers who planned service-learning projects with their student teachers. In most cases, the student teachers did more of the planning and thus the classroom teachers did not feel that planning the service-learning projects took more of their time.

things from here, put a sheet together, and spent a lot of time brainstorming ideas." Part of her brainstorming strategy involved having students peruse the phone book for service ideas and inviting community members to come to class and talk about their areas of expertise. Whether the project idea emanates from the students, the teacher, or a community concern, planning service-learning projects usually involves considerable time, a variety of materials, and some creative thinking on the part of the teacher.

Working With Others

Most of the service-learning projects involved others in the school or community. School personnel included in the projects were other classroom teachers, music and art specialists, school counselors, principals, and even cooks, bus drivers, and custodians. For example, a fifth-grade service-learning project at a nursing home involved the school guidance counselor (in preparing the students for interacting with the seniors), the music teacher (who taught the students some old time songs to sing to the seniors), the art teacher (who helped the class prepare a craft project to make with the seniors), and the school principal (who videotaped the participants and served ice cream at the last visit of the year). Parents were also involved in this project, as they were in many projects, by helping with transportation or providing snacks or needed supplies.

Given the nature of service-learning activities, many agencies and businesses from the community were involved in the projects. These ranged from agencies to which services were provided (e.g., nursing homes, an animal shelter, food banks, a domestic violence center, Headstart preschool, a neighborhood center) to businesses who contributed goods, services, or consultation for the projects (e.g., landscaping businesses, banks, grocery stores, department stores, book stores).

In addition, teachers often called on individuals with expertise, such as a farmer, an environmentalist, a forester, or a nursing home activity director, to help with the project. A junior high teacher of students with behavior disorders, attributing her collaboration with the director of a community agency as essential to her success with placing her students at various sites, stated, "(She) really helped me because she had so many contacts in the community."

Another person who was extremely influential for 5 of the 10 teachers interviewed was the district's service-learning coordinator. All five of the teachers attested to her help with planning and carrying out the projects. "She does all the organizing and planning," stated one teacher. "She does a previsit. She comes out with slides ... She arranges school buses, everything." One of the teachers asserted that the coordinator was a "catalyst" who "made it all seem possible. She made me think, gosh, this would be easy to do even in the context of the classroom."

The coordinator also influences the types of projects teachers choose to participate in, as illustrated by the following two examples. As part of an in-service session focused on integrating community service with whole language, the coordinator took the participating teachers to a youth shelter. A fourth-grade teacher who attended this session based her service-learning project on helping children at the youth shelter. When a new coordinator was hired, a sixth-grade teacher stated, "Partly we didn't go to the nursing home (this year) because we have a new facilitator just getting her feet wet. ... If she would have pushed the nursing home we would have gone there."

For the most part, teachers' collaborations with other school personnel, community members, and parents enriched their service-learning experiences. Two drawbacks cited were difficulty in making contacts with those outside of school and someone not following through on an agreed on task. However, the success of the service-learning activities was largely enhanced through the combined efforts of the participants.

The Rewards of Service-Learning

These midwestern teachers find many aspects of their service-learning activities rewarding. The gratifying aspects of service-learning include: student motivation and learning, recognition from colleagues, administrators, and parents; public attention in the media; and the benefits they perceive resulting from the service activity for the community. Consistent with the research on rewards of teaching in general (Feiman-Nemser & Floden, 1986; Fullan, 1991; Jackson, 1968; Lortie, 1975), the greatest reward is seeing positive changes in their students in conjunction with service-learning. Most teachers have observed increases in student enthusiasm and motivation to learn, as well as their improvement in self-esteem, academic learning, and social skill development. In my interviews with teachers, they often bring up stories of student success and excitement, even when I ask other kinds of questions.

Whereas the teachers note that almost all students are motivated by and learn from service-learning activities, some appear to be particularly impressed by the benefits for individual students. For example, a junior high teacher was excited about being able to recommend one of her students with a behavior disorder for a paying job after a positive community experience. A fifth-grade teacher was gratified that a few of her students continued visits to seniors in a local nursing home throughout the summer following their monthly school year visits. A number of teachers commented on the student who typically misbehaved but was a "model child" while out in the community working with others.

Many of the teachers enjoyed the recognition they received from others in the school and community as a result of the service-learning project. Frequently, service-learning projects were noticed by colleagues and parents. A sixth-grade teacher, who had completed a service-learning project with his morning science class, quickly added the experience for his afternoon science class, as well, after a parent request. Many parents were very enthusiastic and willing to help out with field trips or food items for bake sales or meals for the homeless. One junior high teacher found that some of her students, in the process of completing their service-learning activities at an agency site, involved the rest of their family members in serving others as well.

Most school principals were supportive of teachers' efforts. Teachers sensed that even when principals were quiet, they were positive about service-learning opportunities for students. A high school teacher's principal wrote on her yearly evaluation, "If you decided not to do peer helpers, I can't think of another staff member who could fill your shoes." One principal who initially questioned a fifth-grade teacher's decision to take her students once a month to the local nursing home, ended up videotaping their last visit of the school year and helping serve ice cream to the residents.

Successful service-learning projects appear to frequently make the news, another source of reward for both teachers and students. Teachers mentioned publicity in the school and district newsletters as well as in local newspapers. One group of students was recognized by the mayor of a small city for their service work; another was featured in a local TV show on service-learning.

Teachers also were gratified by the community benefits resulting from their service-learning activities. They cited improvements in the environment, food and supplies for those in need, and the enrichment of nursing home residents' lives. Siegel (1995), in one of six case studies of service-learning teachers from her doctoral dissertation, discussed the benefits one teacher perceived for an elderly woman of a weekly crochet class with her sixth graders:

> At the nursing home we had the idea that maybe we should see if the older people can offer the kids something ... So one of the ladies crocheted. And we asked her if she could teach the girls how to crochet. They (the staff) said that she would talk all week about oh Thursday, she had to get ready for Thursday because her crocheting class was coming. I mean she sits in that nursing home with nothing to do, and now she has something to think about all week ... that really made her time worthwhile.

Although there are undoubtedly other rewards that teachers experience in concert with service-learning activities, those discussed here were most frequently cited. It is important to note that although teachers enjoy recognition from their colleagues, administrators, and parents, and value the benefits service-learning offers the community, the most rewarding aspect of service-learning for almost all of the teachers is the benefits they observe in their own students. The outcomes teachers cited for students—enthusiasm, motivation to learn, academic gains, improvement in self-esteem, and the development of social skills—have all been noted as prominent outcomes in research on K–12 students' service-learning involvement (Conrad & Hedin, 1991).

Despite the many rewards for teachers, service-learning is not without its challenges. I turn now to a discussion of the problems and stresses teachers may encounter in community service-learning activities.

Problems With Service-Learning

Although there are many different types of problems teachers might experience in conjunction with service-learning, most of their concerns can be linked with one critical factor: time. Of the many ways that service-learning activities differ from traditional academic instruction, three have particular significance for teachers in terms of the time problems they experience.

First, most service-learning activities cannot be taught directly from a curriculum guide or textbook. Because service-learning projects must address a school or community need, teachers usually need to develop tailor-made plans for the project and seek creative ways to tie the service activity to the academic curriculum. Reflection lessons must also be developed specific to the project and students' experiences. Service-learning curriculum materials (e.g., Cairn & Coble, 1993; Iowa Service-Learning Partnership, 1995; Maryland Student Service Alliance, 1992; Novelli & Chayet, 1991) can give teachers useful ideas but rarely can form the basis for the curriculum in the way that a math textbook or a children's literature series can. "The thing that is hardest for us is to come up with the ideas," confirmed one junior high teacher.

Second, almost all service-learning projects involve collaboration with others. In many cases, this collaboration involves individuals outside of the school, such as community agency workers and parents. Most teachers do not have phones in their rooms; nor are they given significant amounts of time during the day to make phone calls or meet with others outside of the school. It is a challenge for teachers to find the time to plan collaboratively and to make needed contacts with community members.

Third, service-learning activities usually involve some unforeseen problems or surprising events. Because most projects involve other people in the school or community and because service-learning centers around trying to change existing problems, time must be spent in addressing the barriers and difficulties that inevitably arise. Just with the logistics of a visit to a service site, many things can go wrong. For example, imagine a fifth-grade class who is going to make and serve a meal at the local homeless shelter. Perhaps some children forget to bring their contribution to the meal or a parent who was supposed to drive now has to stay at home with a sick child. When the students arrive at the service site, they may find 50 more mouths than expected to feed or that miscommunication with the agency director has resulted in no one providing the drinks. Any one of these problems is enough to create additional stress for a classroom teacher who may already feel that his or her teaching days are harried.

Although time is the most often mentioned problem in service-learning, it is important to note that some of the teachers indicated that planning for service-learning activities did not take more time than planning for other subject areas in their classrooms.[3] There was a great deal of diversity in the amount of time teachers spent on their service-learning activities. Planning time ranged from 30 minutes to 30 hours for a semester long project, with the average being slightly over 6 hours. Actual time spent working on project activities both in and outside of the classroom ranged from 15 minutes to 40 hours with the average being a little over 9 hours.

Time is certainly not the only problem that these teachers encountered. Other occasionally mentioned problems with service-learning included: student misbehavior out in the community, the need for additional project funds or help with transportation, students' apprehensions about working with the elderly or individuals with disabilities, parent complaints, lack of colleagues' or administrator's support, and students' lack of motivation.

---

[3] All but 10 of the teachers were given financial and personnel assistance with their service-learning activities through a university-sponsored grant funded by the Corporation for National Service's Learn and Serve Higher Education program or the Fund for the Improvement of Post Secondary Education (FIPSE). It is probable that without this support more of the teachers would have experienced time or lack of project money as a problem.

Siegel (1995) noted that two middle school teachers she studied had problems with student motivation and ownership of the project because it was largely teacher planned and directed. They also experienced how too many students involved in an outside activity can lead to havoc, making the project unmanageable. They also discovered the difficulty of sustaining student interest over time.

All of these problems are ones that teachers might realistically encounter in service-learning projects. Yet, with the exception of time, the vast majority of the teachers discussed here did not experience them. In most cases, teachers noted the prevalence of student enthusiasm, collegial and administrative support, and the personal satisfaction of assisting students in helping others and learning through service.

IMPLICATIONS OF TEACHERS' EXPERIENCES FOR SERVICE-LEARNING PROGRAMS

The issues discussed in this chapter in relation to teachers' experiences with service-learning hold important implications for coordinators of service-learning programs, teacher educators, in-service trainers, and teachers of service-learning themselves. These implications are discussed here in relation to three key goals of many service-learning programs: recruiting new teachers, providing support for initial implementation of service-learning projects, and fostering teachers' commitment to service-learning over time.

Recruiting New Teachers

Most of the teachers discussed in this chapter chose to participate in a university-sponsored service-learning program that offered in-service training, project supply and transportation funds, teacher education student assistance, and in some cases, a personal stipend for their planning time. Although most of the teachers indicated that they chose to participate in the program for reasons other than these factors, it is likely that the support and organization of the program were contributing factors as well. Some of the teachers did indicate that they might not have participated without the personal stipend or the project funds.

Service-learning programs aimed at recruiting new teachers should consider up front the different types of support that might be provided. In addition to the above, our program offers paid planning workshops at school sites and kits of resource materials developed around service-learning themes (e.g., intergenerational, environmental, poverty/hunger; Iowa Service-Learning Partnership, 1995). These are ideas that were generated by teachers in the program.

The findings here point to three other promising strategies as well. First, successful teachers of service-learning may be one of the best resources for recruitment. A number of the midwestern teachers became involved in service-learning on the recommendation of a colleague. Also, encouraging teachers to consider their personal, social, and academic goals for students and letting them know how service-learning can help to meet those goals is a useful strategy. Third, asking teachers to reflect on their prior service experiences in their families, communities, and schools, may enable them to develop a conscious awareness of the value of service.

Supporting Initial Implementation

In addition to the types of financial, training, and personnel assistance just mentioned above, service-learning program coordinators are likely to be more successful if they take a flexible, individualized approach to supporting teachers in their initial attempts at service-learning. The variance in how teachers plan for service-learning activities attests to the fact that there is no one right way to begin a service-learning project. Some teachers want to begin with a small, manageable project that does not extend beyond the school grounds. Others want to jump in and, as the Nike slogan goes, "Just do it!" Teachers should be encouraged to allow the project to develop from their own interests, student initiative, their curricular goals, and/or a current community need.

Regardless of how a project idea is initiated, program leaders should inform new teachers about three critical elements of successful service-learning efforts: student ownership, teacher creativity, and collaboration with others. Student ownership of the project will vary depending on the type of project, the grade level of the students, the degree of curriculum integration, and the process by which the project idea was generated. In all projects, however, teachers should endeavor to give students opportunities to make choices and decisions that affect the course of the project and thus enhance their ownership of the service-learning experience.

Teacher creativity (or teacher agency) appears to be essential in most service-learning projects. Teachers should know that they are unlikely to be able to take a service-learning project directly from a book and implement it in their classrooms. Programs should provide teachers with resources on service-learning as well as a variety of other curriculum materials they can use to plan service projects that will meet important community needs and enhance student learning from the service experience.

Teachers should also be encouraged to consider carefully who in the school and community could help them plan and implement their service-learning projects. Ideally, community agencies and service recipients should be involved in planning the project. Parents, businesses, and experts from the community can also be instrumental. Communicating with administrators and parents and carefully delineating various responsibilities for project activities among all those involved in the school and community are also necessary ingredients for success.

Time is a critical issue for teachers as they implement service-learning for the first time. A service-learning coordinator can be extremely helpful in planning and coordinating project activities as well as encouraging teachers to engage in specific types of projects. In programs without a coordinator, teachers should be encouraged to set aside time for planning and begin with a small project rather than become over committed and burned-out on service-learning after the first experience.

Fostering Teachers' Commitment

After the initial enthusiastic experience, what is likely to sustain teachers' involvement in service-learning? What measures will prevent potential backsliding and weak levels of implementation (Huberman & Miles, 1984) or simply giving up on service-learning? Given the lack of long-term studies addressing these questions, my speculations are informed only by the teachers' service-learning experiences as described here and the literature on teachers as curriculum makers.

Some turnover among teachers who participate in a service-learning program seems inevitable. There will always be teachers who tried it only to find out that it was too difficult, too time consuming, or otherwise not worth the effort. At the same time, teachers who are committed to service-learning over a number of years are vital to the development of a quality program. It is these teachers who can provide expertise, inspiration, and consultation to others who choose to become involved.

Program coordinators would be wise to consider the three components of Doyle and Ponder's (1977–1978) practicality ethic in relation to teachers' service-learning experiences. The congruence aspect involves the fit between service-learning and the teacher's goals and teaching philosophy. Helping teachers become aware of the multiple goals they have for students and how service-learning can foster some of these goals should contribute to long-term commitment.

The second aspect of the practicality ethic, instrumentality, points to the importance of providing teachers with in-service training, curriculum resources, and personnel support. In-service training must not be just a one time event. After the implementation phase, teachers need to regroup for follow-up sessions focused on assessing the benefits of their service-learning activities for their students and the community. These sessions can also serve to give teachers a chance to share in celebrating their projects, to reflect on their service-learning efforts, and to discuss ways to improve the overall service-learning program. As a program coordinator, I have found these sessions to be essential for both teacher and program success.

The third aspect of the practicality ethic, cost, involves teachers' assessments of the benefits versus the costs of service-learning. Again, at follow- up sessions or through interviews or surveys, teachers should be encouraged to assess both the problems and the rewards of service-learning. For almost all of the 84 midwestern teachers, the benefits of student enthusiasm and learning and community benefit outweighed the difficulties with finding time for service-learning or communicating effectively with others in the school and community. A recent survey study has revealed that more than half of these teachers have continued to include service-learning projects in their curriculum, up to a year and a half later than their official involvement in the university-funded program. Although time will always be an issue in service-learning, as it is with much of teachers' work lives (Fullan, 1991; Huberman & Miles, 1984), service-learning is clearly an innovation that can involve the excitement, mastery, and accomplishment that serve as powerful incentives for trying new pedagogical practices (Huberman & Miles).

CONCLUSION

Service-learning is a complex and exciting endeavor for teachers and students. Teachers who choose to participate in service-learning programs value their students' personal, social, and academic growth as well as believe in the importance of social responsibility in the curriculum. Based on their own experiences with community service, their personal desires to make a contribution, or their concern for students' development of empathy and social responsibility, these teachers take the time and effort to plan projects that both meet important community needs and foster student enthusiasm and learning. Time and coordination of service-learning projects are challenges for most teachers, yet with creativity, skill, and energy, teachers can bring about powerful experiences benefiting their students, schools, and communities.

REFERENCES

Anderson, J., & Guest, K. (1994, April). *Meeting the needs of children and youth: A community service-learning program for preservice teachers.* Paper presented at the annual meeting of the American Educational Research Association, New Orleans, LA.

Anderson, J., & Guest, K. (1995). Linking campus and community: Service leadership in teacher education at Seattle University. In B. Gomez (Ed.), *Integrating service-learning into teacher education: Why and how?* Washington, DC: Council of Chief State School Officers.

Berman, P., & McLaughlin, M. (1977). *Federal programs supporting educational change, Vol. VII. Factors affecting implementation and continuation.* Santa Monica, CA: Rand Corporation.

Cairn, R. W., & Coble, T. (1993). *Learning by giving: K–8 service-learning curriculum guide.* St. Paul, MN: National Youth Leadership Council.

Clandinin, D. J., & Connelly, F. M. (1991). Teacher as curriculum maker. In P. W. Jackson (Ed.), *Handbook of research on curriculum* (pp. 363–401). New York: Macmillan.

Conrad, D., & Hedin, D. (1991). School-based community service: What we know from research and theory. *Phi Delta Kappan, 72*(10), 754–757.

Doyle, W., & Ponder, G. (1977–1978). *The practicality ethic in teacher decision making. Interchange, 8*(3), 1–12.

Erickson, J., & Bayless, M. A. (1996). Integrating service-learning into teacher education. In B. Taylor, (Ed.), *Expanding boundaries: Serving and learning* (pp. 10–14). Washington, DC: Corporation for National Service.

Feiman-Nemser, S., & Floden, R. E. (1986). The cultures of teaching. In M. Wittrock (Ed.), *Handbook of research on teaching* (pp. 505–526). New York: Macmillan.

Flinders, D. J. (1988). Teacher isolation and the new reform. *Journal of Curriculum and Supervision, 4*(1), 17–29.

Fullan, M. G. (1991). *The new meaning of educational change.* New York: Teachers College Press.

Greene, M. (1978). Teaching: The question of personal reality. *Teachers College Record, 80*(1), 23–35.

Grundy, S. (1987). *Curriculum: Product or praxis.* Philadelphia: Falmer Press.

Hodgkinson, V. A., & Weitzman, M. S. (1992). *Giving and volunteering in the United States.* Washington, DC: Independent Sector.

Huberman, A. M., & Miles, M. B. (1984). *Innovation up close.* New York: Plenum.

Iowa Service-Learning Partnership. (1995). *Joining hands community service-learning resource kits.* Iowa City: University of Iowa College of Education.

Jackson, P. W. (1968). *Life in classrooms.* New York: Holt, Rinehart & Winston.

Little, J. W. (1990). The persistence of privacy: Autonomy and initiative in teachers' professional relations. *Teachers College Record, 91*(4), 509–536.

Lortie, D. (1975). *School teacher: A sociological study.* Chicago: University of Chicago Press.

Maryland Student Service Alliance. (1992). *The courage to care, the strength to serve: Draft instructional framework in service-learning for middle school.* Baltimore: Author.

Nathan, J., & Kielsmeier, J. (1991). The sleeping giant of school reform. *Phi Delta Kappan, 72*(10), 739–742.

Novelli, J., & Chayet, B. (1991). *The kids care book: 50 class projects that help kids help others.* New York: Scholastic Instructor Books.

Paris, C. L. (1993). *Teacher agency and curriculum making in classrooms.* New York: Teachers College Press.

Root, S. (1994). Service-learning in teacher education: A third rationale. *Michigan Journal of Service Learning, 1*(1), 94–97.

Rosenholtz, S. (1987). Workplace conditions that affect teacher quality and commitment: Implications for the design of teacher induction programs. *The Elementary School Journal, 89*(4), 421–440.

Rosenholtz, S. (1989). *Teachers' workplace: The social organization of schools.* New York: Longman.

Seigel, S. (1995). *Community service-learning as empowering pedagogy: Implications for middle school teachers.* Unpublished doctoral dissertation, University of Massachusetts, Amherst.

Selke, M. (1996). Student teacher involvement in service-learning: Anticipating potential areas of concern. In B. Taylor, (Ed.), *Expanding Boundaries: Serving and learning* (pp. 26–28). Washington, DC: Corporation for National Service.

Shumer, R. (1994, April). *A report from the field: Teachers talk about service-learning.* Paper presented at the annual meeting of the American Educational Research Association, San Francisco.

Wade, R. C. (1993). Social action: Expanding the role of citizenship in the social studies curriculum. *Inquiry in Social Studies: Curriculum, Research, and Instruction, 29*(1), 2–18.

Wade, R. C. (1995a). Developing active citizens: Community service-learning in social studies teacher education. *The Social Studies, 86*(3), 122–128.

Wade, R. C. (1995b). Community service-learning in the University of Iowa's elementary teacher education program. In B. Gomez (Ed.), *Integrating service-learning into teacher education: Why and how?* (pp. 41–55). Washington, DC: Council of Chief State School Officers.

Wade, R. C., & Anderson, J. (1996). Community service-learning: A strategy for preparing human service-oriented teachers. *Teacher Education Quarterly, 23*(4), 59–74.

Wade, R. C., & Eland, W. M. (1995). Connections, rewards, and challenges. *National Society for Experiential Education Quarterly, 21*(1), 4–5, 26–27.

7

The Role of Student Characteristics in Service-Learning

Alan S. Waterman
The College of New Jersey

In considering the ingredients for successfully initiating, sustaining, and improving programs in service-learning, it is necessary to consider not only the specific characteristics of various programs but also the roles played by the teachers and the students. Janet Eyler and Dwight Giles (chap. 5) have examined aspects of service-learning programs contributing to success, and Rahima Wade (chap. 6) has looked at the programs from the perspective of the teachers. In this chapter, I examine the role of student characteristics in these programs.

There are two hypotheses drawn from the field of personality psychology that provide the basis for the perspective advanced here:

1. Students will differ in their motivations for participation in service-learning programs and these differences will effect both how students involve themselves in service activities and what they derive from such activities in terms of both affective changes and cognitive growth and learning.

2. Student development, in both the affective and cognitive realms will be enhanced when there is a good "fit" between student characteristics (including motivations) and the nature of the service experiences provided to the students.

Whereas there is substantial evidence of the impact of service-learning programs on student development and attitude change, the existing research on service-learning has not provided the means for assessing the role of student characteristics as input variables in such programs. There is, however, a body of research literature on the role of participant characteristics in volunteer service activities that can be used to evaluate the two hypotheses just offered. The review of this literature, with few exceptions, is limited to the coverage of studies involving volunteers of high school and college age; samples corresponding to those involved in service-learning programs.

Four questions drawn from the research on volunteer service are the focus of attention here:

Question 1: How do students who engage in volunteer service differ from those who do not? (Studies addressing this question involve comparisons of service providers and non-providers.)

Question 2: What factors play a central role in the motivation to engage in volunteer service activities?

Question 3: Among service providers, what characteristics are associated with the level of involvement, in terms of hours of service, devoted to helping others?

Question 4: Among service providers, what characteristics are associated with sustaining volunteer service over time, as opposed to terminating such activity?

In addition to a review of the literature on each question, I summarize the findings emerging from my own work on these questions.

HOW DO STUDENTS WHO ENGAGE IN VOLUNTEER SERVICE DIFFER FROM THOSE WHO DO NOT?

Research Findings

College students who engage in volunteer activities have been found to differ from comparison samples not engaged in volunteer activities on a range of measures. Serow (1991) compared the values held by college students involved in community service volunteer activities with those not participating in such programs. As would be expected, the volunteers more strongly endorsed the value of helping others, but rated the value of family lower than did the nonparticipants. Students' approach to religion was found to be related to participation in volunteer activities, with those involved in volunteer service scoring higher on a measure of intrinsic religiosity (i.e., genuine commitment without regard to personal benefits), whereas no difference was found regarding extrinsic religiosity (Bernt, 1989). Knapp and Holtzberg (1964), in a study of male college students serving as companions for chronically ill mental patients, found the volunteers to be more compassionate, more religiously oriented, and more morally concerned, than a comparison group of students not engaged in the program. The volunteers expressed less concern about economic success and related values.

Turner (1973) surveyed students, all of whom expressed an interest in volunteering for a campus "hot line" program and attended an initial meeting. The students actually agreeing to participate in the program were then compared with those who indicated that they would have no further involvement. The volunteers were found to be more self-controlled, more tolerant, and more dedicated to social improvement.

The successful psychological functioning of individuals engaged in volunteer service was documented by Tapp and Spanier (1973) who found volunteers at a suicide prevention and crisis service to score significantly higher on a measure of self-actualization in comparison to a relatively well-matched sample of college students. Hersch, Kulik, and Scheibe (1969), in a comparison study of college students volunteering in a mental hospital with other students who did not volunteer, reported greater flexibility in thinking and a stronger drive for creative achievement among the volunteers. And Evanoski (1988) found that college students engaged in an on-campus volunteer program described their college experiences as more fulfilling, satisfying, useful, and important than did nonvolunteers. The volunteers also reported more positive self-evaluations, indicative of higher self-esteem.

In my own program of research, I have been primarily concerned with the nature of optimal experiences (Waterman, 1990, 1992, 1993). Because "helping others" is one type of activity consistently described as giving rise to optimal experiences, I have undertaken a series of studies on student involvement in volunteer service activities. The findings from that research are relevant to developing answers to the four questions posed earlier.

In four undergraduate courses and one graduate course at Trenton State College, I surveyed students with regard to their involvement in volunteer activities during the past year, their motivations for such service, and their intent to continue with their service. The participants also completed a series of other questionnaires:

1. A background questionnaire tapping demographic information.
2. The Personally Expressive Activities Questionnaire (PEAQ; Waterman, 1993) designed to tap four aspects of optimal experience: feelings of personal expressiveness, feelings of flow (Csikszentmihalyi, 1975), combined levels of challenges and skills associated with activities (Csikszentmihalyi, 1990), and opportunities for the development of one's best potentials.
3. The Extended Objective Measure of Ego Identity Status (Bennion & Adams, 1986), an instrument designed to assess the ways in which individuals develop a sense of personal identity.
4. The Work Preference Inventory (Amabile, Hill, Hennessey, & Tighe, 1994), a measure of the respondents' intrinsic and extrinsic motivations regarding education.

Of 243 students surveyed, 165 (67.9%) reported engaging in some form of volunteer service during the preceding year. The proportions of males and females engaged in such activities were quite similar. Comparisons of volunteers with nonvolunteers revealed the following differences:

1. With regard to optimal experiences, on the PEAQ, volunteers were found to be significantly more likely to be engaging in activities giving rise to experiences of personal expressiveness than were nonvolunteers. There were also statistical trends indicating they were more frequently experiencing feelings of flow and engaging in activities that afford opportunities for the development of their best potentials. No

difference was found for the level of challenges and skills involved in the activities rated on the PEAQ.

2. Volunteers differed from nonvolunteers with respect to the manner in which they approached the task of identity formation, with nonvolunteers significantly more often reporting that they adopted a strategy that did not entail active, reflective consideration of alternative potential identity-related goals, values, and beliefs.

3. Volunteers also reported significantly greater intrinsic motivation toward their education than did nonvolunteers, but the groups did not differ in the extent of their extrinsic motivations.

Implications for Service-Learning Programs

Because the studies discussed here involve comparisons between students already engaged in volunteer service with those not volunteering, the research does not permit a determination of whether the differences observed predated involvement in the service activities, and may have played a role in the original decision to volunteer, or were a product of the service activities themselves. Both alternatives appear plausible, and they are not mutually exclusive. With respect to service-learning programs, where courses at the high school or college level are optional, the students choosing to enroll in the programs can be compared with those drawn from the general student population to assess the extent to which they are similar to, or different from the average student. The existence of notable differences between students who self-select service participation from those who do not, has important implications in instances where there is a desire to make service participation a requirement for all students. A service program demonstrated to be effective with self-selected students may not work as effectively for students whose personal characteristics differ substantially from those choosing to participate on an elective basis. On the other hand, if there are few prior differences between students who do and do not choose to enroll in service-learning courses, then the likelihood is higher that the differences that have been observed between volunteers and nonvolunteers are a function of the service experiences themselves. This would remove one source of concern when considering instituting a general service-learning requirement.

WHAT FACTORS PLAY A CENTRAL ROLE IN THE MOTIVATION TO ENGAGE IN VOLUNTEER SERVICE ACTIVITIES?

Research Findings

A traditional distinction made with respect to motivations to engage in volunteer service activities pertains to differences between altruistic and egoistic motivations. *Altruistic motivations* refer to engaging in helping behaviors exclusively, or at least primarily, because of the benefits generated for other people. *Egoistic motivations* are self-serving in nature, that is, a person engages in behaviors to help others in the expectation that some personal benefit will be obtained. Such benefits may include such things as the development of personal skills, recognition from one's family or from community leaders, and increased employment opportunities. Because it is recognized that helping others may generate good feelings in oneself, these two categories of motivations should not be viewed as mutually exclusive. There has been considerable research conducted with regard to whether altruistic or egoistic motivations predominate.

Among studies of high school and college students on this question, Wiche and Isenhour (1977), surveying junior volunteers, ages 12 to 17, at a Voluntary Action Center, found the reasons for volunteering, in the order of their importance, to be: altruism, personal satisfaction, self-improvement, and demands from outside. Gillespie and King (1985), in a study of current and former Red Cross volunteers, reported that among 18 to 25 year-olds, the three principal reasons for volunteering were to help others, to obtain job training and skills, and to contribute to the community. When Fitch (1987) asked members of college service organizations their reasons for becoming involved in these activities, the four reasons rated most important were; (a) "It gives me a good feeling or sense of satisfaction to help others"; (b) "I am concerned about those less fortunate than me"; (c) "Of the people I meet and friendships I make with other volunteers"; and (d) "I would hope someone would help me or my family if I/we were in similar situations." Thus, both altruistic and egoistic motives are prominent in the motivations for undertaking volunteer service. Given that both types of motives may be simultaneously present, these studies have not succeeded in providing a basis for reaching a conclusion about their relative importance within this age group.

In my own research on volunteer activities (Waterman, 1997), I have found it useful to distinguish between intrinsic versus extrinsic motives, a distinction that cuts across the altruistic—egoistic motive distinction. Intrinsic motivations for volunteering reflect a direct and inherent connection between the activity of helping others and qualities of the individual enacting the service. Extrinsic motivations entail rewards for volunteer service that bear little or no direct connection to enacting helping behavior.

The scale of intrinsic motivations I employ is composed of items relating to the importance of the following: (a) learning about oneself (self-exploration), (b) making effective use of one's talents, (c) expressing one's religious or ethical beliefs, (d) feeling good about oneself, (e) making a contribution to others, and (f) enjoying the challenge entailed in volunteer service. Viewed this way, intrinsic motivation for volunteer service simultaneously provides for both benefits to others and self-realization.

The scale of extrinsic motivations involves items relating to the importance of the following: (a) obtaining course credit or satisfying a school requirement, (b) responding to parental encouragement, (c) making contacts that could lead to future employment, (d) as a way to fill time and keep from being bored, (e) as a way of being with friends, and (f) helping to build a résumé useful in obtaining further education or finding employment. Presumably, these extrinsic rewards may be obtained from a relatively wide array of activities that do not entail helping others.

In a study of college undergraduates and graduate students at Trenton State College, I found the four motives for volunteer service rated highest by service providers to be in the intrinsic category: making a contribution to others, feeling good about oneself, enjoying the challenge entailed in volunteer service, and making effective use of one's talents. Each received an average rating above 5 on a 7-point scale. The highest rated extrinsic motive: as a way of being with friends, had an average rating just below 4, the midpoint of the scale. Thus, it is evident that intrinsic factors, both altruistic and egoistic, play a far stronger role in motivating volunteer service than do extrinsic factors.

In this study, the extent to which the respondents were motivated by intrinsic motives was found to be correlated with a variety of personality variables associated with effective functioning. Significant positive correlations indicated links between intrinsic motivation toward volunteer service, and such variables as intrinsic motivation toward one's education, a more reflective approach in the development of one's identity commitments, and greater success in identifying activities that gave rise to optimal experiences (i.e., experiences of flow and personal expressiveness; Waterman, 1997).

Implications for Service-Learning Programs

With the multiplicity of student motives for engaging in volunteer service, it follows that participants in service-learning programs are seeking to achieve varying objectives from their involvement in service. In line with the "student-placement fit" hypothesis introduced at the start of this chapter, we can anticipate both greater involvement in, and greater benefits deriving from such programs when the students perceive their objectives for participation are being satisfied. One purpose for classroom reflection sessions can be to focus the students' attention on their motivations for service involvement and whether their objectives are, or are not, being met through their service experiences.

It should also be remembered that student motivations for participation may change over the course of the semester or school year. Some of these changes may occur due to what takes place during the service activities and some through hearing other students talk about their motivations and experiences. The result should be greater self-awareness on the part of the students and a broader appreciation of the benefits of community service. From the teacher's standpoint, the information gained from such discussions can be used to plan more effectively for ways to satisfy the array of student motivations identified.

AMONG SERVICE PROVIDERS, WHAT CHARACTERISTICS ARE ASSOCIATED WITH THE LEVEL OF INVOLVEMENT, IN TERMS OF HOURS OF SERVICE, DEVOTED TO HELPING OTHERS?

Research Findings

Whereas this question has received scant attention in the research literature, it has been one focus of my own studies on volunteering (Waterman, 1997). One of the strongest predictors of the number of hours of volunteer service is the student's level of intrinsic motivation in helping activities. The stronger the confluence of motivations for helping others and self-realization, the more time is devoted to helping. The level of extrinsic motivation was found to be unrelated to the hours of volunteer service. Furthermore, the hours of volunteer service was significantly correlated with each of the four aspects of optimal psychological functioning: combined levels of challenges and skills, feelings of flow, scores on the personal expressiveness scale, and the opportunities to develop one's best potentials. A significant correlation between the reflective development of the student's sense of personal identity was also obtained. Finally, hours of service were significantly correlated with intrinsic motivation toward one's educational studies. In sum, those students most characterized by qualities associated with successful self-realization devote the most time to being of help to others.

Implications for Service-Learning Programs

Service-learning programs differ very widely with respect to the extent of community service expected of the students. Programs vary from a one-time, one-day experience, through requiring a specified number of hours over the course of the school year (with the pattern of engagement in service determined by the student), to weekly community involvements carried out throughout a semester or academic year. One implication of the research on volunteerism is that student characteristics, both motivations and personality, may play some role in student attitudes toward programs involving differing levels of involvement, and in the educational benefits to be derived from the programs.

AMONG SERVICE PROVIDERS, WHAT CHARACTERISTICS ARE ASSOCIATED WITH SUSTAINING VOLUNTEER SERVICE OVER TIME, AS OPPOSED TO TERMINATING SUCH ACTIVITY?

Research Findings

Although the research by Snyder and Omoto (1992) on AIDS volunteerism involves a general population of volunteers unrestricted with regard to age, it has provided the most direct evaluation of this question and warrants discussion here. In a 1-year longitudinal study of volunteers, comparisons were made of those who did, and did not, continue their service. Those who did and did not continue did not differ with respect to their reported satisfaction with their service or their support for the purposes of the AIDS organizations with which they were involved. Those who terminated their service felt it had taken up too much of their time and had encountered greater costs to their participation, including such costs as embarrassment, discomfort, and stigmatization.

The volunteer's motives for helping also served to distinguish continuers from noncontinuers (Snyder & Omoto, 1992). Continuers were more likely to be motivated by esteem enhancement or personal development, rather than by community concerns, values, or gains in understanding or knowledge.

Additional evidence of the role of volunteer motivations in the decision to continue or drop out of service activities was provided by Fretz (1979). For college students involved in a paraprofessional program with children, those choosing to continue their involvement were more likely to express motivations to increase self-understanding and improve or expand their interpersonal relationships, than were students dropping out of the program. Those dropping out were more likely to have expressed a motivation to understand others. Further, continuers scored significantly higher than dropouts on a measure of self-actualization.

In my own research (Waterman, 1997), students who intended to continue with their volunteer service were characterized by intrinsic motivation for such service to a significantly greater degree than were those who did not intend to continue. Extrinsic motivations did not serve to distinguish between the two groups. Differences between continuers and noncontinuers were also found with respect to two aspects of optimal psychological functioning: combined levels of challenges and skills and feelings of flow.

Implications for Service-Learning Programs

One of the frequently listed goals for service-learning programs is promoting good citizenship and community responsibility. Gains in this area can be documented by the decisions of students to continue on a volunteer basis the type of community involvements begun during their service-learning experiences. The data, indicating that both volunteer motivations and volunteer characteristics predict to continuing involvement in service, provides teachers with a basis for assessing, during school programs, the likelihood that citizenship objectives are being realized. For example, evidence of sustained or increased intrinsic motivations for service involvement suggests that students will be interested in the continuation of such activities beyond the completion of a course requirement.

THE STUDENT-PLACEMENT FIT HYPOTHESIS

The research evidence documenting a range of student motivations for involvement in volunteer activities provides a foundation for the input side of the student-placement fit hypothesis. Similarly, the range of student effects observed in studies of the impact of service-learning establishes the differential-outcomes side of the hypothesis. There is, however, very little research currently available that can be used to evaluate the proposition that matching student interests and motivations with placement characteristics actually makes a difference in the outcomes obtained.

A study by Clary and Miller (1986), relevant here, focused on the relationship of matching volunteer backgrounds with the orientation program provided by a volunteer telephone crisis counseling agency. The volunteers ranged in age from 17 to 49 and involved both students and nonstudents. The research documented that an orientation program promoting group cohesiveness would result in greater sustained service activity for volunteers thought to be high in "social-adjustive" motivations. This supports a functional view of volunteer activity (Clary & Snyder, 1991).

Sergent and Sedlacek (1990) set out to test a version of the student-placement hypothesis developed by Henderson (1980). They found that college student volunteers participating in four organizations doing different types of service activities differed significantly in their personality types based on high-point scores on Holland's (1985) Self-Directed Search and a measure of Murray's (1938) need categories. The particular patterns of differences observed were consistent with the nature of the environments afforded by the various organizations, thus supporting the student-placement fit hypothesis. Additional evidence for the hypothesis was obtained by Fretz (1979) who found that college students who dropped out of a volunteer program involving helping children had been less interested in learning about children at the start of the program than were those who stayed with the program. Similarly, Hersch, Kulik, and Scheibe (1969) found students volunteering in a mental hospital to have a stronger dedication to mental health work than other college students.

Service-learning programs appear to offer valuable opportunities to obtain additional empirical evidence regarding the student-placement fit hypothesis. If subsequent research provides substantial support for the hypothesis, this will offer a framework for efforts to maximize the value of service-learning placements.

FURTHER IMPLICATIONS OF THE RESEARCH ON VOLUNTEER CHARACTERISTICS FOR SERVICE-LEARNING PROGRAMS

This review of the research literature on student volunteer activities carries a variety of implications relevant to the development and refining of service-learning programs. The evidence is consistent in indicating that students who; (a) are intrinsically motivated to engage in volunteer service, (b) are concerned about their personal development, (c) have gone through a reflective process in identifying their interests and identity-related goals, values, and beliefs, and (d) have identified activities in their lives that give rise to feelings of personal expressiveness, flow, and self-actualization are the most willing to engage in volunteer service, will devote more time and effort to such services, and will sustain such activity over a longer period of time. It can be anticipated that students with these qualities will be the ones most likely to participate in elective service-learning programs and will derive the greatest benefits from participation in either elective or required programs. It follows that to the extent that teachers and service-learning supervisors can promote such qualities through the service experiences they provide to students, the overall value of the programs will be increased.

In addition to the recommendations previously offered, the following suggestions regarding service-learning programs can be derived from the review of literature on volunteer motivations and characteristics:

1. Given the multiplicity of motives for service, teachers and supervisors working with students enrolled in a service-learning program may be better able to plan projects and other activities for their students if they are aware of each student's motivation for participating in the program. As the research indicates, altruistic and egoistic motives, and intrinsic and extrinsic motives are not mutually exclusive and may be present simultaneously. Teachers may wish to vary assignments and follow-up reflection activities so as to acknowledge and support the full range of student motivations for service involvement.

2. When recruiting students for elective service-learning programs, the use of a broad array of motivational inducements will likely create a broader pool of participants than will inducements that fall primarily in a single category. However, because intrinsic motivations were considered significantly more important to students than were extrinsic motivations, and were associated with more extensive and more sustained service, these should be emphasized.

3. If an elective service-learning program is oversubscribed, awarding limited spaces to intrinsically motivated students may result in the maximization of educational gains as a function of the program.

4. Consistent with the student-placement fit hypothesis, where possible, it is advisable to match students with placements that will best satisfy their particular motivations for participation. This will more likely be accomplished if there is a broad array of service opportunities, rather than a single experience provided to all participating students, or only a narrow range of available options.

5. Continuing efforts to improve service-learning programs will be enhanced by follow-up assessments of the extent to which the student's initial motivations were satisfied. Attention should also be devoted to identifying the ways in which the nature of the student's motivations changed from the period prior to the program, through the time when service was provided, to the completion of the student's participation. Future students participating in the same service placements may be cued to anticipate particular patterns of changes in motivation, based on what earlier cohorts of students had experienced.

REFERENCES

Amabile, T. M., Hill, K. G., Hennessey, B. A., & Tighe, E. M. (1994). The Work Preference Inventory: Assessing intrinsic and extrinsic motivational orientations. *Journal of Personality and Social Psychology, 66*, 950–967.

Bennion, L. D., & Adams, G. R. (1986). A revision of the extended version of the Objective Measure of Ego Identity Status: An identity instrument for use with late adolescents. *Journal of Adolescent Research, 1*, 183–198.

Bernt, F. M. (1989). Being religious and being altruistic: A study of college service volunteers. *Personal and Individual Differences, 10*, 663–669.

Clary, E. G., & Miller, J. (1986). Socialization and situational influences on sustained altruism. *Child Development, 57*, 1358–1369.

Clary, E. G., & Snyder, M. (1991). A functional analysis of altruism and prosocial behavior. In M. S. Clark (Ed.), *Prosocial behavior; Vol. 12; Review of personality and social psychology* (pp. 119–148). Newbury Park, CA: Sage.

Csikszentmihalyi, M. (1975). *Beyond boredom and anxiety*. San Francisco: Jossey-Bass.

Csikszentmihalyi, M. (1990). *Flow: The psychology of optimal experience*. New York: Harper & Row.

Evanoski, P. O. (1988). An assessment of the impact of helping on the helper for college students. *College Student Journal, 22*, 2–6.

Fitch, R. T. (1987). Characteristics and motivations of college students volunteering for community service. *Journal of College Student Personnel, 28*, 424–431.

Fretz, B. R. (1979). College students as paraprofessionals with children and the aged. *American Journal of Community Psychology, 7*, 357–360.

Gillespie, D. F., & King, A. E. O. (1985). Demographic understanding of volunteerism. *Journal of Sociology and Social Work, 12*, 798–816.

Henderson, K. A. (1980, September). Programming volunteerism for happier volunteers. *Parks and Recreation*, 61–64.

Hersch, P. D., Kulik, J. A., & Scheibe, K. E. (1969). Personal characteristics of college volunteers in mental hospitals. *Journal of Consulting and Clinical Psychology, 33*, 30–34.

Holland, J. L. (1985). *The Self-Directed Search professional manual*. Odessa, FL: Psychological Assessment Resources, Inc.

Knapp, R. H., & Holtzberg, J. D. (1964). Characteristics of college students volunteering for service to mental patients. *Journal of Consulting Psychology, 28*, 82–85.

Murray, H. A. (1938). *Explorations in personality*. New York: Oxford University Press.

Sergent, M. T., & Sedlacek, W. E. (1990). Volunteer motivations across student organizations: A test of person–environment fit theory. *Journal of College Student Development, 31*, 255–261.

Serow, R. C. (1991). Students and voluntarism: Looking into the motives of community service participants. *American Educational Research Journal, 28*, 543–556.

Snyder, M., & Omoto, A. M. (1992). Volunteerism and society's response to the HIV epidemic. *Current Directions in Psychological Science, 1*, 113–116.

Tapp, J. T., & Spanier, D. (1973). Personal characteristics of volunteer phone counselors. *Journal of Consulting and Clinical Psychology, 41*, 245–250.

Turner, J. R. (1973). Personal and situational determinants of volunteer recruitment for a campus "hot-line" program. *Journal of the American College Health Association, 21*, 353–357.

Waterman, A. S. (1990). Personal expressiveness: Philosophical and psychological foundations. *Journal of Mind and Behavior, 11*, 47–74.

Waterman, A. S. (1992). Identity as an aspect of optimal psychological functioning. In G. R. Adams; T. Gullotta, & R. Montemayor (Eds.), *Identity formation during adolescence. Advances in adolescent development* (Vol. 9, pp. 50–72). Newbury Park, CA: Sage.

Waterman, A. S. (1993). Two conceptions of happiness: Contrasts of personal expressiveness (eudaimonia) and hedonic enjoyment. *Journal of Personality and Social Psychology, 64*, 678–691.

Waterman, A. S. (1997). *On the paradoxical relationship of individualism and interdependence: Research on helping others*. Manuscript in preparation.

Wiche, V. R., & Isenhour, L. (1977). Motivation of volunteers. *Journal of Social Welfare, 4*, 73–79.

Part III

Research on the Contexts
for Service-Learning

8

Service-Learning in Support of Rural Community Development

Bruce A. Miller
Northwest Regional Educational Laboratory

INTRODUCTION

Rural schools and communities face unique problems that differentiate them from their metropolitan counterparts. For example, rural communities tend to be geographically isolated, tend toward low population density, and often suffer from declining economics and a loss of job opportunities. Many rural communities have no dentists, factories, radio stations, or movie theaters. There are minimal social services available and, often, a single grocery store serves the community. Moreover, changes in world economic patterns place pressure on schools and communities to prepare youth for work in a global community, further complicating life in rural areas. Low-skilled jobs are declining, especially in rural settings where the traditional dependence on resource-based employment is no longer viable and low-level manufacturing jobs have all but disappeared. No longer is a traditional, basic-skills education enough to secure meaningful employment (Harrington-Lucker, 1993; O'Hare, 1995).

Currently, rural America suffers from the highest unemployment rates in the United States, a rate of poverty that is growing twice as fast as that found in metropolitan areas, a 10% decrease in median family income, and a wide-scale exodus of the young and educated seeking employment in metropolitan centers (Fuguitt, 1995; Jensen & McLaughlin, 1995; McGranahan, 1992; Miller, 1991). These changes have triggered the decline of once viable communities.

Research and development efforts are underway in many rural areas of the United States to help address these critical needs (Nachtigal, Haas, Parker, & Brown, 1989). One promising area of work has focused on how rural schools can serve the social, economic, and environmental development needs of their communities. Many meaningful opportunities for the substantive engagement of youth in community service-learning activities can be fostered through effective and holistic community development.

This chapter describes research and development activities conducted by the Northwest Regional Educational Laboratory to engage rural schools, especially youth, in service-learning opportunities that help their rural communities address community-wide goals.

TWO FORCES WEAKENING THE BONDS OF COMMUNITY

Two forces have disrupted many close-knit communities. First, when young, educated residents work and socialize in nearby metropolitan areas; they no longer identify with the local community, its values, or its people (Bryant & Grady, 1990). As a result, relations between generations lose their vitality and the bonds that once held communities together weaken.

A second source of disengagement arises from the rapid growth of communication technology. In the past, communication was directed primarily inward toward community members. However, communication technologies such as radio, television, and videos have shifted communication outward. According to Coleman (1987), "these new sources of communication, unconstrained by the norms that once dominated the community, now offer values that deviate sharply from those and provide a base of legitimization for the deviant values" (p.199). Where rural parents once could insulate their children from the harsh realities of the outside world, media have brought those realities into the living room.

Healthy, self-sufficient rural communities are an endangered species. They straddle two worlds: On the one hand, they strive to maintain a world characterized by small-town values where residents look out for one another and where kinship and friendship run deep. On the other hand, they face the continual encroachment of urban America and the need to somehow adjust to impending change. Monk and Haller (1986) conducted detailed case studies of rural towns and their schools. They have found a sobering picture.

> In some respects the image Americans have of their small towns—shaded, tree-lined streets; a solid sense of community identity; friendly, caring neighbors; a reasonably stable economic base oriented to the surrounding farms; and a shared set ... of values—describes the villages we visited. ... In every locality, the economy presented problems. The root of these problems was perceived to be the gradual drain of business and industry out of the community ... whatever the cause, it was clear that each village was in some economic difficulty.
>
> This difficulty manifested itself in numerous ways. Perhaps the most obvious was a generally high rate of unemployment. ... The state of the local economies also had less obvious consequences ... a drain of youth out of these villages to areas that offer greater economic opportunity ... people drive, sometimes lengthy distances, to work in neighboring small cities. (pp. 25–28)

Probably the most significant theme to emerge from these researchers' case studies was the central role of the school. It remained one of the only viable institutions in these economically declining communities. The school served as a gathering place, a key recreational facility, and an employer. Perhaps most important, it fostered "a stable pattern in the web of social life that binds individuals together. It is what makes a community something more than an aggregation of people" (Monk & Haller, 1986, p. 28). Interestingly, Monk and Haller did not find the school acting in a central role in community survival. The role of the school in these communities existed more by default than by intention. However, schools can play an intentionally significant role in supporting rural community revitalization.

THE SCHOOL AND THE
IMPORTANCE OF COMMUNITY

Schools have come to symbolize the identity and survival of many small, rural communities (McCracken, 1988; Peshkin, 1978). The ramifications of this central role have come under considerable attention in recent years as rural communities find themselves distressed by economic and social changes occurring at the state, national, and international levels of government (Hobbs, 1995; Rosenfeld, 1985).

Although significant gains in understanding, model development, and implementation have been made in linking schools to their communities, school personnel and local community residents generally fail to recognize school–community interdependency and the synergistic benefits of collaboration. In so doing, they often miss the opportunity to meaningfully engage youth in community-based learning experiences.

Rural Community–School Collaboration and Social Capital

Mutual survival has become a compelling reason for communities and schools to work collaboratively. It also makes good economic and educational sense, especially when students play active roles that help them develop a sense of appreciation for their rural community. Social capital is the investment in the community's ability to collectively act toward improving community well-being. When students are given substantive roles in community-based learning experiences and are directly involved in the decision-making process, the growth of social capital is promoted.

Social capital, according to Putnam (1993), "refers to features of social organization, such as networks, norms, and trust, that facilitate coordination and cooperation for mutual benefit" (pp. 35–36). Flora and Flora (1993) used the terms Entrepreneurial Social Infrastructure (ESI) to describe their view of social capital, which involves three interrelated elements. The first element reflects a climate of inclusiveness, where the diverse elements of the community are viewed as valuable and necessary to successful community. The second element involves investing resources collectively and at the local level. The last element refers to the networks within the community and between the community and the outside world that facilitate the flow of information.

Coleman (1987), described social capital as resources that are imbedded in the social structure itself such as norms, social networks, and interpersonal relationships that contribute to a child's growth. Unlike Flora and Flora and Putnam, whose emphasis centers around social capital and its relationship to community development, Coleman emphasized the impact of social capital on children. Taken together these authors provide a conceptual foundation about the importance of schools in the development of social capital and the role youth might play in helping to revitalize rural communities.

Some rural schools have begun collaborating with their communities to ensure that there is a variety and quality of service reflecting local and societal needs and that responsibilities are provided to children and adults. These have ranged from general education to lifelong learning, from day-care programs to meals for the elderly, and from vocational training to small business development (Hobbs, 1995; Miller, 1991; Rosenfeld, 1985; Wall, Luther, Baker, & Stoddard, 1989).

Two isolated, rural school districts in the Northwest have developed noteworthy collaborations with their communities. In Saco, Montana, students have developed a recreation center in a building on Main Street that is open to everyone in the community. Working with faculty advisors, students have formed a community advisory committee, developed a governance structure, and written successful grants to remodel the facility. Using computer drafting programs, students have designed plans for remodeling. Students also took correspondence courses in interior design and used the recreation center project as a real-life opportunity to apply what they had learned. Community volunteers taught students to hang and prepare sheetrock for painting, wire electrical fixtures, and install plumbing (Miller, in press).

In the north central cascades of Washington State, the Methow School District implemented a comprehensive community-based learning project entitled *Community as a Classroom*. A local resident coordinates more than 200 activities and classes taught by community volunteers to high school students. For eleven weeks during the fall and winter, students are dismissed for a half-day each week to participate in the Community as a Classroom. The program is organized around four strands: (a) career/jobs skills; (b) leisure and recreational time activities; (c) informational classes; and (d) community service. In the spring, they participate in an intensive 2-day experience that may range from fire fighter training with the Forest Service to backpacking and survival. The success of the program can be attributed to the overwhelming level of community involvement and support, the fact that all students in the high school participate, and that students are actively involved in planning and choosing activities and classes. The program is in its 4th year and continuing to grow (Miller, in press).

Both Saco and Methow School Districts represent rural communities overcoming their isolation through establishing collaborative relationships with their respective communities. In so doing, they open the way for students to engage in meaningful community-based learning and service experiences where students, working along side community adults, gain an increased appreciation of their communities while contributing to a sustainable future.

THE COMMUNITY–SCHOOL DEVELOPMENT PARTNERSHIP

In 1992, the Rural Education Program at the Northwest Regional Educational Laboratory began pilot testing a rural community development model in three small, isolated rural communities in the Northwest. The model, Community–School Development Partnership (CDP), was designed to build local capacity for renewal and growth by using local school district resources—such as students, teachers, facilities, and equipment—as development resources.

Student involvement provided an opportunity for youth to work alongside adults and to develop skills and competencies required for successful citizen involvement. Although three communities participated successfully in the pilot effort, only the community of Broadus, Montana, demonstrated extensive student and teacher involvement. The other two sites, Tonasket, Washington, and Cottonwood, Idaho, are touched on briefly in order to help clarify the development process and outcomes.

CDP Goals and Building Local Capacity

The CDP model was designed to facilitate the accomplishment of three goals: (a) Create a community structure that would empower the community and the local school district to address community development issues; (b) develop the knowledge and skills important for community renewal; and (c) implement a plan that engages the community and the school district in a partnership to achieve community-defined needs.

Each goal was believed attainable by students working in conjunction with the adults in their communities. Because students hold the potential for becoming tomorrow's leaders, it became critically important that they be engaged in substantive ways. This is especially true in rural settings such as Broadus, where students represent a continuity with the historical past of their communities and a transition to its future survival.

Clearly, leadership plays a central role in community development. Leaders evolve through training, practice, and exposure to successful leadership models and experience. Therefore, it becomes critically important that leadership be redefined as a shared responsibility rather than a divine right held in the hands of a few elected or hired individuals.

In CDP, leadership skills are taught to a broad range of the community, including students, and then applied to real-life situations that address community-identified needs. As will be seen in the community of Broadus, students demonstrated remarkable responsibilities, insights, and leadership. However, they are often overlooked. In rural communities, where the tasks needing to be done often outweigh the available adult population, students represent a hidden resource.

TABLE 8.1
CDP Process Overview

Readiness Conduct initial orientation and obtain agreement to participate	• Meet with potential process sponsors and describe purpose and event of the program • Describe expectations for involvement • Obtain agreement to participate
Event 1 Select Process Coordinator	• Sponsors select a coordinator to manage process • Notify NWREL • Identify key individual to accompany coordinator to leadership training
Event 2 Attend Process Coordinator training	• Training focuses on developing skills in communication, group process, decision making and conflict resolution • Learn how to select and implement a Community Council
Event 3 Conduct community meeting to introduce process and select Community Council	• Hold community meeting • Select Community Council using a role sampling process designed to involve as many people as possible
Event 4 Convene Community Council for orientation	• Define role • Confirm who will represent the various interest of the community • Set time and date for day-long training
Event 5 Conduct Community Council training and planning	• Learn team building and communications skills • Learn about rural issues • Plan for community meeting on visioning and goal setting • Learn about data collection using focused interviews
Event 6 Conduct community meeting for vision development and goal setting	• Describe assets of the past • Categorize desired assets for the future • Develop a goal for each category • Decide whether to implement the goals
Event 7 Conduct community meeting for action planning	• Review goals and establish task force for each one • Conduct an analysis of community–school strengths • Develop one month short-term action plans for each goal that builds on strengths or eliminates weakness • Seek sponsor review, endorsement and commitment of resources
Event 8 Conduct community meeting for evaluating progress and long-range planning	• Review short-term plan results and celebrate successes • Review and revise goals as needed • Develop long-range plan with a 3 to 5 year timeline • Each task force develops new one-month action plan. Seek sponsor review, endorsement and commitment of resources

Key Events in the CDP Process

Table 8.1 provides an overview of the key events and activities in the CDP process. The process begins with a readiness session designed to assess the level of support from community leaders for a CDP. The initial point of contact is with the school superintendent, who helps identify a group of community leaders whose support is necessary for the CDP project to succeed.

In rural communities, established leaders are often involved in so many activities, they are reluctant to take on one more. As a result, it is important that they know they are not expected to be directly involved in the project. Like the sponsors of a little league baseball team, they support the process but do not directly play the game.

The community development game is played by the community itself. To coordinate, encourage, and keep the community focused, a process coordinator is selected (i.e., Event 1), a Community Council chosen (i.e., Event 3), and timelines established for completing a cycle of community meetings and activities.

A key premise of the CDP process revolves around the concept of place and the importance of a sense of community held in the beliefs and values of rural people. They choose to live in a small, rural community because there is something they value about the place.

They may value the environment, the people, the isolation, the opportunity to be self-sufficient, the small size, or a combination of these. Whatever the reason, place, and what that place has come to mean, provides fertile ground for building a solidarity of purpose. Developing a recognition of this common ground provides a motivational basis on which to unite the community in action.

The CDP model incorporates a vision and consensus-building strategy designed to unite the community. It is believed that by actively involving students in these activities, they will develop not only the skills to be effective members of a community, but also positively strengthen their rural identities and their future employability.

High school students from the Powder River County High School in Broadus were involved in the CDP project from its inception. In addition, both elementary and high school teachers participated in all aspects of the project. Program evaluation data showed that the projects were part of course objectives, involved offering school credit, using in-school time, and that the teacher or other significant adult involvement was essential for the sustained involvement of students. This was especially true in terms of incentives, such as providing guidance and encouraging students to follow their own ideas to completion (Miller, 1993a, 1993b).

PILOT SITE SELECTION

In order to test the CDP model, three pilot sites were selected based on low population density, geographic isolation, incorporation as a small town, and evidence of social, economic, or environmental distress. In addition, student achievement data were considered an indicator of distress if school averages fell consistently below the national norms.

After initial contact, discussion, and, in some cases, on-site presentations with the school district superintendent and community residents, three communities were selected. Table 8.2 provides an overview of each community. Pilot-site sponsors made a commitment to pilot test the CDP process (i.e., Readiness). A CDP-sponsoring group in each community then selected a Process Coordinator from their respective communities. The Process Coordinator, along with the school district superintendent, attended a 3-day leadership development institute, where participants learned about the CDP process, effective communication, running meetings, group facilitation, and related topics.

Although all three communities instituted important changes in their communities and schools, only the community of Broadus significantly involved teachers and students throughout the duration of the pilot phase and sustained that engagement well after the pilot phase ended. Tonasket, Washington and Cottonwood, Idaho were unable to involve students and teachers because of many complex and interrelated factors. For example, the Tonasket School District draws from a large geographic area consisting of many diverse cultural and political groups such as ranchers, town dwellers, alternative lifestyle folks, environmentalists, and Hispanics. There is also the school-related staff.

Historically there has not been good communication or relations among all these groups. There has been a conspicuous absence of a collective sense of community. Moreover, there has not been much value placed on education. For the school district, this has meant levies and bonds seldom pass. A new school board and superintendent saw their involvement in pilot testing CDP as an opportunity to change relations between the school and the community. In part, they were successful.

The district passed a bond to build a new elementary and high school. Several task-force groups were formed to improve relationships among businesses and

TABLE 8.2
Demographic Characteristics of Three Selected Pilot Sites

| Community | Size of Town | Isolation | Distress Factors | | | |
			Low Tax-Base	Student Decline	Population Decline	Student Achievement
Broadus, Montana	<550	85 miles from nearest town of 2,500 or more	yes	yes	yes	no
Cottonwood, Idaho	<800	75 miles from nearest town of 2,500 or more	yes	yes	yes	yes
Tonasket, Washington	<1000	120 miles from a town of 2,500 or more	yes	yes	yes	yes

between the school and the community. These resulted in a community cultural center being developed, a downtown newsletter created, and numerous new alliances formed around community needs. Few of these service opportunities involved students or teachers, even though efforts were made to include them. In part, this failure appeared to be the result of numerous historical conditions. For example, the school staff and administration had not viewed schooling as something directly related to the community. As a result, incentives such as class time or credits were not provided to students. Disappointingly, a local business task force wanted students to help write and publish a newsletter as a service project, but not one teacher was willing to take advantage of the opportunity.

Similar results were found in Cottonwood. Efforts were initially made to involve students, but because of historical tensions between teachers and the community, few teachers were willing to become involved or to help involve their students. Like Tonasket, the school had seldom ever passed a levy to support school programs and staff. This resulted in teachers refusing to get involved. But the community did have some positive results. For the first time, community and school volunteers offered a 1-week summer recreation program for all ages. It was held in the school and sustained itself 3 years after the pilot phase ended. However, students did not play any active roles in planning, organizing or supervising.

In both Tonasket and Cottonwood, there appeared to be an historical malaise between the community and the school that limited their willingness to work together. Over the 4 years of pilot work, numerous positive changes happened in these two communities, but only in Broadus, Montana were substantive changes made that involved students in community-based service learning activities. Moreover, each community used a coordinator to manage and encourage involvement in the CDP work but only in Broadus was the coordinator effective in engaging both students and teachers.

THE BROADUS COMMUNITY

Broadus, Montana, the county seat for Powder River County, is a small western town located on U.S. Highway 212 that connects southeast Montana with South Dakota. Rolling prairie, cattle, sagebrush and antelope are common sights as you drive through the area into town. Large freight trucks drone on day and night as they haul their payloads to destinations far beyond Broadus. Gillette, Wyoming, population of 23,200, is 86 miles south of Broadus. Miles City, Montana and its 9,600 residents, is 85 miles east. Billings, the largest town in Montana with a population of 80,500, is a 3-hour drive from Broadus, barring bad weather conditions. Isolation creates unique needs for the citizens of Broadus, but it also provides a valued way of life.

Broadus has both a county and a local elementary school district. The county high school is situated on the same campus as the elementary school. The buildings are relatively modern, with new additions having been built with oil money during the early 1970s. Government, education, ranching, farming, and small service businesses are primary sources of employment, with small plane chartering, hunting guide services, and the development of a wagon train tourist event emerging in recent years. The school district is the second largest employer in the county, with the county ranking number one. Student population has been on a steady decline since the 1980s. In 1985, the high school enrollment peaked at 171. By 1993, enrollment had dropped to 127, a 26% decline. Teachers remain some of the highest paid people in the county.

Many family histories go back to early settlers and homesteads. People live in the area because they value the small size, clean environment, and freedom associated with open spaces. However, the viability of the area has been threatened by the same economic downturn that has affected many rural areas in the nation. Stores and small shops have closed while medical and social services and employment opportunities have been radically curtailed. When issues of local economic and social distress were presented to local business and education leaders, there was an immediate agreement that something needed to happen. As a result, a small group of local leaders agreed to sponsor the community's involvement in the CDP pilot project.

By the time Community Meeting 4 was held, all task-force groups had carried out several short-range action plans, including the development of a long-range plan. The Broadus community received an $8,000 grant from the local Coal Board as a result of student testimony regarding the impact of student involvement in community development. This grant was used for continuation of the use of a professional architect and community planner to work with students and community representatives in redesigning Broadus. This activity was coordinated by the local art teacher and the county extension agent who also used the services of a local artist-in-residence to help students produce a community mural and sculpture. The education task force worked with school officials to implement a course on rural development in the high school and a program for students to shadow employers for a day. In addition, a cross-age tutoring program grew from the interests of a primary teacher who requested high school students be given credit for working with her students. In both the career shadowing and tutoring programs, students helped design the program and presented their plans to the school board for approval.

Student Involvement, Service, and Learning

What specific ways have students been involved in community development? What have they learned? How do students perceive the benefits and challenges of their involvement? How has the community and school benefited? What have students learned that will equip them for life after high school?

Student involvement in community development activities increased over time. Initially, only one student appeared to have the time and interest to participate. However, the number of students began to increase as goals developed around their interests.

Teacher involvement also tended to facilitate student interest and participation. For example, after Community Meeting 2, where citizens created a vision of what they desired their community to be like in 5 years, a high school senior, with the support of the social studies teacher, facilitated the development of a student vision for the future. Based on this senior student's interest, the entire senior class became involved.

The high school principal and the social studies teacher said they had never seen the senior class as motivated and on task. In part, they attributed this motivation to the highly active nature of the "vision activity," the fact that it was led by a respected student, and that it had immediate connection to the students' lives. In an interview conducted by the local newspaper, the student facilitator commented on student motivation and involvement: "The kids really are interested and involved and are ready to do some projects. [They] went through the same process that was involved in the last Town Meeting—we took the seniors clear through it."

Out of this student vision activity came a set of goals that nearly matched those of the community. This encouraged the students and gave them a sense of confidence. By the last two community meetings, students participated on an equal basis with adults. For example, students facilitated brainstorming and planning sessions and presented reports to the 80 citizens in attendance at Community Meeting 4. For many students, it was their first active involvement with adults and presentation before a large gathering. Presenting before a large audience, working in teams, facilitating planning, and developing reports are all highly desired skills for the workplace. Students mastering these skills will have a head start on employability.

Out of these initial community meetings emerged a realization that students could be valuable resources in helping set goals, developing action plans, and actively participating in community and school development. Table 8.3 provides an overview of key activities students and teachers have been involved in and what students have learned. Workplace competencies identified as important for the workplace of the future by the Secretary's Commission on Achieving Necessary Skills (SCANS, 1991) have been used to help delineate student learning. The checks (✓) indicate that a primary feature of the activity corresponded with one or more of the competencies.

In the following section, each activity is discussed, describing in detail how SCANS competencies were addressed. It is important to keep in mind that these activities have grown out of community needs and an emerging realization on the part of educators and community residents that education can occur in meaningful ways outside the four walls of the school.

Community–School Development Partnership (CDP).   Many of the processes and activities used in implementing the CDP served to pull the diverse energies in the community into a unified effort, driven by a common vision. This has led to a spill-over phenomena where previously unrelated curriculum and community activities have been explicitly focused on community development. For example, students from primary classrooms have often visited a local retirement home on field trips. With the advent of the CDP, such activities have taken on the importance of helping achieve community development goals. Students have become more aware of their community and the needs of its citizens.

TABLE 8.3
The Relationship Between Broadus Activities and Scans

| | School/Community Activities | | | | |
Competency Areas	CDP Activities	Task force Commitee Activity	Career Shadowing	Community Developent Course	Cross-Grade Tutoring
Resources—allocating time, money, materials, space, and staff	✓	✓		✓	✓
Interpersonal Skills—working on teams, teach others, service customers, leading, negotiating, and working well with people from culturally diverse backgrounds	✓	✓		✓	✓
Information—acquiring and evaluating data, organizing and maintaining files, interpreting and communicating, and using computers to process information	✓	✓	✓	✓	✓
Systems—understanding social, organizational, and technological systems, monitoring and correcting performance, and designing or improving systems	✓	✓	✓	✓	✓
Technology—selecting equipment and tools, applying technology to specific tasks, and maintaining and troubleshooting technologies	✓	✓		✓	
Basic Skills—reading, writing, arithmetic and mathematics, speaking, and listening	✓	✓	✓	✓	✓
Thinking Skills—thinking creatively, making decisions, solving problems, seeing things in the mind's eye, knowing how to learn, and reasoning	✓	✓	✓	✓	✓
Personal Qualities—individual responsibility, self-esteem, sociability, self-management, and integrity.	✓	✓	✓	✓	✓

Another example is the use of a computer-based thinking development program called Talents Unlimited. The content of this program has shifted toward community-based problem solving. The elementary principal facilitated this shift because he felt teachers were more likely to become involved in community development if they built on existing strengths (Talents Unlimited) rather than taking on a new set of responsibilities.

Many other examples of how community development provides service opportunities, while at the same time developing useful life skills, can be found throughout the school district. Students worked with the business teacher to develop a database of local talent, including the design of data input fields and entering appropriate information regarding skills, talents, and worker volunteers in the community. In order to improve communication among various community development groups, the English teacher worked with students to produce a local one-page newsletter that reports local news such as meetings, games, and important events. The newsletter is distributed by the publication class to all local cafés, businesses, and other public gathering places.

The business task force published a directory of local businesses and organizations serving the public. Students surveyed community businesses and organizations to solicit their participation in the project. This led to a publication with more than 35 entries describing services available in the area. The supervising teacher said students were shocked at the number of services available in their small, rural community.

Local service organizations and businesses indicated they were quite pleased that students sought their involvement. Students have also been active in improving recycling in the community by helping the task force on civic pride raise money for a cardboard bailer. This project was coordinated with the local grocer and a committee on recycling.

Elementary students clipped coupons and redeemed them for cash toward the bailer. Students also helped organize and provided goods for a "white elephant" sale that raised $5,000. In total, students and adults raised $8,000 for the cardboard bailer.

Task-Force Committee Work.   A core group of about eight students served as members of various community development task-force groups. The purpose of each task force was the development and implementation of action plans aimed at reaching community-defined goals. The greatest number of students signed up for the recreation task force, with the others choosing to work on the community beautification and education committees.

Students and adults received training in group facilitation skills, recording group comments and ideas on chart pack, and arriving at decisions through consensus. Students also had opportunities to observe a range of organizational and management skills from community leaders, consultants, and local citizens.

More important, they were given the opportunity to assume leadership roles such as facilitating problem-solving sessions, recording group ideas, and carrying out responsibilities critical for task completion.

An especially noteworthy example emerged out of the work of the task force on education, reinforcing the value to be gained by involving students. A student member pointed out that students could learn a great deal about different professions by spending time in local businesses and organizations while receiving credit.

The idea was adopted by the task force after this same student presented the idea to more than 75 local residents attending a community meeting. During the presentation, she told members of the task force on business enhancement that they would gain much by hosting students for a day. "You know, if you had us spend a day in your businesses, you might get a full day of free student help," she said. Everyone laughed and nodded in appreciation. As a result, the school has implemented a student-intern program in the high school where students can spend a day in a business or organization of their choice.

The administration worked with students to develop the program and had students present it to the school board. This gave students the opportunity to plan, develop, and present their ideas before a governing body, thus helping them to understand the role of policy and governance in school district organizations.

The task force seeking to beautify Broadus provides yet another example of how students and the school can serve as a valuable resource for community development and have students learn and practice new competencies and skills. In this case, the task force contracted a rural planner and architect, along with several graduate students from a state university, to help redesign the community in ways that would make it a more inviting place for tourists and local residents. Task-force members sought the help of teachers and students to participate in a community design project. The local art teacher saw it as an opportunity to involve her students in real-life applications of art principles.

As a result, more than 30 students helped draw pictures of buildings, streets, and parks of a redesigned Broadus. Students also designed a three-dimensional model of a recreation building. Costs for the planning consultants came from the school, the county commission, service club donations, city government, and a Coal Board grant. The Coal Board decided to fund the project after hearing the impassioned speech of a high school senior who said that before her involvement in community development, she held little hope for her community. "Broadus was a dead-end, a place without any hope," she said. "Now I feel there is hope, that by working together as a community, we can bring about changes in the community to make it a better place to live. To make it a place I could move back to and raise a family."

Students also worked with an artist-in-residence program to design and create a sculpture and a mural on the side of a building depicting the flora and fauna indigenous to the local environment. The mural and sculpture helps beautify downtown while providing students with experiences of scale drawing and painting in large formats. Both the architect and the artist-in-residence helped students learn the skills while engaging in highly motivational projects.

Several offshoots of this community beautification activity emerged. Vocational education students videotaped the downtown area and used the video to draw the town to scale in the motif of an early Western frontier town. Other students cleaned a vacant lot and converted it into a park, an effort that included gaining permission to use land belonging to a local landowner. Interestingly, teachers and administrators told students to give up because the property owner would not cooperate. Students chose to ignore the advice and contacted the landowner who wholeheartedly endorsed the student project. Student optimism and persistence paid off. As a result, the school provided release time for a community project that allowed a group of students to clean the vacant lot, including the removal of a dilapidated building.

The task force on tourism also sought the help of students, who will help the committee design postcards. The school's art teacher worked closely with other teachers on the tourism task force and made student involvement a part of class time and credit.

Broadus County High School Community Development Course.   A community development course was established for the 1993–1994 school year as an outgrowth of the school's commitment to community development. The course provides a structure for students and staff to pursue community development goals within the existing structure of the school. As such, the course provides incentives for student involvement through credit and time.

The course is taught by two teachers who had been actively involved in the CDP project. During interviews, both teachers characterized themselves as being "action types of people." This has resulted in a course unlike any other. One of the teachers characterized students as a "structured implementation force" for community development needs.

Students design, build, and carry out projects that come from their own interests, as well as the interests of others, such as the student council, school board, and teachers. Students are gaining valuable skills for making the transition to postsecondary life. They are learning valuable lessons in planning, time management, interpersonal communication, and problem solving.

Students are given a great deal of freedom to choose projects they care about. But they also are expected to take on projects that will help the school or the community be a better place. The community development course, although still in its infancy, is creating innovative curriculum content. The following provides an overview of the types of projects, activities, and processes found in the course.

Two students voiced a concern about the amount of litter found in the school. In part, their interest related to administrative comments about keeping the student recreation area clean. However, the two students also felt a better job could be done keeping litter picked up throughout the school. Students, using teachers as resource guides, decided they needed more information about the amount and location of the litter. A map of the school was divided into areas for monitoring purposes. For 2 weeks, students kept count of the amount of litter by area of the map. From these data, they were able to determine that litter concentrated in several areas of the school. After further analysis, they hypothesized the lack of trash cans contributed to the problem. The students discussed their insights with the custodian, who told them that he had requested new trash cans over a year ago. Surprised by this long delay, students decided to go directly to the principal with the trash problem and their supporting data. Their compelling case led to trash cans being ordered immediately and put in place. For 2 more weeks, students continued to monitor the amount of litter to determine the effectiveness of their intervention. They observed a reduction of trash in these areas. However, they also concluded more effort needs to be made by students to pick up after themselves throughout the school.

An outgrowth of the community development project was a goal to provide more recreational opportunities for youth and adults. In 5 years, students envision a recreation center in the community. However, after discussion and consultation with task-force members, the students decided that a good starting point would be the development of a recreation center within the school that would provide a place for students to mix and socialize during and after school. This approach would help sustain student motivation and involvement. In addition, the school administration had already set aside an area designated for students.

When school started, the student area contained a student store, soda machines, a table, and barren walls. The community development class decided to take this area on as a project. They began by brainstorming about what needed to be done. For example, they felt the area needed to be made visually attractive, comfortable, and entertaining. Ideas such as new paint, a pool table, video games and foosball, a sofa, and the removal of unneeded tables were presented. An action plan was developed and presented to the administration for approval that included what would be done, a time frame, who would be responsible, necessary resources, and other groups or individuals who needed to be involved. By analyzing who else should be involved, new partnerships were formed and the work was distributed across the student body, thus helping to build ownership.

However, conflict arose because the student council viewed the recreation center as a project they had begun the year before. Neither the administration nor the community development class knew of the council's plans. After bringing the groups together, they decided that the community development class and the student council needed to improve their communication. As a result, a student council member sits in on the community development class and a member of the class sits in on student council meetings.

Another recreation-related activity center project focuses on raising money for field trips to visit other student-initiated recreation projects. One such project is in Saco, Montana, an isolated rural community northeast of Broadus. Several discussions have been held between Saco and Broadus students regarding the development of recreation opportunities. Two students from the community development class have begun a winter firewood business to raise money for a trip to Saco. They cut, split, and supply wood to the community. Transportation and related overhead costs were removed from their income and the remainder put into the field trip fund.

These students are learning to manage time and resources, to work with the public, and to experience the rewards associated with volunteering. They are also learning the value of self-initiative and hard work. A student involved in the firewood sales project said he had learned "to get along with a partner and to work with money." Students also said the project helped them learn to manage business affairs.

The community development course is not without challenges. Scheduling students into the class is difficult when there are so many other activities and required courses in the school. Another scheduling problem is the 50-minute period that divides the day. Often, projects require sustained periods of time longer than 50 minutes. Lastly, the course appeared dependent on the leadership of individuals with a strong belief in the importance of service, without whom it is unlikely the course will continue.

Cross-Grade Tutoring.   Another outgrowth of the community development partnership was a focus and redefinition of the concept of community. Several teachers from the elementary school and the high school saw a possible link between the two schools that would build a greater sense of community within the school district. The result was the development of a cross-age tutoring program where high school students tutor students in the elementary school and receive credit and training for their involvement.

The high school principal, who had been successfully involved in a similar effort at another school, took direct responsibility to work closely with teachers and students in designing and implementing the program. A proposal was collaboratively developed and approved by the school board for implementation during the 1993–1994 school year.

As reported in the local newspaper, "High school students volunteering for the program give up three days of weekly study hall time in exchange for one-quarter semester credit ... the tutors receive a monthly evaluation from the supervising teacher as an effort to continually improve the program and their efforts" (*Powder River Examiner*, 1992, p. 7). Moreover, the high school principal reported, "The program is currently a big success for both the high school tutors and the elementary children." One key element of this success has been the organization and structure that clearly lays out guidelines and expectations for those involved.

Guidelines specify credit requirements, student responsibilities, attendance and consequences for failing to live up to agreed-on expectations. A contract signed by the student, teacher, and principal specifies guidelines. Because this project is in its formative stages, teachers are learning how to effectively use tutors and develop training activities to facilitate a smooth transition for tutors into the classroom. Tutors are learning how to work with young children while gaining insight into the work life of teachers.

In this way, they are providing meaningful assistance while learning valuable workplace skills such as scheduling, working with adult supervisors, being a positive role model, and the flexibility necessary when working with young children. They may be learning whether or not they would like to be a teacher. "Since I started tutoring," said one student, "I've been thinking about going into something similar for college. Going up to the elementary school is always a learning experience for me as well as the kids. I learn patience, how to get organized, and how important it is for children to have heroes, or at least someone to look up to."

Moreover, for those involved in the community–school, the big payoff may be a closer working relationship among teachers, administrators, and students, leading to a greater sense of community.

CONCLUSION AND IMPLICATIONS

Broadus and the Powder River region of southeast Montana, like many Western rural communities, face hard times. With fewer opportunities for employment, rural communities are seeing the out-migration of their youth, especially those with high school degrees and postsecondary education. Many rural youth feel they do not have a choice but to leave. Moreover, they often have come to believe staying in their rural community symbolizes failure.

If rural communities are to be seen as viable and meaningful places to live, rural youth must learn to see their communities as a positive choice among many in which to live and work. This can be accomplished by providing youth with service-learning opportunities to become active, responsible members of a community that works together.

Broadus did not consciously set out to provide service-learning activities for its youth when town leaders chose to become involved in community development. They started from the premise that their community faced difficult economic times; without the school and community working together, their mutual survival would be in jeopardy. This context presented an opportunity to explore ways students and the school could address community needs while helping students learn valuable life skills.

Interviews conducted with educators, students, and residents indicated wide-scale support for involving students in community-based learning. More important, there was a nearly unanimous opinion that involving students provided invaluable experiences that would help them prepare for their future. For example, one senior was asked, "How will your involvement in community development be of benefit 5 years from now?" The student responded: "You're learning teamwork. You're learning how to negotiate. You're learning how to talk with people. I mean it's better than anything going on in school because it's hands-on, and you learn from your mistakes and you learn from the things that you do right. So it's very educational."

Observations by residents and educators substantiate much of what this student said. For example, one parent felt student involvement helped change the way students relate to their community: "I feel real thrilled with what they have done. The students have been just so enthusiastic and they have come up with many ideas of what they would like to do. I just feel like they are able to relate to the community in a better way because of this—and thinking what they can do to better it."

Another resident who serves on the tourism task force describes how students learned to translate their ideas into visual forms for presentation to the public: "The students drafted their own image ... they drafted their own map and layout of what they thought the town of Broadus (which still has a city square with the businesses around the square) might look like in the future ... they drew maps, redesigned streets, made boulevards, and wanted to plant trees—just beautify, fix up what we have."

The high school principal describes how involving students in real-life planning not only helps them develop important skills, but also creates pride in who they are as members of a community:

Students helped plan town improvements. An architect came in and worked with them. They went downtown and said, "Now how could we improve the looks of our town?" and came up with, "We've got really wide streets in our town. We could put a divider in the middle of the street and plant flowers and things like that." I think the students buying into that—being a part of the planning process—that's going to be their pride in their community. They will come back 10 years from now and say, "I was one who helped do this."

As many residents of the Broadus area have pointed out, the community and school are just at the beginning of what can be accomplished when parents, students, educators, and the general public set their minds to work together. The Broadus community received substantial help from their involvement in the CDP project. This raises the important issue of whether other rural communities can replicate their experiences without outside intervention.

The activities occurring in Broadus do not appear very different from what happens in many small, rural schools. What makes the Broadus experience unique is the change in perspective regarding the important contributions students can make to their community, while simultaneously addressing academic goals. Unlike the other two pilot sites, the Broadus community and school were able to develop a collective vision about the significant role students could play in their communities. Furthermore, the project coordinator had the skills to encourage and sustain the involvement of key stakeholders over time.

REFERENCES

Bryant, M. T., & Grady, M. L. (1990). Community factors threatening rural school district stability. *Research in Rural Education, 6*(3), 21–26.

Coleman, J. S. (1987). The relations between school and social structure. In M. Hallinan (Ed.), *The social organization of schools: New conceptualizations of the learning process* (pp. 177–204). New York: Plenum.

Flora, C. B., & Flora, J. L. (1993). Entrepreneurial social infrastructure: A necessary ingredient. *The Annals of the American Academy, 529*, 48–58.

Fuguitt, G. (1995). Small communities in the northwestern United States also declining. Rural Development Perspectives, 9(2), 29–32.

Harrington-Lucker, D. (1993, November). Preserving American know-how. *American School Board Journal*, 29.

Hobbs, D. (1995). Capacity building: Reexamining the role of the rural school. In L. Beaulieu & D. Mulkey (Eds.), *Investing in people: The human capital needs of rural America* (pp. 259–284). Boulder, CO: Westview Press.

Jensen, L., & McLaughlin, D. K. (1995). Human capital and nonmetropolitan poverty. In L. Beaulieu & D. Mulkey (Eds.), *Investing in people: The human capital needs of rural America* (pp. 111–138). Boulder, CO: Westview Press.

McCracken, J. D. (1988). Community leaders' perceptions of the importance of rural community schools. *Journal of Rural and Small Schools, 3*(2), 12–15.

McGranahan, D. (1992). Key challenges facing rural America (Appendix III, pp. 59–61). In *Rural development: Rural America faces many challenges,* Washington, DC: U.S. General Accounting Office (GAO/RCED-93-35).

Miller, B. A. (in press). *School- to-work transition in rural communities: Lessons from the field and strategies for change.* Charleston, WV: ERIC Clearinghouse on Rural Education.

Miller, B. A. (1993a). *Community/school development partnership (CDP) project: Evaluation conference report.* Portland, OR: Northwest Regional Educational Laboratory.

Miller, B. A. (1993b). *Community/school development partnership (CDP) project evaluation report of first-year pilot sites.* Portland, OR: Northwest Regional Educational Laboratory.

Miller, B. A. (1991). *Distress and survival: Rural schools, education, and the importance of community.* Portland, OR: Northwest Regional Educational Laboratory.

Monk D. H., & Haller, E. J. (1986). *Organizational alternatives for small rural schools: Final report to the legislature of the State of New York.* New York: Cornell University.

Nachtigal, P. M., Haas, T., Parker, S., & Brown, N. (1989). *Noteworthy.* Aurora, CO: Mid-Continent Regional Educational Laboratory.

O'Hare, W. (1995). People with multiple disadvantages live in rural areas, too. *Rural Development Perspectives, 9*(2), 2–6.

Peshkin, A. (1978). *Growing up American: Schooling and the survival of community.* Chicago: University of Chicago Press.

Powder River Examiner. (1992, November 5). Students involved with community planning process. *Powder River Examiner,* p. 7.

Putnam, R. D. (1993). The prosperous community: Social capital and public life. *The American Prospect, 13,* 35–42.

Rosenfeld, S. (1985, Summer). The high school in a rural economy. *Foresight, 3*(2), (Institution: Southern Growth Policies Board sponsored by U.S. Department of Agriculture, Washington, DC, Office of Rural Development Policy).

SCANS. (1991). *What work requires of schools: A SCANS report for America 2000.* Washington, DC: Secretary's Commission on Achieving Necessary Skills, U.S. Department of Labor.

Wall, M., Luther, V., Baker, K., & Stoddard, S. (1989). Schools as entrepreneurs: Helping small towns survive. *The Rural Educator, 10*(3), 14–17.

9

Doing Service Projects in Urban Settings

Novella Zett Keith
Temple University

Since the publication of the Coleman Report (Coleman et al., 1966), educators and advocates have searched for ways to demonstrate that good urban schools could make a difference, in spite of the overwhelming odds facing them and their students. This seminal report, it should be recalled, marshalled considerable evidence demonstrating that family and social factors, rather than educational inputs, were largely responsible for students' ultimate success or failure.

The effective schools "movement" and related initiatives that followed represented a kind of educators' retort, a search for the power inherent in the educational process, when organized appropriately, to promote success regardless of the students' background, social class, and environment. These approaches led to significant efforts to transform school climate and restructure schools through the mechanisms of transformational leadership, schools within schools, teacher involvement, and the like.

In the last decade, however, the search for effective urban schooling has lead back to the world beyond school walls. This does not imply a cyclical fad—no one is suggesting that schools' efforts to increase involvement in learning or achieve a positive school climate (two of the characteristics of effective schools) be abandoned. Rather, it speaks of a growing sense of urgency among actors at different levels of the system, counseling the need for concerted and integrated efforts to address the inescapable nexus between school, community, and society. This is the context that now provides support for community-based service-learning.

This chapter surveys several areas of research that are relevant for service projects in urban settings, in order to answer two questions: What contributions can service-learning make to improving student achievement in such settings? How can the research help us design and implement successful service projects for these environments? I also provide some examples of projects that conform to this research and thus are apt to make the greatest contribution to enhancing learning in urban schools.

URBAN EDUCATION DEFINED

Urban education is not a unitary phenomenon; rather, it can be defined as the intersection of a number of factors. Identifying these factors will help direct us to the educational and social issues that service-learning might address; in the end, however, each service project must take into consideration the particular school–community environment in which it dwells. Table 9.1 summarizes the identifying characteristics of urban education, grouping them under two headings.

In the first set, labeled "traditional perspective," are descriptors that have familiar sounds, such as poverty, social problems, low attainment, deficits; these support the perception that urban education is a *problem*, whose origins lie mainly in urban youth and neighborhoods. The second set includes descriptors that emphasize alternative perspectives on urban youth and communities: Here, the main focus is not so much on deficit as on difference, on community and young people's capacities and resilience (in spite of very real needs), on the need for true partnerships for change, and on systemic factors as an important source of problems—for instance, on the negative effects of organizational, political, and economic environments, of segregation, and of social distance between educators and urban students. Of course, such binary oppositions do not mirror real life. Whether one sees one set of descriptors or the other is a matter of perspective and interpretation: which "facts" one looks at and how one interprets them.

Subscribing to one or the other perspective, however, has profound implications for service-learning. For instance, a traditional orientation might eschew service projects in partnership with the local community, preferring to work with agencies and organizations that can help students make the transition to mainstream values, employment, and so on; alternative orientations might, instead, integrate parts of both approaches (e.g., traditional and alternative interventions at the economic level), and include the local community in empowering ways.

Table 9.1 also alerts us to new organizational trends in urban education. Fiscal stringencies, scathing national reports, pressures to "do more with less," and trends in the business community are serving to promote a shift from what had been the major organizational approach in urban school systems since the turn of the century; although the final outcome remains uncertain, the shift is away from bureaucratization and its attendant propensity to homogenize and control and toward district decentralization, school-based decision making, school choice, and small learning communities with a diversity of approaches to teaching and learning.

Accompanying this movement is an increasing emphasis on "partnerships"—the involvement, in and with schools, of business, higher education, service agencies, parents, community members, and other "stakeholders"; indeed, the concept of

TABLE 9.1
Urban Education Defined

Areas of Functioning	Characteristics	
	Traditional Perspectives	*Alternative Perspectives*
Organization/ Management	Bureaucratic centralization; standardization and control.	Learning communities; local decision making; teacher and community participation.
Learning environment	Low attainment & high attrition; compensatory, deficit approaches; emphasis on isolated basic skills and fragmented knowledge.	Low attainment results from student resistance, disengagement, lack of resources; diversity as strength; need knowledge in context and culturally appropriate curriculum/pedagogy.
Social environment	Social disorganization; deviance, poverty, social problems; change through mainstream partnerships and professional services ("service to").	Resilience; barriers due to racism/classism; social distance between school and community calls for "bridges" across "borders;" change through partnerships between community and resource provider/ professionals ("service with").
Cultural environment	Impoverished; "culture of poverty"; isolation; deviance and criminal subcultures.	High degree of diversity means potentially rich cultural mix; local cultures devalued/not recognized by mainstream; resistance to privileging of mainstream cultural norms leads to oppositional cultural norms.
Political environment	Large number of political constituencies (state legislature, business community; middle-class taxpayers; etc.); complex, competing claims; political "apathy" of poor/minorities.	Local community involvement and leadership; partnerships needed to support schools and gain equitable share of resources.
Economic environment	Economic shift to high tech/services demands highly skilled workforce; develop closer linkages between schools and industry; focus on science, math, high technology, and learning to learn.	Eroded fiscal structure but increased environment needs for services; loss of cities' economic base; dual labor market and scarcity of jobs for urban/minority youth in primary sector; need both traditional and innovative economic outlets (i.e. small business, informal economy).

community schools is enjoying a resurgence (Dryfoos, 1994). Such trends can become important carriers for service-learning, as they expand the arena for learning to the world outside school. It should be emphasized, however, that approaches to partnerships also betray the divergent orientations highlighted in Table 9.1 and thus carry different implications for service-learning programs (see Keith, 1996).

PREMISES

The human sciences are multiple paradigm sciences: Researchers work within different traditions that are informed by different sets of premises. This does not invalidate all research efforts, nor does it suggest that we should abandon all attempts to search for accumulated knowledge to guide educational practice. Rather, it calls for caution in interpretation and counsels the need to make explicit the basic premises guiding one's search.

My basic premises start with the assertion that all people have culture, and all have strengths and capacities, potential as well as actual. However, the recognition given to such cultures, strengths and capacities is differentially distributed. Those who belong to the "mainstream" or to groups that have dominant social positions (by virtue of their class, race, gender, culture, job title, age, profession, etc.) are more likely to be recognized and develop identities as holders of culture and knowledge than those who do not. Furthermore, these dynamics operate not only at the personal and interpersonal levels, but become embedded in the workings of organizations (i.e., schools) and social structures (i.e., differentiated curricula); these, then, "advantage" some people and "disadvantage" others. It does not mean, of course, that the first group has nothing to offer, but that expertise can come from different sources, including a first-hand knowledge of an urban neighborhood and its workings.

The understanding of learning that is emerging from neo-Vygotskian researchers and related work on multiple intelligences supports these premises (Gardner, 1993; Rogoff and Lave, 1984). Briefly, the human mind is elastic and its capacities are not fixed. Development occurs in interaction with one's environment and through the use of tools and signs that are not universally given, but are culturally or environmentally situated; multifaceted and malleable, intelligence develops through attempts to solve problems and negotiate one's environment. Where multiple cultural environments (and/or subcultures) exist and are hierarchically arranged, people who are exceedingly "able" in one setting (i.e., the home community, the peer group) may be "failures" in another (i.e., the school).

In my search through the literature, I have sought studies that build on these premises. This search yields findings that are significant enough to support the call for a shift from seeing urban communities primarily in terms of their deficits, to seeing them as "different" and "capable." In particular, they provide a rationale for opening what have been near-impenetrable "borders" between urban schools and their neighborhoods. A border exists when cultures are seen not only in terms of difference, but in terms of hierarchies. Making urban schools into fortresses (or, in a more benign perception, "oases") in which professional experts could enforce the "one best way" of teaching, unhampered by community concerns and local politics, these borders have reinforced prevailing deficit perceptions of students and their communities among educators and stakeholders at large. They have thus severed students and schools from the organic supports for learning that come from connecting school learning with community life, culture, and knowledge. Service-learning can help reestablish this vital link and contribute to a revisioning of urban communities. The fundamental approach to service-learning that is derived from these assumptions is "service with" rather than "service to": Service must be based on reciprocity.

I do not advocate that, in moving away from deficit approaches, we discount the dangers and devastation in so many urban neighborhoods, nor the imperative that schools and families protect youth from such dangers. Nor can we ignore the degree of community destruction that has occurred as part of processes leading to the formation of the "underclass" (i.e., deindustrialization and loss of jobs in urban centers) and, therefore, the need for outside resources and the formation of broader social networks (Wilson, 1987). We do, however, need to perceive such neighborhoods not only as places of needs, deviance, and dangers but also as places where diverse cultures exist and where knowledge, problem solving, and resilience are developed.

SERVICE-LEARNING IN URBAN SETTINGS: A SKETCH AND SOME PRINCIPLES

The research suggests several principles for sound service-learning programs. The following sketch—a composite of several programs—meets these principles and serves as an introduction to the research. In reading it, one should keep in mind three areas of schooling in which service-learning can play a supportive role: pedagogy, curriculum, and community building (both within the school and between school, neighborhood, and others).

Our composite program has been designed with the full input not only of teachers but also of students (even young ones), parents and caregivers, and community members. It involves students at different levels, according to their ages and preferences—for instance, high school students are engaged in young adult roles, assuming responsibility for the learning of younger students and for community improvements and the like. Students may also collect information about the neighborhood, such as people's skills and oral histories, work on community-based projects in areas such as housing, the environment, health, culture, recreation, and so on. With their service, they forge links between the local and wider communities, expanding their own vistas as well as their social networks. In many cases, they work in groups.

Back in the school, students continue working in cooperative groups, using reflection to derive lessons about their community, its culture, knowledge, and assets, as well as its relationship to the larger sociocultural environment, publishing the "stories" they have learned, and integrating this knowledge and academic subjects. The high standards to which their work is held (and to which they hold themselves) are clear and public, because their work itself usually leads to usable, public "products."

Students practice long hours to perfect their work, with encouragement and support from teachers, families, mentors, and neighborhood members. There develops a synergy between school and community. The substance of many of these projects becomes the stuff of new learning and of community building and development—that is, activities that physically and socially improve the neighborhood also strengthen community ties (Bingham & Meier, 1993). It appears in school–community newspapers and other aids to learning that are developed jointly by students and teachers; further evidence comes through improvements in the neighborhoods, achieved through collaborative efforts that also include outside resources.

The general principles underlying this sketch can be summarized under three headings:

Principle 1: Instruction.   Service-learning practice matches research findings that stress the importance of alternative learning environments and learning styles, learning in context, real-life tasks and assessments, collaborative work, and multiple opportunities for success. Service-learning programs should be group-oriented and should lead to tangible or visible student "products." Emphasizing community-oriented, culturally relevant service can further enhance student motivation and engagement.

Principle 2: Curriculum.   Service-learning can facilitate the development of curricula that value local knowledge. It fits research findings supporting the value of curricula that are intrinsically meaningful, connected to life experience, committed to change, and respectful of the historical contributions of minority communities—in other words, curricula that are thought provoking, culturally relevant, and committed. Service-learning programs therefore should build on students' experiences, orientation, and local knowledge; they should involve students in real life, community issues they perceive as important; and they should stress not only inquiry approaches to the learning of relevant knowledge, but the use of that knowledge to improve the life of the community.

Principle 3: Community Building and Development.   Service-learning can support the kinds of in-school and school–community relationships that enhance learning in urban schools. To counteract the emphasis on control that characterizes relationships in urban schools, the learning environment and school–community relations must foster mutual respect and knowledge. When implemented in ways that allow personal contact to lead to dialogue and mutual learning, service-learning fosters positive relationships. Programs, therefore, should have as their express goals the building of "two-way bridges" across the bounds of diversity, facilitating cross-cultural understanding, relationship building, and the creation of communities of support.

RECONCEPTUALIZING BARRIERS TO LEARNING FOR URBAN STUDENTS

Validating service-learning as an effective approach for urban schools involves, as a first step, reconceptualizing the causes of school failure. I focus in this section on issues involving school organization and learning environment, addressing school–community relations, and the responsiveness of schools to the community environment in the next.

The Effective Schools Movement

The vast majority of urban schools today are heavily influenced by what is known as the effective schools research and its attendant "movement" (Firestone, 1991). Promoted since the 1970s through the work of Edmonds (1982), Levine (1994), Lezotte (1992), and others, this movement sought to identify uncommonly effective urban schools (as measured by high and equitable test scores), with the goal of replicating them. Equity here is defined as reducing the influence of social class on test scores. The key concern was to demonstrate that good schools could indeed counter the barriers to success constituted by low socioeconomic status and other factors associated with poverty. The school could not change the neighborhood, but it could remake itself so as to promote success in spite of the external environment, indeed, compensating for it.

The idea that success might be within reach of the educational practitioner had great appeal, especially among practitioners (Firestone, 1991). Given the focus of this chapter, perhaps the most important aspect of the movement is its emphasis on school-wide factors and, implicitly, on barriers to learning that reside at the level of school organization. The "effective schools correlates" (i.e., organizational factors associated with school effectiveness) usually include the following: a positive school environment, high expectations for learning, instructional leadership, clear and focused goals, opportunity to learn, frequent monitoring of student progress, and parental involvement.

These correlates are not frozen in time. One of the movement's founders, Lezotte (1992), observed that student monitoring is shifting from reliance on standardized test scores in the basic skills to "authentic" assessments that include higher order learning. Parental involvement is now understood as requiring a "true partnership" more than one-way supports; in tandem, "positive" school environment, originally construed as "safe and orderly," is being reconceptualized to include a sense of caring and community within the school, which necessarily involves multicultural sensitivity. Continuing research has confirmed the importance of factors such as teacher expectations, parental participation, and academic focus. It is also clear that what works in some schools does not work as well in others. For instance, Newmann (1991) found that in schools where the student body is largely minority and of low socioeconomic status, effective principals are not only strong instructional leaders, but are also moderately authoritarian; furthermore, they are strong spokespersons for their schools, able to negotiate the system on the school's behalf.

These shifts in perspective suggest that the movement stimulated, through the work of both proponents and detractors, the search for a reconceptualization of the dynamics of school success and failure for urban students. Needed were theories of learning and of school functioning that might link research findings and, by pointing in promising directions, continue to advance reform efforts. Whereas the original effective schools movement did not offer much scope for service-learning, these shifts create the opportunity for it to contribute to reform efforts.

School Culture and School Restructuring

Purkey and Marshall (1982) offered the concept of school culture as a way of organizing and making sense of the effective school correlates. As they suggested, "The school culture model … assumes that changing schools requires changing people, their behaviors and attitudes, as well as school organization and norms. It assumes that consensus among the staff of a school is more powerful than overt control, without ignoring the need for leadership" (p. 68).

Given the present emphasis on school change through teacher teams, school councils, schools within schools, and Total Quality Management (TQM), it is clear that Purkey and Marshall's observations are part of a perspective on school reform that is gaining currency. Of course, embracing such approaches does not mean abandoning old ones, and urban schools often meld the two.

Service-learning may contribute to improving school culture through its beneficial effect on teacher–student relationships. Attitudes and understandings are formed in "discourse communities" that involve relationships; to change these, new communities and new relationships must be forged. Rather than engaging in blaming teachers, students, or parents, community-based service-learning can help forge solutions that involve changing these larger structures.

Although the research has established the importance of positive relationships for enhancing the quality of learning for minority students (Vasquez, 1994), staff consensus in urban schools may typically solidify around deficit perspectives and the imperative of control, yielding a school culture that is fundamentally disabling. For instance, feeling beleaguered and hampered by lack of resources, high school staff may develop a consensus that high dropout rates in the 9th and 10th grade are essential to the smooth and effective functioning of the school (Fine, 1992). Urban educators, who are more often than not of "mainstream" (i.e., middle-class White) backgrounds, are usually disconnected from the local neighborhood, and not only because contacts beyond school walls tend to be minimal: The research on prospective and actual teachers suggests that the vast majority, regardless of class of origin and ethnic or racial affiliation, would prefer to teach in a mainstream, suburban setting and view students in poverty from a deficit perspective (see Gomez, 1993, for a review). Of course, a preference for suburban settings is quite rational when one considers the poor work conditions and bureaucratized environment of most urban schools.

Negative attitudes tend to be strengthened rather than abandoned as a result of teaching in urban schools; programs that focus on preprofessional training and professional development do not easily lead to change, in part because such attitudes are supported by social and organizational arrangements (see, e.g., Sleeter, 1992). The induction of teachers into urban schools thus produces teacher–student relations that often follow a pattern identified by Williams (1989). The teacher's attempts to "be nice" (first stage) result in chaos (second stage). Subsequent attempts to reassert authority (third stage) lead to an uneasy truce that involves a "contract": Successful teaching is no longer measured by high academic expectations and achievement, but by the relative quiet of halls and classrooms. This fourth stage is the most common form of adjustment between urban teachers and their students; only rarely is a fifth and final stage achieved, that involves respect and mutual learning (also see King, 1993).

The extensive literature on teacher expectations reveals that urban students' social class, race, and prior academic achievement are strongly correlated with low teacher expectations and impoverished, less demanding and more controlling educational environments (Proctor, 1983). Where control is an issue (this is common in large group settings, with students for whom one has low expectations), teachers will tend to inhibit student initiative and participation (Cooper & Good, 1983). But even where such issues are not primary and the school environment appears friendly and warm, teacher (and student) expectations may remain quite low, as social concerns take precedence over academic ones.

A key issue in urban school reform, therefore, relates to the factors that might support movement toward Williams' fifth stage. This suggests that the focus should not be on school culture per se (which often stops at measures of teacher participation and team building among staff), but on school culture and organization as it relates to high teacher expectations, sound teacher–student–parent relationships, student engagement and—the key factor—high levels of learning (see, e.g., Weinstein, Madison, & Kuklinski, 1995). Service-learning may contribute, in this context, through its potential for supporting a more engaging, performance-based curriculum and "authentic" pedagogy; these are the foundations for high quality learning that have emerged from large-scale studies of restructured schools—the vast majority of which are urban (Newmann & Wehlage, 1995).

Curriculum and Pedagogy:
Authentic, Culturally Relevant, and Committed

An extensive literature demonstrates that, for overwhelming numbers of urban students, schools achieve the opposite of engagement (see e.g., D'Amato, 1993; Ogbu, 1990). As Newmann (1991) aptly observed, "large numbers are so alienated from schools that almost any activities which fall under school sponsorship are suspect" (p. 65). Newmann's work locates student engagement within a theory of the environment and culture that are likely to promote it. He relates engagement to three broad factors: the extent to which (a) the students' need for competence is supported by (b) the quality of school membership (a sense of schooling as legitimate, a sense of integration and belonging) and (c) the quality of tasks. Importantly, he observes that the usual extrinsic rewards (grades in the immediate and jobs in the long-run) cannot serve to motivate students in a context of prevailing unemployment, racism, and poverty. This puts a greater premium on the intrinsic value of academic tasks. According to Newmann, the factors likely to enhance student interest include the opportunity to express diverse forms of talent, a sense of ownership, authenticity, fun, and social supports.

Building on this work, Newmann and Wehlage's (1995) analysis of recent research on successful school restructuring revolves around the concept of "authentic" intellectual work. High and equitable levels of learning are achieved by all

students, regardless of social background, when instruction and assessment emphasize three factors: (a) knowledge construction (students analyze, organize, evaluate
information and consider alternatives), (b) disciplined inquiry (students use an
established knowledge base, develop in-depth understanding of problems, and use
elaborate language to communicate findings), (c) value beyond school (students
link "substantive knowledge and either public problems or personal experience,"
p. 17). It should be self-evident that service-learning provides an excellent vehicle
for such pedagogy.

Other researchers, who focus specifically on the learning of African-American
students, would likely agree with Newmann and Wehlage's quest for "authenticity"
but question its definition: how should members of minority groups, whose cultures
have been rendered invisible by ethnocentrism and assimilationist biases, undertake
the construction of knowledge, for instance? Should authenticity not require a quest
to legitimate subculturally appropriate attitudes, knowledge, and behaviors (e.g.,
high levels of expressivity and "verve" in interaction) vis-á-vis those of the
mainstream? If these are marginalized and summarily labeled deviant, the result is
the alienation of potentially high achieving students, whose critical intelligence
leads them to question school norms and knowledge, and to see schools less as
vehicles for learning than as agents of control (the "hidden curriculum"). In her
study of urban school dropouts, Michelle Fine (1992) found these students to be
more aware and often more intelligent than the ones who stayed in school.

What would lead to high levels of learning for such students? Research on
effective teachers of African-American students provides support for a curriculum
that is both multicultural (in the sense of fully integrating the life, experiences, and
worldview of diverse groups) and committed to the uses of knowledge as a
mechanism for self-understanding and community change. For instance, Michelle
Foster conducted a number of studies of African-American teachers termed "exemplary" by their former students (see Foster, 1994); there emerges a picture of
"connection, affiliation, and solidarity with the pupils they teach" (p. 228). Concerned with more than academic learning, these teachers convey to their students
"the personal value, the collective power, and the political consequences of choosing or rejecting academic achievement" (p. 237). Their classroom activities and
pedagogy incorporate the norms and values of the African-American community:
social equality, egalitarianism, mutuality, all connected to a group orientation rather
than an individual ethos.

The successful teachers of African-American students in Gloria Ladson-Billings' (1994) study identified the following paths to successful learning: first,
parents and community members should have the power to affect schools (educational self-determination); second, the students' home culture must be honored and
respected—this does not mean supplanting the whole curriculum, but understanding the "wealth and strength of African American culture" rather than deni-
grating it; third, students must acquire the knowledge and attitudes "to struggle
successfully against oppression" (p. 139).

In other words, the relevance of school knowledge does not reside so much in
its generically intellectual or immediately practical applicability. Rather, for these

authors, knowledge and pedagogy are authentic if they enable knowers to recognize themselves, name their experiences, and learn how to change existing conditions for themselves as well as for others in the community: Knowledge, in other words, must be emancipatory. Political commitment or "realism" (see Lawrence, 1995) is a major theme. Successful teachers acknowledge the societal barriers that face poor, minority children—naming racism, classism, and injustice, for instance—but, instead of reacting with pity, acceptance, cynicism and the like (which lead to lowered expectations and performance—see Graham, 1989), they strive to develop communities of support to overcome such barriers. The importance of community and group strength—of empowerment—as a path to success for subordinated minorities tends to elude mainstream educators, who prefer to focus on individually based interventions and, in tandem, improvement in psychological functioning (e.g., self-esteem). This may be due to the fact that living in the mainstream facilitates taking for granted the supports provided by existing social arrangements; indeed, it renders them invisible.

Service-learning that is group- and community-oriented begins to build those supports, contributing to peer group norms and values that define school as a place for meaningful learning and community problem solving. Service-learning is also a valuable tool for promoting a sense of agency in students (e.g., being able to act rather than being acted upon). It does so by opening the school door to activities that potentially can change the quality of relationships between students and teachers (Shumer, 1994): leveling power differences, it helps promote the reciprocity and cooperation that facilitate mutual learning. When the focus of service or other student–teacher experiential learning is on community knowledge and community development, the potential for improving relationships broadens further, reaching from the school to the local community (see Harkavy & Puckett, 1991).

Although these comments apply specifically to African Americans, they receive support from a growing literature on the learning environments in which minorities are more likely to succeed. Reviews by Banks (1994), Boykin (1994), Levine (1994), Losey (1995), and Vasquez (1994) concluded that schools should be responsive to diverse styles of learning, cognition, and motivation. The minority students studied tended to learn more when knowledge was presented in context ("field sensitive"), when the learning process was collaborative, when they could see the relationship between their efforts and accomplishments, and when they engaged in activities that allowed repeated experiences with success and therefore promoted patterns of internal attribution. Finally, as learning involves more than learning tasks, relationships were also important: More learning occurred when teachers were perceived as caring.

Boykin (1994) found that when tasks stressed cooperation rather than individualistic competition, performance outcomes between Euro-American and African-American students were reversed, with the latter doing better than the former. Research on the school experiences of Hawaiian children led D'Amato (1993) to conceptualize a key distinction between competition and rivalry: Rivalry consists of groups competing to equalize results, whereas competition involves working, at either the group or individual level, at surpassing others' performances. Cooperative learning fits well in environments, such as urban neighborhoods, where rivalry is prevalent, more than the individualistically competitive environment typical of mainstream society and classrooms. This suggests that the factors at work are not just cultural but also entail environmental adaptation: the urban, inner-city world is a world of street life, of peer groups, of rivalry; it is a world of action and verbal contests. All these can be used to enhance learning. The literature provides many examples of successful teaching and learning when local cultural knowledge is appropriated and becomes a valued bridge to and context for school knowledge—an approach that is often termed "teaching the culture of power" (see Delpit, 1988; McCaleb, 1994).

Further support for culturally contextualizing learning comes from research conducted by Tharp (1995) and others associated with the National Research Center for Cultural Diversity and Second Language Learning. Researchers reviewed 18 projects across the United States serving Native Americans, Latinos (mainly of Mexican origin), Koreans and other Asians. Designed to explore the classroom conditions that improve the school performance of minorities, the research led to four principles of effective instruction:

1. Developing competence in the language of instruction should be the over-reaching goal of all instructional activities, throughout the day.
2. Teaching, the curriculum, and the school must be "contextualized" by reference to the experiences, skills, values, and norms of the community.
3. Teaching and learning should occur in the context of joint productive activities with one's peers and with teachers.
4. The basic form of teaching should involve a dialogue between teachers and learners.

All the earlier findings dovetail well with the aims and approaches of service-learning: They lend support to the collaborative work, community orientation, experience, and reflection that are the markers of good service-learning programs. They also attest to the validity of integrated learning experiences that draw from the community and other experiential involvements outside the classroom. Indeed, the comments of a service proponent seem to be written with these research findings in mind:

> Service-learning involves and immerses students in relational learning environments and engages multiple senses and intelligences. Learning becomes more accessible by expanding the definition of competence and redefining the relationship of teacher to student and student to learning. The teacher, rather than simply being the provider of information and the evaluator of competence, is the creator of environments where students learn by doing, working with others, and reflecting on their experiences. (McPherson & Nebgen, p. 1)

In the urban environment, the benefits of service-learning are even greater: where many widely different ethnic and cultural groups attend the same schools, educators must devise new ways of learning about these groups and integrating their experiences and knowledge into culturally appropriate pedagogies. By bringing teachers and students together in a process of discovery and a context in which the teacher is not the depository of all knowledge, service-learning can provide a vehicle for validating students' experiences and thus bridging the cultural divide between school and neighborhood. Additional opportunities for learning occur when teachers work as partners with community leaders who facilitate students' community involvement or collaborate in the collection and interpretation of information about the neighborhood.

Building Communities of Support

At the beginning of this chapter, I pointed to the current interest among urban school reformers in creating "partnerships" that reach beyond school walls—and that these constitute a supportive climate for service-learning. We can envision a number of different approaches to partnerships. First, as should be clear from the previous discussion, improving learning and relationships in urban schools requires building bridges to the local community and bringing local culture and knowledge into the school. Second, ameliorating difficult life circumstances calls for creating supportive environments in school and community. Third, increasing community social and economic resources means that school improvements must be linked to community development. Thus partnerships need to include parents and the local community on the one hand, and agencies, organizations, and influential individuals in the larger community on the other. A "capacities" approach means that these partnerships are guided by the goal of bridging existing divisions and "flattening" hierarchies.

It is possible and desirable that each of these partnerships include service-learning involving students (at all levels, including college and teacher preparation), teachers, parents, community members, and members of service agencies and other organizations (i.e., businesspersons, workers, professionals, etc.). The discussion that follows focuses on issues related to developing ties to the local community; partnerships with other entities (and involving service-learning placements in health agencies, businesses, and other mainstream organizations) are more common and do not require a special discussion.

It is difficult to imagine urban schools engaging in authentic pedagogy, as redefined earlier, without also changing the way they relate to students, families and caregivers and, more generally, to the local neighborhood or community. Bridges need to be created over existing "borders," and appropriately organized service-learning projects can help in the process. We should recall that borders are present whenever different cultures come into contact in the context of hierarchy: with regard to urban schools, borders come about because the "world" of school (e.g., the values, attitudes, behaviors, norms it expects and rewards) generally constitutes itself as separate from and superior to the "world" of the neighborhood—of peer groups and, often, of home (Phelan, Davidson, & Yu, 1993).

The issue here is the obstacles such borders constitute for urban students and their communities. Tersely put, students who experience a high degree of consistency among their worlds (and this is more typical in mainstream environments) find it easier to conform to social expectations than those who do not. Conformity is also facilitated, as in the case of many "voluntary minorities" (see Ogbu, 1990), when the native and mainstream communities support or do not resist assimilation. In the mainstream, congruence between school and community norms is often the result of a community's ability to enforce the dominance of its norms in the schools, rather than the other way around; importantly, if teachers enter such environments with divergent expectations, attitudes, and repertoires of skills, it is they, rather than the students, who are required to change in order to conform to school norms.

When these supports are not available, when the borders are impassable, students are faced with difficult choices among their worlds: For instance, will they perfect the role of successful students or that of valued members of their peer group? The teen mother must forego being a student. In urban neighborhoods, a "good home" is often one that helps youth choose education, by being very strict, structured, and protective—including "protection" from the influence of an undesirable peer group. Success, as Richard Rodriguez' (1981) well-known autobiography, *Hunger of Memory*, reveals, may require alienation not only from peers, but also from home and community. These are enormous sacrifices, such that we do not ask of White middle-class students.

From the youth's perspective, school failure and the process of dropping out can now be seen as one of gradual disengagement and can be conceptualized in terms of the cultural dissonance of the "different worlds" to which they belong (Gordon & Yowell, 1994), and of identity politics: schools and other mainstream institutions often fail to accommodate different lifestyles (Wehlage, Rutter, Smith, Lesko, & Fernandez, 1989) and provide support for the development of talents and positive identity for lower class, minority youth; disengaging from such negative environments, many of these youth then resort to peer groups and nonmainstream inner-city institutions (e.g., gangs) for support, developing oppositional identities in the process. The causes of failure thus reside both in social structures (including schools) that send subtle and not-so-subtle messages of inadequacy and "difference-as-deficit" and in the response and resistance to such messages by inner-city youth and adults.

The question, then, is how schools and communities in urban settings might support their students by increasing the congruence between their worlds and building border-crossing bridges of support. Of course, this perspective adds significance to culturally relevant curricula, which we can now understand as one possible border-bridging strategy. Border-bridging is not an easy task, however. Mainstream (deficit) worldviews are not a matter of individual beliefs but have their roots in dominant ideologies that are upheld by social institutions, such as the media and education; they are further propagated through government programs and other societal arrangements, including discourse communities—that is, groups that perpetuate particular interpretations of reality through linguistic interaction. Contacts between educators and neighborhood members often confirm these views of "reality." It requires a conscious effort, buttressed by systematic supports, to envision poor urban, and especially inner-city residents, as possessing strengths and capacities.

Yet, there are sources of hope and possibilities for change. Dominant perceptions of inner-city residents can be dispelled through exposure and relationship building that give outsiders an "inner" understanding of these neighborhoods. Conversely, programs that identify, value, and strengthen community members' capacities empower them to address school and community issues. By linking with these possibilities and creating in-school supports as well as bridges to the outside worlds, schools can begin to enact new tales of hope. Successful strategies that can dovetail with service-learning include reorganizing the school so as to support the different lifestyles of the students (i.e., by accommodating teen parents—see Wehlage et al., 1989); and inviting a genuine partnership with parents and community members, which might involve both the presence of parents in the school and that of educators in the household and community (Delgado-Gaitan, 1993; Keith, 1996; McCaleb, 1994; Moll, Amanti, Neff, & Gonzalez, 1992;).

There is significant research on the strength and capacities many inner-city youth and adults possess. Resilience, which consists of psychosocial factors that protect children who are "at risk," is fostered when children have opportunities to participate and make meaningful contributions, and when the activities in which they are engaged give them a sense of responsibility (Werner & Smith, 1992). A good relationship between children and at least one adult—a potential outcome of service-learning—also fosters resilience.

Opportunities to participate are available in urban settings and urban minority youth are more active than is generally recognized. A 1990 survey found that 11% of African-American 10th graders engaged in service, as against 9% of all urban students and 7% of all 10th graders (Lewis, 1992). Participation may be even higher if we assume that many service activities go unrecorded (McClure, cited in Davis, 1980). The synthesizing work of Kretzmann and McKnight (1993) uncovered large numbers of local initiatives in many cities across the nation, built around and drawing strength from community assets, including local organizations and individuals. Based on these findings, the authors developed the concept of "community assets maps" as alternatives to the more common "community deficits maps." Further support for capacities approaches comes from the continued successes of organizations such as the Industrial Areas Foundation and projects sponsored by foundations such as the Poverty and Race Research Action Council.

McLaughlin, Irby, and Langman's (1994) extensive study of *urban sanctuaries*—successful inner-city organizations for youth—offers additional evidence of strengths. Their research strongly suggests that youth behaviors such as community service, volunteering, and the taking of responsibility become quite common when organizations offer "support and optimism, fun and friendship," rather than being premised on preventing at-risk behaviors (p. 8). They asserted that: "The public's discouraging conclusions and myths about the interests, motivation, and capacities of inner-city youth are in urgent need of revision. Many adolescents *do* want to belong to organizations that help them escape inner-city despair, imagine and move toward positive, hope-filled futures" (McLaughlin, Irby, & Langman, pp. 5–6).

Successful youth organizations create environments that provide an alternative to affiliation with undesirable groups and their destructive norms, at the same time replicating aspects that make such groups attractive and successful. For instance, they provide strong supports for developing positive identities; youth are seen as capable and able to prove themselves; there is a "career ladder" that brings increasing responsibility and rewards. Some researchers suggest that inner-city youth organizations should learn from the successes of gangs, in both the social and economic sphere (Fine & Mechling, 1993). The adults who work successfully with neighborhood organizations are themselves bridges between worlds: Knowledgeable about local culture, they are also at ease in mainstream settings, able to use their networks and contacts to bring resources into the inner city (McLaughlin, Irby, & Langman, 1994). Community leadership by former gang members provides additional local knowledge useful in creating responsive and inviting organizations (Vigil, 1993).

These comments alert us to the fact that more deviant behaviors are also potential assets. Assertive cultural, art and music forms such as rap, breakdancing, graffiti murals, and the like, speak of a creativity that persists in the midst of want (Lusane, 1993; Miller, 1993). These activities are not just individual, but are supported by peer groups, which call forth extraordinary commitment. This is not to romanticize such involvements, the darker side of which is gang membership; it is merely to call attention not only, as is common, to their deviance, but also to their capacities. Recent peace initiatives by gangs demonstrate that these groups have organizational talents that may at times be put to the use of community development. It is by building on such strengths, for instance, that the Nation of Islam security patrols in low-income projects are able to succeed where mainstream approaches have failed miserably.

The conclusion is that there is strong support for school–local community partnerships built on a foundation of reciprocity rather than on compensatory or at-risk models. When working with parent and community involvement, capacities or empowerment approaches have been successful where models that emphasize the transmission of school practices have not (McCaleb, 1994). Community-based service-learning projects can thus proceed with assurance that building from the ground up is not required. The issue is not whether sound foundations already exist: they do. Rather, it involves what is seen and how educators "construct" the local community.

How can educators appreciate and learn to make use of positive attributes of urban residents and neighborhoods? Although there is no single answer to this question, it is clear that service-learning has a valuable role to play. Ensuring that preservice teachers experience life in such communities may provide one avenue, by creating opportunities for challenging their uncritically held views (Gomez, 1993). A teacher preparation program in Texas discovered that immersing prospective teachers "in a culture in which they become the Other" (Gomez, 1993, p. 467) was a key ingredient of successful bridge building. Another such program learned that many students' "first awareness of social and economic injustice in U.S. society came about while engaging in the required community service work. Only then did these students begin to question how and why Others end up on public assistance or in poverty rather than in the work force" (Gomez, p. 466).

The conclusion is that programs aiming to foster teachers' understanding of diversity need to develop genuine partnerships with both individuals and institutions in the communities of origin of their students.

CONCLUSION

Service-learning can be an important catalyst in breaking down the barriers between school and community, making the school a bridge between the local community and the outside world, and reintegrating the school as a community institution; it can do so by contributing to the understanding of local knowledge and local ways, and by building on them.

Given the effort involved, service-learning should not be limited to individual projects by individual teachers but should build sustained institutional commitment to engaging community members in a process of community building and development. It is important that such a vision be considered in the beginning, when planning for service-learning community outreach projects. Only if service-learning is inserted into a larger vision can it contribute to it; otherwise, its potential may not be fully realized.

Ultimately, the vision and direction for the future is one where schools become better at being what they are supposed to be, developing young adults who have not only the skills to succeed in the world, to earn a living, but also young adults who understand the value of knowledge, accept their social responsibilities, and have learned that it is possible to change one's environment, to be agents rather than objects. If we succeed in this task, we will promote the education for citizenship and democracy on which this country was founded.

DESCRIPTION OF SELECTED PROGRAMS

The following list of programs is meant to be suggestive rather than all-inclusive.

Community Service Academy. Salome Urena School (IS 218), 4600 Broadway, New York City. Naomi Smith, Teacher Director. Member, Coalition of Essential Schools.   Salome Urena School was opened 5 years ago as a middle school (Grades 6–8) with "academies"—specialized "schools-within-the school"—serving a total of 1,400 students. The Community Service Academy involves approximately 420 students and 22 teachers in 15 classes. All the teachers chose the academy, knowing that it would mean involvement with the community. Students are mostly Latino, with a few African Americans, Asians, and other minorities and the staff is diverse. Each class undertakes two projects each year, with students spending a few hours a week involved in service. The projects are conducted through advisory groups, constituted by 1 teacher and 15 students, thus providing the advantages of small size and continuity. The teacher accompanies the students in the field.

Service projects were developed initially by teachers and members of community organizations, with teachers and students subsequently building on this foundation. Community projects include the development and staffing of a child-care center in a welfare office and cross-cultural education for the police. Proposed by a student "Peace Team" in the context of police–community tensions, the latter project now features students as teachers of police officers, for both Spanish language and Latino culture. Students also work with pre-K children in a learning center and old people in a geriatric center; they have cleaned up a subway tunnel and empty lots, planted trees, and created community gardens. Also included are internships at community organizations, museums, politicians' offices, and others. Although all projects involve reflection, integration into the curriculum occurs at different levels, through a natural process of development. Students involved in the pre-K project have their entire curriculum centered on the project; integration for other students is partial. These projects, many of which also involve community participation, have had significant community impact and have created in the students a strong sense of being role models.

Urban Academy. 351 West 18th Street, New York City (see Raywid, 1994). Member, Coalition of Essential Schools. This "school-within-a school" for students in Grades 9–12 relies extensively on service-learning. All students spend an afternoon per week involved in community service. The pedagogical focus of the curriculum is on "problematizing of all school work" (Raywid, 1994, p. 108). Most classes integrate academic knowledge and issues that concern and challenge urban students. For instance, in a course on popular culture, students studied data on cassette and CD sales to draw inferences about musicians' popularity (Raywid, p. 96). On "research days" when all staff is involved in intensive and extensive conferences with students, students spend their time outside conference in service activities such as reviewing a controversial book and developing an argument on its appropriateness for children's reading.

Dewey Center for Urban Education. 3550 Lodge Drive, Detroit, MI. Francis Parker, Principal. Located in downtown Detroit, this pre-K–8 school caters to 600 students, all of whom participate in service-learning. The center's philosophy is that knowledge should be used to improve society and its major goal is community improvement. Each year, teachers receive a small budget and develop a plan for service in collaboration with their students. Students in fifth and eighth grades participate in a "rite of passage" ceremony that lasts the whole term and involves fulfilling a contract to improve self, family, and community. Service projects are age appropriate: Service might start, for young students, with making placemats and artifacts highlighting different cultures, for use in senior centers; other projects have included peer tutoring and mentoring (i.e., "book buddies"); community clean-ups; work in nursing homes, TV station, and other organizations; creating brochures to improve community health; and creating and distributing "community services" maps so that transient residents (who do not know the neighborhood) can find services and other community help. Because of these projects, the community presence in the school is strong and teachers have a good knowledge and understanding of the community.

Cambridge Service Corps. Cambridge Rindge and Latin High School, 459 Broadway (R-101), Cambridge, MA. John Shea, Social Studies teacher. T h i s program is featured because for a number of interesting aspects that are applicable to an urban setting; even though the school body is diverse, Cambridge does not, strictly speaking, fit the "urban" mold. John Shea teaches a community service class that includes a diverse group of 17 from all grades and groups in the high school (Community Problem Solving 101). The class provides a context for learning core academic subjects. For the first half of the year, students learn about neighborhood critical issues through service placements in especially selected agencies and community groups: AIDS support group, homeless shelter, substance abuse task force, Economic Opportunity Commission, and so on. By sharing their experiences in the class, all students learn about a broad range of issues in the community. Then, the group as a whole identifies a particular project and recruits others in the school (teachers and students) to carry it out. During the first year (1995–1996), the project involved creating a Community Resource Center in the school, to provide information and resources for the school and the community.

Feinstein Institute for Public Service. Providence College, RI. Rick Battistoni, Director. The Institute has developed a college major and a minor in public service. Preservice elementary education teachers learn to use service-learning as a pedagogy for urban schools and serve as classroom resource persons for teachers whose students undertake service-learning. College students have, for instance, obtained input from the community on designing an appropriate curriculum. With regard to school activities, the aim of service projects is to bring parents and community members into the schools and to enable children to express in different ways aspects of their own cultures. Students work with teachers to identify projects of importance to them. Initially, the school was defined as the community to be served and many projects were school-based: cleaning gang graffiti from school walls and windows, addressing vandalism in the school; establishing a "peace site" to address violence (the peace site is attached to a conflict resolution program). Later projects have involved more teacher-initiated contacts and collaboration with the larger community (e.g., creating community gardens). Projects have been presented to community members (e.g., senior centers).

Shriver Center. University of Maryland, Baltimore. James Price, Director.
The Center was created as a holding company for initiatives that address and solve the problems of the city. Projects involving service-learning were developed on the basis of assessment of community needs and capacities and the development of community-driven areas of priority. Current priorities include juvenile justice and funding. A range of programs are in operation. The center has developed its own

program for choice middle schools, which includes an integrated approach to service delivery and advocacy. College students are involved in service-learning in a number of ways (e.g., as tutors and mentors).

West Philadelphia Community Improvement Corps (WEPIC). Penn Program for Public Service, University of Pennsylvania. Joan Weeks, Director, WEPIC Replication Project. WEPIC is a project of neighborhood revitalization initiated by the University of Pennsylvania in the West Philadelphia neighborhood in which it is located. The partnership involves the University, the School District of Philadelphia, and community organizations. Service-learning, sponsored through Penn courses, brings Penn students into the schools; school students undertake service in other schools (e.g., as peer tutors) and the community. Two high schools and two middle schools are most heavily involved in community-based service-learning: University City High School, West Philadelphia High School, Turner Middle School, and Shaw Middle School.

WEPIC schools strive to involve community members and students in identifying community projects and in-school activities. Students have undertaken such projects as creating community gardens, renovating houses, building projects for a nursery school, collecting oral histories, and writing newspapers. High school students also work as apprentices (e.g., in the building trades) through the Philadelphia Community Development Corporation.

REFERENCES

Banks, J. (1994). Ethnicity, class, cognitive, and motivation styles: Research and teaching implications. In J. Kretovics & E. J. Nussel (Eds.), *Transforming urban education* (pp. 274–290). New York: Teachers College Press.

Bingham, R. D., & Meier, R. (Eds.). (1993). *Theories of local economic development; Perspectives from across the disciplines.* Newbury Park, CA: Sage.

Boykin, A. W. (1994). Harvesting talent and culture; African-American children and educational reform. In R. J. Rossi (Ed.), *Schools and students at risk; Context and framework for positive change* (pp. 116–138). New York: Teachers College Press.

Coleman, J. S., Campbell, E., Hobson, C., McPartland, J., Mood, A., Weinfeld, F., & York, R. (1966). *Equality of educational opportunity.* Washington, DC: U.S. Government Printing Office.

Cooper, H., & Good, T. L. (1983). *Pygmalion grows up: Studies in the expectation communication process.* New York: Longman.

D'Amato, J. (1993). Resistance and compliance in minority classrooms. In E. Jacob & C. Jordan (Eds.), *Minority education: Anthropological perspectives* (pp. 181–207). Norwood, NJ: Ablex.

Davis, K. E. (1980). An alternative theoretical perspective on race and voluntary participation. *Journal of Voluntary Action Research*, 126–142.

Delgado-Gaitan, C. (1993). Research and policy in reconceptualizing family–school relationships. In P. Phelan & A. L. Davidson (Eds.), *Renegotiating cultural diversity in American schools* (pp. 139–158). New York: Teachers College Press.

Delpit, L. (1988). The silenced dialogue: Power and pedagogy in educating other people's children. *Harvard Educational Review, 58,* 280–298.

Dryfoos, J. G. (1994). *Full-service schools; A revolution in health and social services for children, youth, and families.* San Francisco: Jossey-Bass.

Edmonds, R. E. (1982). Programs of school improvement: An overview. *Educational Leadership, 40*(3), 4–12.

Fine, M. (1992). *Framing dropouts.* New York: Teachers College Press.

Fine, G. A., & Mechling, J. (1993). Child saving and children's cultures at century's end. In S. B. Heath & M. W. McLaughlin (Eds.), *Identity and inner-city youth* (pp. 120–146). New York: Teachers College Press.

Firestone, W. A. (1991). Introduction. In J. R. Bliss, W. A. Firestone, & C. E. Richards (Eds.), *Rethinking effective schools; Research and practice* (pp. 1–11). Englewood Cliffs, NJ: Prentice Hall.

Foster, M. (1994). Educating for competence in community and culture; Exploring the views of exemplary African-American teachers. In M. J. Shujaa (Ed.), *Too much schooling, too little education; A paradox of Black life in White societies* (pp. 221–244). Trenton, NJ: Africa World Press.

Gardner, H. (1993). *Multiple intelligences: The theory in practice.* New York: Basic Books.

Gomez, M. L. (1993). Prospective teachers' perspectives on teaching diverse children: A review with implications for teacher education and practice. *Journal of Negro Education, 62,* 459–474.

Gordon, E. W., & Yowell, C. (1994). Cultural dissonance as a risk factor in the development of students. In R. J. Rossi (Ed.), *Schools and students at risk; Context and framework for positive change* (pp. 51–69). New York: Teachers College Press.

Graham, S. (1989). Motivation in Afro-Americans. In G. L. Berry, & J. K. Asamen (Eds.), *Black students: Psychosocial issues and academic achievement* (pp. 40–68). Newbury Park, CA: Sage.

Harkavy, I., & Puckett, J. (1991). *Academically based public service in a university's local community as a possible strategy for integrating teaching, research, and service.* Paper presented for the Wingspread Conference on Setting the Agenda for Effective Research in Combining Service and Learning in the 1990s. Racine, WI: Johnson Foundation.

Keith, N. Z. (1996). Can urban school reform and community development be joined? The potential of community schools. *Education and Urban Society, 28,* 237–268.

King, S. H. (1993). The limited presence of African-American teachers. *Review of Educational Research, 63,* 115–149.

Kretzmann, J. P., & McKnight, J. L. (1993). *Building communities from the inside out.* Evanston, IL: Northwestern University, Center for Urban Affairs and Policy Research.

Ladson-Billings, G. (1994). *The dreamkeepers; Successful teachers of African-American children.* San Francisco: Jossey-Bass.

Lawrence, C. (1995, April). *The three R's revisited: Toward an emancipatory pedagogy for Black learners—Implications for curriculum, classroom practice, and community.* Paper presented at the annual conference of the American Educational Research Association, San Francisco.

Levine, D. U. (1994). Instructional approaches and interventions that can improve the academic performance of African American students. *Journal of Negro Education, 63,* 46–63.

Lewis, A. (1992). Urban youth in community service: Becoming part of the solution. *ERIC Clearinghouse on Urban Education Digest, 81* (EDO-UD-92-4), 1–2.

Lezotte, L. W. (1992). Correlates of effective schools: The first and second generation. In L. W. Lezotte & B. C. Jacoby (Eds.), *Sustainable school reform; The district context for school improvement* (pp. 238–245). Okemos, MI: Effective Schools.

Losey, K. M. (1995). Mexican American students and classroom interaction: An overview and critique. *Review of Educational Research, 65*, 283–318.

Lusane, C. (1993). Rap, race and politics. *Race & Class, 35*, 41–56.

McCaleb, S. P. (1994). *Building communities of learners; A collaboration among teachers, students, families, and community.* Hillsdale, NJ: Lawrence Erlbaum Associates.

McLaughlin, M. W., Irby, M., & Langman, J. (1994). *Urban sanctuaries; Neighborhood organizations in the lives and futures of inner-city youth.* San Francisco: Jossey-Bass.

McPherson, K., & Nebgen, M. K. (1991). Setting the agenda: School reform and community service. *Network, 2*(3), 1, 4.

Miller, I. (1993). Guerrilla artists of New York City. *Race & Class, 35*, 27–40.

Moll, L. C., Amanti, Co., Neff, D., & Gonzales, N. (1992). Funds of knowledge for teaching: Using a qualitative approach to connect homes and classrooms. *Theory into Practice, 31*, 132–141.

Newmann, F. M. (1991). Student engagement in academic work: Expanding the perspective on secondary school effectiveness. In J. R. Bliss, W. A. Firestone, & C. E. Richards (Eds.), *Rethinking effective schools; Research and practice* (pp. 58–75). Englewood Cliffs, NJ: Prentice-Hall.

Newmann, F. M., & Wehlage, G. G. (1995). *Successful school restructuring.* Madison: Center on Organization and Restructuring of Schools, College of Education, University of Wisconsin–Madison.

Ogbu, J. U. (1990). Cultural model, identity, and literacy. In J. W. Stigler, R. A. Shweder, & G. Herdt (Eds.), *Cultural psychology: Essays on comparative human development* (pp. 520–541). New York: Cambridge University Press.

Phelan, P., Davidson, A. L., & Yu, H. C. (1993). Students' multiple worlds: Navigating the borders of family, peer, and school cultures. In P. Phelan & A. L. Davidson (Eds.), *Renegotiating cultural diversity in American schools* (pp. 52–88). New York: Teachers College Press.

Proctor, C. P. (1983). Teacher expectations: A model for school improvement. *The Elementary School Journal, 84*, 469–481.

Purkey, S. C., & Marshall, S. S. (1982). Too soon to cheer? Synthesis of research on effective schools. *Educational Leadership, 40*(3), 64–69.

Raywid, M. A. (1994). A school that really works: Urban Academy. *Journal of Negro Education, 63*, 93–110.

Rodriguez, R. (1981). *Hunger of memory.* Boston, MA: D. R. Godine.

Rogoff, B., & Lave, J. (Eds.). (1984). *Everyday cognition: Its development in social context.* Cambridge, MA: Harvard University Press.

Shumer, R. (1994). Humanizing education. *Journal of Adolescence, 17*, 357–367.

Sleeter, C. (1992). Resisting racial awareness: How teachers understand the social order from their racial, gender, and social class locations. *Educational Foundations, 6*(2), 7–32.

Tharp, R. G. (1995). Principles of instruction for multicultural classrooms. *Focus on Diversity, 5*(2), 4, 7–8.

Vasquez, J. A. (1994). Contexts of learning for minority students. In J. Kretovics & E. J. Nussel (Eds.), *Transforming urban education* (pp. 291–300). New York: Teachers College Press.

Vigil, J. D. (1993). Gangs, social control, and ethnicity: Ways to redirect. In S. B. Heath & M. W. McLaughlin (Eds.), *Identity and inner-city youth* (pp. 94–119). New York: Teachers College Press.

Wehlage, G. G., Rutter, R., Smith, G. A., Lesko, N., & Fernandez, R. (1989). *Reducing the risk; Schools as communities of support.* New York: Falmer.

Weinstein, R. S., Madison, S. M., & Kuklinski, M. R. (1995). Raising expectations in schooling: Obstacles and opportunities for change. *American Educational Research Journal, 32,* 121–159.

Werner, E. E., & Smith, R. S. (1992). *Overcoming the odds; High risk children from birth to adulthood.* Ithaca, NY: Cornell University Press.

Williams, M. R. (1989). *Neighborhood organizing for urban school reform.* New York: Teachers College Press.

Wilson, W. J. (1987). *The truly disadvantaged.* Chicago: University of Chicago Press.

Conclusions

10

Evaluating Service-Learning: Toward a New Paradigm

L. Richard Bradley
The Ohio State University

When asked about evaluating programs in their schools, teachers and school administrators often answer, "If it ain't broke, don't fix it." Asked for specifics, they say things like "Well, it seems to be working," or "the students like it," or "Maybe next year."

The problem with this is that "next year" hardly ever comes. But not evaluating what you do can lead to bigger problems down the road. As Osborne and Gaebler (1993) stated:

- What gets measured gets done.
- If you don't measure results, you won't know success from failure.
- If you can't see success, you can't reward it.
- If you can't reward success, you are probably rewarding failure
- If you can't recognize failure, you can't learn from it.
- If you demonstrate success, "the people will come."

Whenever parents ask why their son or daughter has to participate in a service-learning activity, it helps to be able to say something like: "Based on our evaluation of programs like this one on other students in this school, your son or daughter is likely to benefit in one or more of the following ways ... " A carefully designed evaluation plan can give you the information for such a statement.

It can also help you answer questions from other key groups such as:

- Administrators who will ask if the educational benefits of service-learning outweigh the costs of implementing it and how we will know if the program works.

- Teachers who will want to know what changes they might expect to see in their students and whether service-learning activities will really benefit certain groups of students.
- Parents and other members of the community who want to know what service-learning has to do with education and what it will do for students and the community, and whether it is worth the trouble.

Finally, an evaluation plan may also be required by your funding agency.

Despite this, there is not a lot of research that supports the claims made by service-learning advocates. One reason for this may be confusion about what service-learning is and is not (Waterman, chap. 1). Another reason may be that the changes researchers are most interested in observing—changes in student attitudes and behaviors—often take more than 1 school year to appear, whereas most service-learning programs run for less than that. A third reason may be what Serow (chap. 2) refers to as an "unduly restrictive view of what constitutes good research and evaluation ... ," (p. 13) which relies almost exclusively on quantitative methods of data collection and analysis. The result is often confusion about what to evaluate and how to go about it.

Choosing an appropriate evaluation strategy can be made easier by careful attention to questions such as:

1. What do you want or need to evaluate? What questions would you like to be able to answer?
2. What is the purpose of your evaluation? To satisfy the requirements of funders? To help you make decisions about whether to continue a program?
3. With whom will the results be shared? Will they be publicly shared or are they primarily for your own use?
4. What resources do you need to conduct your evaluation?

Relationships between the questions you want answered and various evaluation strategies are shown in Table 10.1.

In weighing the relative merits of each of these approaches, a decision must also be made as to whether the evaluation is to be external or internal. There are advantages and disadvantages to each.

External evaluations are typically done by someone outside your organization who is hired to evaluate your program. To the extent that the results of your evaluation are to be made public, it may be to your advantage to hire a nonbiased outsider whose presence will lend greater credibility to the results. Chief disadvantages have to do with cost and availability of a qualified person in your area.

Internal evaluations are typically done by someone from within your organization who has the necessary expertise. Advantages are familiarity with critical aspects of your program and lower cost. The disadvantage is that the findings of your program may not be as widely accepted, no matter how objective your evaluator is.

With these considerations in mind, are there alternative ways to evaluate the very real impact service-learning programs appear to have on students, schools, and communities? Given the insights contained in the previous chapters of this book,

TABLE 10.1
Comparisons of Evaluation Strategies in Relation to Service-Learning

Questions You Want Answered	Type of Evaluation	Ways to Do This
• Are you doing what you said you were going to do in your proposal or program description? • Is your program operating efficiently and in a timely manner?	Formative or Process [primarily qualitative]	• process observation • interviews with program staff & administrators • questionnaires for staff & administrators • minutes of meetings
• How well are your program goals and objectives being met? • What impact is your service-learning program having on student skills & knowledge, attitudes & behaviors?	Summative or Outcome [qualitative or quantitative depending on evaluation design]	• checklists of goals & objectives • surveys • observation • self-reflective tools such as journals • pre/postservice assessments on key indicators, such as GPA, behaviors & attitudes • statistical analysis
• How many students participated in your service-learning project? • How many hours of service did they give? • Who were the primary beneficiaries? How many beneficiaries were there? • How much did it cost?	Descriptive [primarily qualitative]	• case studies • surveys • observation • statistical analysis
• Do programs which integrate service into the curriculum have a greater impact on students than those which are not curriculum based? • What impact does service-learning have on the attitudes & behaviors of "at-risk" youth?	Experimental [qualitative or quantitative depending on evaluation design]	• surveys • observation • self-reflective tools such as journals • pre/postservice assessments on key indicators, such as GPA, behaviors & attitudes • statistical analysis

what kinds of questions need to be asked? Are there ways to do this that do not downplay or overlook potentially useful information? Most important, can this be done in ways that are "user friendly"?

TOWARD A NEW PARADIGM

Perhaps it is time to propose a new paradigm for the evaluation of service-learning; one that takes into account the interests of everyone involved as well as the limitations of current research and evaluation methods.

The traditional method of scientific inquiry—which begins with observation of some phenomenon, proceeds to the formation of a reasonable hypothesis, then to the design of experiments to disconfirm it, and finally to revisions in the original hypothesis—has the following characteristics:

- Linearity (i.e., A - B - C - D, etc.).
- Causality and predictability (based linearity).
- Assumes that the system in which the researcher is interested can be isolated from other systems (which is to say, you can hold all the variables except the one in which you are interested constant).
- Proportionality (i.e., the solutions to linear equations can be added together to produce other solutions).
- Objectivity.
- Reductionistic (i.e., some information may be overlooked in order to get the best "fit" between theory and fact).

The problem has been what to do with data that falls outside the boundaries of accepted explanations. For example, within the field of psychology, Kohlberg's (1981) theory of moral development and Levinson's (1978) "Stages in the Adult Cycle," were developed using all male samples. Until fairly recently, differences between male and female development were typically dismissed as being unimportant or irrelevant. Data that did not fit the theories that had been proposed were routinely overlooked or dismissed.

Although the shortcomings of the traditional scientific method have long been recognized, only recently did a new paradigm begin to emerge—first in the work of people like Edward Lorenz (Gleick, 1987). His attempts to write equations allowing for more accurate weather predictions resulted in the startling discovery that even small variations in the initial conditions made for big differences later on. At the same time, Lorenz also found that, no matter how long his computer-generated weather simulations went on, the resulting differences all fell within the boundaries of the same, butterfly-shaped figure. Two important concepts emerge from the work of Lorenz and others: sensitive dependence on initial conditions and constrained randomness.

This new model of scientific inquiry is characterized by:

- Nonlinearity.
- Unpredictability (within the boundaries of "constrained randomness").
- Nonadditive (i.e., if two events are added together, the resulting effects may be greater than expected—the proverbial "straw that broke the camel's back").
- Systems are interactive and cannot be isolated from one another.
- Inclusive and expanding (look for ways to include all the information).

The approach of nonlinear science parallels the approach of Barbara McClintock, who in 1983, at the age of 81, won a Nobel prize for her discovery that the genes in corn are capable of jumping from one chromosomal site to another

(Horning, 1995). She described her approach as one of "listening to the material, of engaging her subject matter on a deeply personal level."

In their book entitled *Fourth Generation Evaluation*, Guba and Lincoln (1989) proposed a similar approach for educational research, suggesting that the evaluator needs to pay careful attention to the context in which a program occurs. Instead of coming to the evaluation with predetermined notions about what is to be evaluated and how it is to evaluated, Guba and Lincoln suggested listening to the various stakeholders involved in a program to see what their needs are. This process begins by asking each of them the following question: "In thinking about the worth and value of your program, tell me the questions you think I should be asking and how you would answer them." Evaluation plans take shape from their responses.

Evaluation based on this approach takes seriously the fact that the word "assessment" comes from the Latin root "assidere," meaning "to sit beside." In thinking about strategies for evaluating the impacts and effectiveness of service-learning programs, "listening to the material" means paying careful attention to the environments—the schools and communities—in which programs happen.

Second, because schools—like the world—are constantly changing, the understanding and meaning attached to particular events can only be determined by watching, learning from, and facilitating the emergence of information from the schools themselves. This means that thoughtful evaluation of service-learning outcomes cannot happen without understanding the concept of sensitive dependence on initial conditions. Schools and students cannot be isolated from their communities. What are conditions like in the school and in the community? What else is going on in the school and community that either helps or hinders efforts to introduce service-learning into the curriculum? What are relationships like between the school and the community which surrounds it?

Third, beyond the variables that are traditionally assessed in educational programs generally, and in service-learning programs specifically, service-learning evaluations might also seek to learn more about the underlying order or constrained randomness of schools and communities.

Fourth, because education is essentially a non-linear process, program evaluators need to be aware that there are multiple paths to desired outcomes. This means it is at least as important to look at the process as it is the outcome.

What is being described here is the kind of holistic assessment suggested by Serow (chap. 2), assessment that seeks to gage the impact of service-learning by examining the changes in participants within the context of their broader life circumstances and communities rather than looking only at attitudinal changes. Holistic assessment focuses on four sets of outcomes:

- Changes in competence (skills).
- Changes in participation (behavior).
- Changes in understanding (knowledge).
- Changes in relationships (attitudes)." (p.19)

In return for being granted access to a full range of potential data sources, researchers should be prepared to accept the obligation to produce usable information that shows the links between service-learning and the curriculum (Serow, chap. 2). Permanent "feedback loops"—between parents and teachers, between students and teachers, between teachers and community members, between administrators and community members—should be established so that everyone involved or affected by the programs benefits from what is being learned, regardless of where or how the learning takes place.

This new approach to evaluation is not intended to replace the more traditional one. However, by taking a more holistic approach to the evaluation of service-learning and by listening more carefully to the environment, we may learn some things about program impacts and effectiveness that we might otherwise miss. In particular, we might be able to learn more about the "initial conditions" that are necessary for high quality, successful service-learning programs. This, in turn, might suggest possible directions for future research and evaluation efforts in the field of service-learning.

Based on what the previous authors have suggested, what variables define the "initial conditions" of successful service-learning programs?

1. The extent to which the service-learning program addresses and meets learning goals students have set for themselves.
2. The quality of the school–community relationship. This is especially critical for urban schools.
3. The appropriateness of the program design and program goals in relation to the duration of the service-learning activity.
4. The types of reflective activities which are used.
5. The extent to which service-learning activities are integrated into the curriculum.
6. The quality of the service site.
7. The level of school and/or teacher "buy-in."
8. The level of parental "buy-in."
9. The level of administrative "buy-in."

DOES THE PROGRAM MEET THE LEARNING GOALS OF THE STUDENTS?

When students are asked why they serve, they routinely respond with answers like:

- An adult asked them to.
- They wanted to develop good communications and saw this as a way to do that.
- Service-learning projects are fun.
- They felt good about being able to contribute.
- They wanted to give something back to their communities.
- They could do it with their friends.

- It helped them on their college applications.
- They wanted to learn more about themselves.
- It gave them a chance to make effective use of their talents.
- It was a way of expressing their religious or ethical beliefs.
- It satisfied course credit.
- They were able to make contacts that might lead to future jobs. (Shumer, chap. 3; Waterman, chap. 1; Wirthlin Group, 1995)

Research by Waterman (chap. 7) suggests that the most important motivators were all intrinsic: Making a contribution to others; feeling good about oneself; enjoying the challenge entailed in serving; and making effective use of one's talents. Other motivators related to student learning goals and student satisfaction had to do with the kinds of relationship students were able to have with adults, previous involvement in service, and the level of family involvement in service activities.

Listening to the Context: Possible Evaluation Questions

- What are the specific learning goals and needs of the students? To what extent was the service-learning activity planned around these needs and goals?
- What input did students have in planning their service activities?
- What were the student's motivations for participating? To what extent did the service meet his or her personal needs and expectations?
- What kinds of relationships do students have with their teachers? With people at the service site? What was the quality of these relationships?
- In what ways did students have opportunities to assume important "adult" responsibilities in their service assignments?
- What is the level of the student's family involvement in volunteer service activities?

ASSESSING THE QUALITY OF THE SCHOOL–COMMUNITY PARTNERSHIP

Meaningful change in students and schools is most likely to occur when all elements of the school and community work together (Keith, chap. 9). This is particularly important for urban schools, where service-learning can either bridge the gaps that separate groups from each other or reinforce the differences (Schneider, 1995). For learning to occur in these settings schools need:

- To be responsive to diverse styles of learning and motivation.
- To present knowledge in the context of how it can be used the service they are rendering is needed (i.e., understanding why people are homeless or sick or jobless).
- To be staffed with teachers who are perceived as caring about families and the community.

When the quality of school–community partnerships is high, the way the school and the community view each other is likely to change for the better. As students work beside adults in the community in service-learning projects designed to meet real community needs, they begin to view themselves as stakeholders in the community's future (Miller, chap. 8). In addition, adults increasingly view students as resources rather than problems.

Listening to the Context: Possible Evaluation Questions

- Who are the important "players" in the community? What efforts have been made to get them "on board" in support of the school's service-learning programs? What were the results of these efforts?
- What factors keep the school from working with others to bring about significant social change in the community?
- How would you characterize the "quality" of the relationship between the school and the surrounding community
- What resources does the school have to offer to the community? How were these identified?
- What resources does the community have to offer to the school? How were these identified?
- To what extent do the school and other mainstream institutions provide support for the development of positive identity for youth?
- To what extent does the service-learning program focus on student and community assets, strengths, and knowledge? How are these assessed? What assumptions about students and the community underlay these assessments?
- In what ways does the service-learning program make these assets, strengths, and knowledge visible?
- In what ways is the community's knowledge incorporated into the curriculum and the school culture?
- In what ways does the service-learning program support efforts to build opportunities for teachers working with students, parents, to learn and incorporate this knowledge into how they think and approach students, so that over time, the "needs/deficit" map of the community is replaced by a community "assets" map (Keith, chap. 9)?
- In what ways are the school's service-learning programs viewed by the community as "part of the solution" and not as "part of the problem"? Do these programs address real community needs? If so, how and by whom were these needs identified? If not, why not? What role do students play in working developing solutions to problems?
- In preparing students for their service, do teachers and other adults adequately prepare them to understand, not only what they going to be doing, but also the context of their service, that is, why it is needed?

APPROPRIATENESS OF PROGRAM
DESIGN AND GOALS

Duration of the Program

In their chapter on "The Importance of Program Quality in Service-Learning," Eyler and Giles (chap. 5), assert that "the things that make a difference in social and intellectual outcomes are the *particular activities* that students participate in, regardless of program type" (p. 63). One factor was the duration of the program. Their research suggests that the highest quality programs were of *long duration*, spanning a year or more, in which students performed their service over and over again with others. The learning from these programs is the result engaging students in activities which allow for repeated experiences with success (Keith, chap. 9). Blyth, Saito, and Berkas (chap. 4) found that students who engaged in 40 or more hours of service were less likely to be involved in "at-risk" behaviors over time. Thus, although shorter programs may help to change attitudes or convey information, they do not have the same impact as longer programs.

The difference in program impact can be illustrated by this example. Suppose that, for their service activity, a group of students are assigned to work at a shelter for battered women. They will be there once a week for 20 weeks. Two versions of their service-learning experience are possible. One would leave them pretty much on their own. They would be told what they were to do and how to do it, but it would be up to them to learn as fast as they could. The other version would require them to learn the same skills but under the watchful and patient eyes of agency staff. In all likelihood, the second version would result in far more learning than the first.

What this means for service-learning programs can be summed up this way. The impact of a program that offers students repeated opportunities (over at least 1 school year), under the watchful eye of a caring adult, to engage in service activities related to an issue about which they care, is likely to be much greater than the impact of a program that happens once or twice, as part of a school assignment, and engages them in service activities related to issues in which they are not interested.

Listening to the Context: Possible Evaluation Questions

- What was the duration of the service-learning program?
- Are program goals appropriate for a program of this duration?
- What evidence is there that efforts are being made to continue service-learning activities beyond year one—across grade levels—so that students have repeated opportunities for service?

Age and Developmental Needs of the Students

Service-learning programs can be introduced at all grade levels (Duckenfield & Swanson, 1992). For elementary school children, service-learning activities can help fulfill the following needs:

- The need for belonging and approval by the group.
- The need for a sense of personal competence and self-worth.
- The need for affection and acceptance by peers and adults.
- The need for challenging experiences at the child's level of ability.
- The need to participate in creative, nonconforming activities.

For middle school students service-learning can provide important opportunities and experiences that may impact attitudes, decisions, choices, and behaviors as students seek to discover for themselves who they are and what they want to do with their lives. Service-learning activities can help to meet the following needs:

- To feel accepted by peers and others whose opinion matters to them.
- To see concrete outcomes from their efforts.
- To have opportunities for self-definition.
- To participate in and be part of a group.
- To learn decision-making skills through experience.
- To explore adult roles and career opportunities.
- To interact with people of diverse backgrounds.
- To take risks within a "safe" environment.
- To make a difference in the community.

For high school students, service-learning activities may provide important opportunities:

- To prepare for adulthood, citizenship, and the world of work.
- To become self-reliant and achieve psychological independence from their parents.
- To expand peer relationships and achieve the capacity for responsible intimate relationships.
- To formulate a personal value system.

Listening to the Context: Possible Evaluation Questions

- In what ways were the service-learning activities appropriate for the age and developmental needs of the students involved?
- How were these needs determined?
- What opportunities did the students have to give feedback on their level of satisfaction with their service-learning activities? What tools were used to assess this?

TYPE OF REFLECTIVE ACTIVITY USED

The importance of postservice reflective activities was commented on in two of the previous chapters. Blyth, Saito, and Berkas (chap. 4) noted that reflection is a big plus. When it is present, students are not as likely to drop out of school. When it is not present, the service program has a negative impact on students, especially if service is required for graduation. They also found that, without reflection, students felt less responsibility toward serving others, toward civic involvement and toward the environment. Clearly, the reflective component helps students to make important connections between what they are doing and what they might be learning. Without reflection, students have no reason to seek the meaning behind what they are doing. It is not surprising that many of these students question the value of the service requirement.

Eyler and Giles (chap. 5) compared two groups of college students involved in service activities. One group engaged in high reflection, involving weekly intensive seminars. Students were required to complete written assignments and projects and to make oral presentations in which they were expected to analyze the meaning of their service experience, based on concepts they had been learning in the classroom. The second group engaged in moderate reflection, meeting occasionally to share feelings and discuss issues and ideas. They kept journals in which they received occasional feedback from the instructor. Only the students in the high reflection group were able to connect what they had learned in the classroom with what they had learned on their service experience.

This suggests that some structure is necessary so that students are encouraged to think about the issues and feelings associated with their service experience. When coupled with structured reflection, the service experience can be the source of the kind of cognitive challenge that may encourage and invite changes in student attitudes and perceptions associated with the service site (i.e., attitudes and stereotypes about the poor, when working at a shelter or food pantry). The questions, coupled with regular feedback on journal entries from the teacher, provide the support that makes change more likely.

Where journals are used, teachers should structure the task so that students are required to observe, analyze, and evaluate their service experience in light of what they are learning in the classroom. Six steps are involved in this process.

- *Knowledge*: What were your first impressions of the service site?
- *Comprehension*: In what ways was the service site the same as (or different from) what you were expecting?
- *Application*: In what ways has your participation in this service activity changed your perspective on the issue(s) involved?
- *Analysis*: What did you do at your service site? What was most challenging to you?
- *Synthesis*: What is the most important thing you learned about yourself as a result of your participation in this project? What will you do differently because of this?
- *Evaluation*: How would you rate the overall quality of your service experience? If you could change one thing about your service site, what would it be?

Listening to the Context: Possible Evaluation Questions

- What kinds of reflection activities were associated with the service-learning project? When and where did reflection usually take place?
- Were reflective activities developmentally appropriate (age, level of cognitive development) for the students involved?

CURRICULUM INTEGRATION

In addition to the importance of reflection, Eyler and Giles (chap. 5) also found that the extent to which the service activity is integrated into the curriculum is a powerful indicator of successful programs. This can be done in one of two ways—either the introduction of an entirely new course that focuses on service or by infusing a service component into an existing course. In both cases, it is important to structure classroom assignments so that students can apply what they are learning in the classroom to their service site and vice versa. It is also important to make sure that agency staff are aware of the academic requirements of the program so that they can collaborate with students and teachers to create meaningful projects that meet the needs of everyone involved.

Listening to the Context: Possible Evaluation Questions

- To what extent are student service activities integrated into the curriculum?
- In what ways are student classroom assignments and service activities related to one another?

THE SERVICE SITE

Another theme addressed in the previous chapters had to do with the importance of matching the service experience to something that the student wanted to learn (Keith, chap. 9). Blyth, Saito, and Berkas (chap. 4) also noted the importance of the service activities in which students engage. They found that students involved in individual placements were more likely to accept diversity, to report higher levels of self-efficacy, and to be more engaged in academic tasks. Students involved in group placements were more likely to gain a sense of responsibility for civic involvement (now and in the future), but less likely to gain a sense of responsibility for helping others.

Given this, it is important to assess, not only the needs of the community, but also the needs of the school and the student (Bradley, 1994). Students will benefit more when their service experiences give them opportunities to utilize diverse skills and result in a sense of ownership in the project.

This suggests that service sites need to be selected with care and that agency staff and site supervisors need to know ahead of time what students hope and want to learn. At the same time students may need help in identifying sites which may maximize their learning opportunities. This means regular evaluations of sites by both students and teachers.

Listening to the Context: Possible Evaluation Questions

- What are the needs of the community? How were they assessed? By whom?
- In what ways are these goals and needs taken into account in matching students with service sites?
- To what extent are the goals and needs of students met by their service experiences (individual, group, or both)?
- What is the nature of the relationship between the school and the service site?
- What is the link, if any, between the kinds of things students do at their service site and what they learn in the classroom?
- What things do teachers do to help students connect what they learn at their service site with what they learn in the classroom?
- Did the students feel that their service was meaningful? If so, in what ways? If not, why not? How was this assessed?

SCHOOL AND TEACHER SUPPORT
FOR THE PROGRAM

Miller (chap. 8) and Keith (chap. 9) found that the level of school and teacher support was a predictor of successful programs. Signs of this support were seen in;

- A positive school environment (safe, orderly, sense of caring and community).
- Teachers who expected students to learn.
- Instructional leadership.
- The school having clear and focused goals.
- Frequent monitoring of students.

A related issue, addressed by Wade (chap. 6), is the background and training of teachers engaged in service-learning activities.

Listening to the Content: Possible Evaluation Questions

- What is the nature of the school environment? What percentage of the students engage in antisocial behaviors? What percentage engage in "risky" behaviors?

- What evidence is there that members of the school (teachers and students) care about each other?
- Does the school have a mission statement? What are some of the major educational initiatives currently underway or being planned in support of this mission?
- In what ways does service-learning relate to and support the school's educational mission?
- What obstacles were encountered in the school's efforts to implement service-learning programs? What was done to address these obstacles? Were these efforts successful or unsuccessful? What else could have been done?
- What kind of training or preparation for service-learning was provided for teachers? Was it adequate from their point of view?
- What kind of training or preparation for service-learning was provided for students? Was it adequate from their point of view?
- Are student suggestions for improving the service-learning program taken seriously by teachers and site staff?
- Who are the teachers who participate in service-learning activities? What are the reasons some teachers participate, and others do not?
- What evidence is there that teachers are given the time they need to plan their projects and make the necessary contacts?
- What evidence is there that collaborative teaching is encouraged and supported at the school?

PARENTAL SUPPORT FOR THE PROGRAM

Another factor associated with successful programs is the level of parental involvement. What is important is developing a true partnership between the school and parents.

Listening to the Context: Possible Evaluation Questions

- Describe the current level of parental support for the program. What has been done to try to increase it?
- What roles do parents play in helping to give shape and direction to the school's service-learning programs?
- To what extent are parents and teachers encouraged and equipped to think developmentally, to think relationships? How is this being done?

ADMINISTRATIVE SUPPORT FOR THE PROGRAM

Miller (chap. 8) also commented on the conditions necessary for successful service-learning programs from an administrator's point of view. Key elements include:

- Board and community support.
- A climate of risk taking within the school and school district.
- Effective communication within the school and between the school and community.
- Adequate resources (dollars, time, staff).
- Ability to provide the necessary training and staff development.
- Student interest and involvement.
- Careful planning.
- Patience.

Listening to the Context: Possible Evaluation Questions

- What evidence is there that school administrators are generally supportive of teachers within the district who want to try out new teaching and methods, such as service-learning?
- In what specific ways is this support made known to teachers, parents, and the wider community?
- What resources (money, staff, collaborative partnerships with businesses/agencies) or other support systems for the successful implementation of successful service-learning programs in the district are already in place?
- What resources still need to be identified and/or developed? Is there a plan for doing this? How was this plan developed? Who was involved in developing it?
- What perceptions do teachers have of the community which surrounds the school? In what ways are these perceptions based on reality?
- What perceptions does the community have of the school in its midst? Of the teachers who teach its children? In what ways are these perceptions based on reality?

SOME OTHER ISSUES FOR
RESEARCH AND EVALUATION

Assuming that service-learning evaluators pay close attention to the "initial conditions for success" outlined earlier, there are at least two other programmatic outcomes that merit careful scrutiny. One is the degree to which service-learning programs support school reform initiatives; the other is the degree to which service-learning programs support school-to-work initiatives.

Because service-learning promotes personal, emotional, and social development of students, it compliments local and national efforts at school reform, such as Goals 2000.

- By connecting academic knowledge and skills to real-life applications, it makes school relevant.
- By providing students with opportunities to practice good citizenship, it is the core element of effective civic and citizenship education.

- By helping teachers and students learn skills and strategies necessary to affect school change, it supports educational reform.
- Studies have also shown service-learning strategies to be highly effective in substance abuse prevention programs and in preventing high-risk behaviors among students who are "at risk."

In reviewing the goals and objectives of several of school reform strategies in wide use across the United Stated, some common themes emerge, shown in Table 10.2, relating to changes in the school, the classroom, the curriculum, teachers, and students and the learning process.

Listening to the Context: Possible Evaluation Questions

1. In what specific ways did the school's service-learning program support efforts to change the school by:
   - implementing and using site-based management styles?
   - increasing the level of meaningful parental involvement in school-related activities?
   - increasing the number of collaborative relationships the school had with outside businesses/agencies?
2. In what specific ways did the school's service-learning program support efforts to change the classroom by supporting and encouraging cross-age and cooperative learning opportunities for students?
3. In what specific ways did the school's service-learning program support efforts to change the curriculum by:

Table 10.2
Change Themes in School Reform

Changes in the School:	• site-based management and shared decision-making • considerably expanded parental involvement • more formalized relationships with a variety of social service agencies geared toward civic responsibility
Changes in the Classroom:	• cross-age tutoring • cooperative learning
Changes in the Curriculum:	• are interdisciplinary and thematic • show clear connections between the classroom and real-world outcomes
Changes in Teachers:	• a collaborative, team approach to teaching • teachers who are as concerned about the personal and social needs of their students as they are about what they learn
Changes in Students:	• a reciprocal approach to teaching and learning • active, self-monitored learning • recognize the strengths of diversity and heterogeneity

- fostering a collaborative, team approach among teachers?
- providing ways for teachers to attend to the personal and social, as well as the cognitive, needs of students?

4. In what specific ways did the school's service-learning program support efforts to change students and the learning process by:
   - supporting a reciprocal and cooperative approach to teaching and learning?
   - helping students to become active, self-monitoring learners?
   - increasing both the number and quality of school–community interactions geared toward civic responsibility?
   - celebrating the strengths of diversity and heterogeneity?

In its 1991 report *What Work Requires of Schools: A SCANS Report for America 2000,* the U.S. Department of Labor identified five competencies and a three-part foundation of skills and personal qualities, shown in Table 10.3, that will be necessary for success in the workplace of the next century.

Because it is a form of experiential learning, service-learning has great potential for helping schools to address development in each of these areas. However, as Barbara Gomez (1994) recently noted in addressing participants at a conference on "Connecting School-to-Work and Service-Learning," "Although the link between service learning and school-to-work seems a logical and natural one, there has been little concrete work or discussion aimed at bringing the two concepts together."

Listening to the Context: Possible Evaluation Questions

Participants at this conference identified several areas meriting further study and evaluation:

1. What evidence—beyond the affective result—is there that service-learning programs support the efforts of school-to-work programs
   - to make the curriculum more relevant for students? In what ways can this be assessed?
   - to keep students in school and motivated to learn? In what ways can this be assessed?
   - to help build meaningful relationships with and in the community?
   - to help students develop basic skills such as reading, writing, mathematics, speaking and listening?
   - to help students develop critical thinking skills such as decision-making, problem-solving, knowing how to learn, and reasoning?
   - to help students learn and practice the interpersonal skills they will need in the workplace?
   - to help students acquire and use information in appropriate ways?
   - to help students develop personal qualities such as individual responsibility, self-esteem, and sociability?

TABLE 10.3
SCANS 2000 Competencies and Skills

Competencies	Skills and Personal Qualities
Resources: Identify, organize, plan, and allocate resources—time, money, materials, human resources.	Basic skills: Reading, writing, arithmetic and mathematical operations, speaking, and listening.
Interpersonal skills: Work effectively with others.	Thinking skills: Thinking creatively, making decisions, solving problems, seeing things in the "mind's eye,," knowing how to learn, and reasoning.
Systems: Understand complex interrelationships and design new systems.	Personal qualities: Individual responsibility, self-esteem, sociability, self-management, and integrity.
Technology: Select appropriate tools and use technologies appropriate to the task.	

CONCLUSION

Challenges Facing Our Schools

The National Commission on Educational Excellence (1983) concluded that America's school were sinking beneath "a rising tide of mediocrity ... " 74% of our teachers and 80% of parents believe that "the quality of education is worse today than it was five years ago" (Carnegie Foundation, 1995). America's schools are failing, "not because they changed, but precisely because they continue to do exactly what they have always done, in exactly the same ways. ... Education for the new century is a life-long process of training the mind to manipulate information, to solve problems, to imagine, to create " ... (Wilson, 1994, p. 2).

Wilson's conclusions are echoed by Lappe and DuBois (1995), in their book *The Quickening of America*, who noted that, "While the world is changing, America's schools are not meeting the needs that are flowing from these changes" (p. 203). In support of their position they give a number of examples. These are reflected in Table 10.4.

Challenges Facing Our Youth

A recent survey by the American Association of School Administrators (1995) found that, if the schools have not changed, "today's young people have." It is becoming more and more common for today's young people to question authority and shun traditional values and responsibilities. The reasons for these changes include:

- An increase in the number of dysfunctional families, resulting in more and more children growing up without the support, guidance, and discipline they need to make responsible choices.

- More and more of our young people are threatened by crime, violence, ignorance, and poverty.
- In the absence of strong positive adult influences, the values of our young people are, more and more, being shaped by their peers.
- The influence of the mass media—our young people have more information at an earlier age, but do not know what to do with it.

Changes Facing Our Communities

Our communities are facing other problems as well:

- Youth alienation from adults.
- Increased antisocial and at-risk behavior among youth.
- Increased use of stereotypes between generations and races.
- Lack of concern for others.
- Lack of motivation to study and learn among many students.

Given all this it is hardly surprising that, when parents are asked about the qualities they would like their sons and daughters to have:

- 91% want them to be self-confident.
- 88% want them to be responsible, dependable.
- 87% want them to be curious, eager to learn.
- 85% want them to be independent and self-directing.
- 84% want them to be sensitive to others.
- 83% want them to be able to work well with others.
- 82% want them to be kind and considerate.
- 74% want them to get good grades. (Schapps, Solomon, Wilson, 1986, p. 35)

TABLE 10.4
Schools and Changes in Today's World

Changes in Today's World	Needs That Flow From These Changes	Instead of Meeting These Needs, Our Schools...
Greater Diversity: More cultures and races interacting	Appreciation of diversity	Isolate students individually from community life
Heightened Interdependence	Interaction skills	Offer little training in team-work and conflict resolution
Spreading Alienation: Growing magnitude and severity of problems	Skills to negotiate interests, hold others accountable, and solve problems	Provide little training in problem-solving skills
Accelerating change in: Technological development, information output processing	Knowing how to learn and how to teach ourselves	Emphasize routine tasks, repetition, and retention of facts and figures

Service-learning is an educationally sound way to combine the needs of schools, students, communities, and parents. Although the power of this approach has been demonstrated in numerous locations around the country, it is still greeted with skepticism by many. The challenge facing service-learning practitioners is, therefore, twofold.

First, careful attention must be paid to the design and implementation of programs that wave the flag of service-learning. It must be clear to students, teachers, and outside observers what quality service-learning programs look like and what they can do for those who are touched by them.

Second, equal attention must be paid to evaluating these programs. Evaluation is not an afterthought, something you do if you have time. It is an integral part of a carefully designed program. Furthermore, in addition to collecting the usual information about the numbers of students involved, the number of hours of service, and so on, evaluators must pay as much attention to the "initial conditions" in which the program happened. In this way practitioners will learn more about the factors that make for programs that have the kinds of impacts they were designed to have.

As evaluators disseminate this information, they will also help to sharpen the image of service-learning as a strategy for educational reform and learning that can move our schools and students forward into the next century with hope and excitement.

REFERENCES

American Association of School Administrators (1995). *How students have changed.* Arlington, VA: Author.

Boyer, E. (1995). *The basic school.* Princeton, NJ: Carnegie Foundation for the Advancement of Teaching.

Bradley, L. R. (1994). *Needs assessment for Learn and Serve America.* Columbus: Ohio Department of Education.

Duckenfield, M., & Swanson, L. (1992). *Service-learning: Meeting the needs of youth at risk.* Clemson, SC: National Dropout Prevention Center.

Gleick, J. (1987). *Chaos: The making of a new science.* New York: Penguin.

Gomez, B. (1994, July). *Summary of the July 24, 1994, discussion and examples of service learning models with a school-to-work focus.* Paper presented at the Council of Chief State School Officers, Washington, DC.

Guba, E., & Lincoln, Y. (1989). *Fourth generation evaluation.* Newbury Park, CA: Sage.

Horning, B. (1993, January). The controversial career of Evelyn Fox Keller. *Technology Review,* 58–68.

Kohlberg, L. (1981). *The philosophy of moral development.* New York: Harper & Row.

Lappe, F., & DuBois, P. (1995). *The quickening of America: Rebuilding our nation, remaking our lives.* San Francisco: Jossey-Bass.

Levinson, D. (1978). *The season's of a man's life.* New York: Ballantine Books.

National Commission on Excellence in Education. (1983). *A nation at risk: The imperative for educational reform.* Washington, DC: U.S. Government Printing Office.

Osborne, D., & Gaebler, T. (1993). *Reinventing government.* New York: Penguin.

The Prudential spirit of community initiative. (1995). Newark, NJ: The Prudential Insurance Company of America.

Schapps,E., Solomon, D., & Wilson, M. (1986, January). A program that combines character development and academic achievement. *Educational Leadership*, 32–35.

Schneider, J. (1995, Fall). Fostering equity through service-learning. *NSEE Quarterly*, 10–11.

Secretary's Commission on Achieving Necessary Skills. (1991). *What work requires of schools: a SCANS report to America 2000*, Washington, DC: U.S. Department of Labor.

Wilson, K. (1994). *Redesigning education.* New York: Rinehart & Winston.

Author Index

Subject Index